全国高等教育英语规划教材

# 新编实用英语语法教程
New English Grammar: A Practical Coursebook

（英文版）

主　编　谢徐萍
编　者　季天祥　宋建清　刘道影
　　　　张海燕　黄立丰　曹金兰
　　　　武　颖　张　艳　何旭良

苏州大学出版社

图书在版编目(CIP)数据

新编实用英语语法教程 = New English Grammar: A Practical Coursebook：英文版/谢徐萍主编. 一苏州：苏州大学出版社,2016.9(2017.12重印)
全国高等教育英语规划教材
ISBN 978-7-5672-1765-2

Ⅰ.①新… Ⅱ.①谢… Ⅲ.①英语-语法-高等学校-教材 Ⅳ.①H314

中国版本图书馆 CIP 数据核字(2016)第 183422 号

---

| 书　　名：新编实用英语语法教程 |
| New English Grammar: A Practical Coursebook |

---

作　　者：谢徐萍　主编
责任编辑：汤定军
策　　划：汤定军
装帧设计：刘　俊

---

出版发行：苏州大学出版社(Soochow University Press)
社　　址：苏州市十梓街1号　邮编：215006
印　　装：宜兴市盛世文化印刷有限公司
网　　址：www.sudapress.com
E - mail：tangdingjun@suda.edu.cn
邮购热线：0512-67480030
销售热线：0512-65225020

---

开　本：787mm×1092mm　1/16　印张：17　字数：400 千
版　次：2016 年 9 月第 1 版
印　次：2017 年 12 月第 2 次印刷
书　号：ISBN 978-7-5672-1765-2
定　价：35.00 元

---

凡购本社图书发现印装错误，请与本社联系调换。服务热线：0512-65225020

# 前言

进入高校各种层次的学生在中学阶段已基本学完英语基础语法,但是很多学生的语法基础并不好,究其原因是他们不甚喜欢语法或语法课。语法以及语法书往往给人枯燥、刻板的印象,语法教学常常流于传授语法的条条框框,缺乏生动有趣的教学方法。我们要改变这一切,就必须从教材的编写开始,从教法开始。

我们的基本观点是:第一,作为人们交流思想工具的语言,总是处于经常的变化之中,按照自己的规律向前发展。语法规则是语言客观实际的反映,语法的任务不是规定语言的发展,而是从不断变化发展的语言现象中归纳总结出客观而科学的规律。教师应该启发学生如何选择恰当的语法形式来表达思想,培养学生的语法学习和使用的"选择意识",着力发展他们的"语法能力"。第二,词法(Morphology)和句法(Syntax)是语法研究的两个方面。经过一千多年的发展,英语已经失去了原有的许多词形变化,由原来的综合性语言演变成分析性语言。因此,在现代英语语法研究中句法显得尤其重要。本教材的语法讲解以句子为基本单位,首先阐释句子的各个组成部分(主语、谓语、宾语、状语、补语等)以及不同语法形式选择在交际上的差异;然后让学生了解重点词法,认识词法和句法是相辅相成的关系,使学生能较熟练地掌握构句规律。第三,语法教学力求体现以学生为主体的教育思想,从学生的学习经历和认知基础出发,通过反思、讨论、探究和实践,启发学生的思维,激发学生的学习兴趣和发现语法规律的欲望。

本教材主要有以下几点特色:

1. 分目科学体系新,循序渐进,易学易用。先以句法为主线(第一部分和第二部分),阐释语法结构,使学生熟练地掌握构句规律;然后让学生全面了解重点词法(第三部分)、掌握词汇意义与语法结构密不可分的关系;最后引导学生认识语法和语篇的关系,在一定程度上提高了英语教学语法和学习语法的广度和深度。

2. 编排简明新颖,启发性、研究性、任务型教学理念贯穿于始终。以设问开头突出每章的内容重点。每个问题就是每小节所要探讨的问题,讲解讨论后所布置的任务则给了学生理论联系实际去解决问题的机会;每章后面所附的综合练习实则让学生自己去查找资料或以小组做研究,以PPT形式相互交流。

3. 注重语法的交际价值,顾及语法信息量的充足性以及语法内容的可理解性和趣味性。改变以往将语法作为抽象语言知识学习的做法。从交际角度比较相似结构之间的差别,关注语法与词汇作为交际手段之间的联系。语料尽量取样于现实生活,丰富多彩。

4. 以中国学生学习英语为出发点和归宿,考虑到母语的正负迁移影响以及学习者学习语言的经验,紧扣英语语法的核心项目,不讲不是很需要讲的内容,预测性地呈现中国学生可能会出现的语法问题。

5. 考虑到语法课开课于第二学期,而第三学期学生将参加英语专业四级考试,因此语法讲解和讨论关注语法练习与专四以及各种语法测试的结合。

6. 采用多媒体和研讨相结合的教学方法。课堂教学利用多媒体教学课件,采用启发式和互动式,既引导学生掌握本课程基本理论知识,又注重学生结合现实解决实际问题的科学研究能力的培养。此外,根据学生的个性和接受能力,可通过网络、邮件等做进一步的沟通和指导。

7. 本教材全程用英语编写,教学课件制作也使用英语,课堂上个别术语或难点可用中文提示,目的是让学生最大可能地沉浸于英语氛围之中,并锻炼他们运用英语的能力。

8. 为了更好地帮助学生掌握语法知识,将第一课堂延伸到课外的第二课堂,本教材配有练习册,师生可以利用课程网站,特别是互动版块,一起讨论有关语法现象,一起去解决语法上的疑难杂症。

本教材分为四个部分,共 16 章。编写工作的具体分工如下:谢徐萍负责设计全书的编写理念、写作思路、单元样本,具体编写第 1—3 章,同时负责其他单元的修订工作,张海燕编写第 4 章,刘道影编写第 5—6 章,季天祥编写第 7—9 章,黄立丰编写第 10 章,曹金兰编写第 11 章,武颖编写第 12 章,张艳编写第 13 章,宋建清编写第 14—15 章,何旭良编写第 16 章。

《新编实用英语语法教程》(New English Grammar: A Practical Coursebook)历经四届任课教师和学生的课堂使用,边用边改进,终于成为一本吸取近年来国内外语法研究的最新成果、自成一体、观点新颖、内容翔实、体系科学、编排合理的较为成熟的英语语法教材。

在本教材编写过程中,我们参考了大量的英语语法著作,例句多选自词典和英语原著,特此说明,并向所引材料的作者表示感谢。

本书如有错误或其他不足之处,希望读者和老师们多提宝贵意见。

成书之际,我们要向我国语法研究专家苏州大学外国语学院贾冠杰教授表示敬意,他在百忙之中通读全书校样稿,提出了许多宝贵意见,并欣然为本书写了推荐意见。作为 2015 年江苏省社科应用研究精品工程外语类课题、2014 年度南通大学教材建设项目、2014 年度南通大学杏林学院课程建设项目,本书的出版得到了以上部门的配套资助,一并致谢。

编者

2016 年 5 月

# Contents

1. Introduction: Grammatical Hierarchy/ 1
   1.1 Morphemes/ 2
   1.2 Words/ 3
   1.3 Phrases/ 4
   1.4 Clauses/ 6
   1.5 Sentences/ 8

## Part One
## The Structure of English Sentences

2. Sentence Components/ 15
   2.1 Subject and Predicate/ 16
   2.2 Object/ 17
   2.3 Complements/ 19
   2.4 Attribute/ 22
   2.5 Adverbial/ 24
   2.6 Appositive/ 26
   2.7 Independent Element/ 28

3. Subject-verb Concord/ 32
   3.1 Person and Number Forms/ 32
   3.2 Three Guiding Principles/ 33
   3.3 Concord with Nouns Ending in -s/ 34
   3.4 Concord with Collective Nouns as Subject/ 37
   3.5 Concord with Coordinate Subject/ 38
   3.6 Concord with Expressions of Quantity as Subject/ 40
   3.7 Other Problems of Subject-verb Concord/ 42

4. Sentence Constructions and Analysis/ 48
   4.1 Sentence Patterns/ 49

4.2 Sentence Transformation and Expansion/ 53

4.3 Coordinate Constructions/ 54

4.4 Subordinate Constructions/ 54

4.5 Existential Sentences/ 55

5. Uses of Sentences/ 59

5.1 Declarative Sentences/ 60

5.2 Interrogative Sentences/ 62

5.3 Imperative Sentences/ 64

5.4 Exclamatory Sentences/ 65

# Part Two
# Predicate and Related Grammatical Categories

6. Tense and Aspect Systems/ 71

6.1 The Tense of Predicate/ 71

6.2 The Aspect of Predicate/ 72

6.3 Present Tense/ 72

6.4 Past Tense/ 75

6.5 Future Time/ 78

7. Voice System/ 87

7.1 Active Sentence and Passive Sentence/ 87

7.2 Transformation of Active Voice into Passive Voice/ 88

7.3 Constraints on Transformation/ 91

7.4 Voice of Phrasal Verbs/ 93

7.5 Uses of Passive Voice/ 95

7.6 Passivity—Form and Meaning/ 99

8. Mood System/ 110

8.1 Types of Mood/ 111

8.2 Be-subjunctive/ 112

8.3 Were-subjunctive/ 114

8.4 Other Forms Expressing Hypothetical Meanings/ 116

# Part Three  Parts of Speech

9. Nouns/ 123

9.1 Classification of Nouns/ 124

- 9.2 Function of Noun Phrases / 126
- 9.3 Number Forms of Nouns / 127
- 9.4 Genitive Nouns / 135

## 10. Determiners / 144
- 10.1 Types of Determiners / 144
- 10.2 Collocations between Determiners and Nouns / 146
- 10.3 Collocations between Determiners / 148

## 11. Verbs / 153
- 11.1 Classification of Verbs (I) / 153
- 11.2 Classification of Verbs (II) / 157
- 11.3 Infinitive / 160
- 11.4 Participles / 164
- 11.5 Notes about Infinitive and -ing Participle / 167

## 12. Adjectives and Adverbs / 172
- 12.1 Classification of Adjectives / 172
- 12.2 Chief Uses of Adjectives and Adjective Phrases / 174
- 12.3 Classification of Adverbs / 179
- 12.4 Chief Uses of Adverbs and Adverb Phrases / 180
- 12.5 Two Forms of Adverbs / 183
- 12.6 Comparison and Comparative Constructions / 185

## 13. Prepositions / 192
- 13.1 Types of Prepositions / 192
- 13.2 Collocation of Prepositions / 196
- 13.3 Roles of Prepositional Phrases in Sentences / 201
- 13.4 Transformation between Prepositional Phrases and Subordinate Clauses / 202

# Part Four  Grammar and Text

## 14. Inversion / 209
- 14.1 Definition of Inversion / 210
- 14.2 Grammatical Inversion / 211
- 14.3 Rhetorical Inversion / 212

## 15. Ellipsis and Substitution / 219
- 15.1 Definition of Ellipsis and Substitution / 220
- 15.2 Grammatical Ellipsis / 220

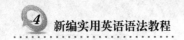

    15.3    Rhetorical Ellipsis/ 225

    15.4    Substitution/ 226

**16. Cohesion in English Text/** 231

    16.1    Definition of Cohesion/ 231

    16.2    Types of Cohesive Devices/ 232

    16.3    Choice of Cohesive Devices/ 236

**Appendix 1    Solutions to Tasks/** 240

**Appendix 2    Glossary/** 252

**References/** 262

# 1. Introduction: Grammatical Hierarchy

## Aims of the Unit

> In this unit we will discuss some general matters about grammar. We are going to discuss six questions in particular:
> - What is grammar? How many ranks are there in it?
> - What is the smallest grammatical unit? What categories are there?
> - What is word? How can words be classified?
> - What is phrase? What phrase types are there?
> - What is the essential feature of a clause? How can clauses be classified according to syntactic functions?
> - What is sentence? What're the two characteristics of a sentence? How to classify sentences?

Language, a tool of social communication, is a system of sound-meaning combination of vocabulary and grammar. Grammar is the structural system of a language. The grammar of the English language is organized into five ranks: the sentence, the clause, the phrase, the word and the morpheme. Each rank is composed of one or more than one grammatical unit of the immediate lower rank. As a grammatical unit, the sentence consists of one or more than one clause; the clause, one or more than one phrase; the phrase, one or more than one word; and the word, one or more than one morpheme. The sentence is the highest rank of grammatical unit while the morpheme is the minimum or the lowest rank.

grammatical hierarchy
语法层次
segmentation
切分法

> **Task 1**
>
> Now that the sentence is the highest rank of grammar, we can break it up into its smallest component—morpheme through **segmentation**. Please try to dissect the following sentence:
>
> *These undergraduates are rapidly improving in their writing.*

## ◆ 1.1 Morphemes

> free morphemes
> 自由词素
> bound morphemes
> 粘附词素
> root 词根
> derivative
> 派生词
> compound word
> 复合词
> prefix 前缀
> suffix 后缀

The morpheme is the minimum or the smallest grammatical unit, also the most basic meaning element of speech. Morphemes fall into two categories: **Free Morphemes** and **Bound Morphemes**.

A free morpheme has a complete meaning and can stand by itself as a simple word like *girl*, *rely* and so on. Free morphemes can serve as **Root** to form **Derivative** by adding **Affix** like: kind*ness*, *un*kind, *un*kind*ness*, kind*ly*; or be used with other free morphemes to form **Compound Word** like *book*mark, *book*worm, *book*shop, *book*stall.

> inflectional affix
> 屈折词缀，包括名词复数标记-s/-es、名词属格标记-'s、第三人称动词单数现在时标记-s/-es、动词过去时标记-ed、动词-ed 分词和-ing 分词标记-ed，-ing、形容词和副词比较级和最高级标记-er，-est等。
> allomorph
> 词素变体

Bound morphemes are mostly the morphemes which are meaningful, but the meaning is not complete in itself unless it is attached to some other form. Therefore, a bound morpheme cannot stand by itself: it only exists as an **Inflectional** or **Derivational Affix**. Derivational affix can be divided into **Prefix** or **Suffix** to form **Derivatives** by combining Root, e.g.

| Prefix | Suffix | Prefix & Suffix |
|---|---|---|
| *anti*war | Marx*ist* | *un*luck*y* |
| *post*war | move*ment* | *co*-existence |
| *pan*-African | care*less* | *pre*-liberation |

In addition, those carrying the same meanings but various forms in different contexts are called **Allomorphs**, e.g.

| in- | im- | il- | ir- |
|---|---|---|---|
| *in*active | *im*mature | *il*legal | *ir*rational |
| *in*experienced | *im*perfect | *il*logical | *ir*regular |
| *in*secure | *im*practical | *il*legible | *ir*responsible |

# 1. Introduction: Grammatical Hierarchy

**Task 2** Work in groups and distinguish free morphemes from bound morphemes in the following words. Try to give reasons for your decision.

| | | | |
|---|---|---|---|
| pro-French | semicircle | likewise | underpay |
| warmth | secondary | international | illegitimate |
| irrelevant | chair | careful | golden |
| critical | fourteen | selfish | unlucky |

## ◈ 1.2  Words

The word is composed of one or more than one morphemes. Words can be classified in two ways: classification in terms of word-formation and classification in terms of grammatical function. In terms of word-formation, words can be divided into **simple words** (like *at*, *up*, *down*, *far*, *near*, etc.), **derivatives** formed by free morpheme or free root plus bound morpheme or derivative affix (like *un*fair, *non*smoker, *dis*cover, *mis*judge, arrange*ment*, happi*ness*, fool*ish*, friend*ship*, etc.), **compounds** (like *deadline*, *world-famous*, *nickname*, *moreover*, *something*, *whenever*, *outside*, etc.). In terms of grammatical function, words can be divided into **Closed Class** or **Function Word** and **Open Class** or **Content Word**.

Closed-class words refer to those sets of words, without complete lexical meaning but with grammatical meaning, whose items are "closed" or limited in number. Closed-class words include:

- Preposition: *in*, *of*, *on*, *without*, *in spite of*
- Pronoun: *you*, *he*, *one*, *which*, *this*, *that*
- Determiner: *a*, *the*, *this*, *some*, *any*, *no*
- Conjunction: *and*, *or*, *but*, *because*, *when*, *if*
- Auxiliary: *do*, *can*, *may*, *must*, *will*

Open-class words refer to those sets of words whose items are indefinitely extendable. New items are constantly being created and old items are giving place to new ones. Open-class words cover:

- Noun: *Smith*, *Paris*, *man*, *chess*, *table*
- Adjective: *old*, *young*, *small*, *big*, *pretty*, *ugly*
- Adverb: *here*, *there*, *early*, *late*, *really*, *fast*

---

simple words
简单词
derivatives
派生词
compounds
复合词

---

closed class
封闭词汇
function word
功能词
open class
开放词类
content word
实义词
cardinal numeral
基数词
ordinal numeral
序数词
interjection
感叹词

- Main Verb: *work*, *give*, *put*, *take*, *talk*

In addition, **Cardinal Numeral**, **Ordinal Numeral**, and **Interjection** are the words between "closed" and "open" words.

**Task 3**  Discuss: What words are they and why?

| make | nice | hand | foot |
| boyhood | belittle | archbishop | coverage |
| wherever | by | throughout | so |
| should | could | might | dare |

## 1.3 Phrases

The phrase is composed of one or more than one word. Generally, the phrase is a group of words organized in a specific way with a key word as its head. The word class of the head determines the class of the phrase and the way in which the words are organized, such as **Noun Phrase**, **Verb Phrase**, **Adjective Phrase**, **Adverb Phrase**, **Prepositional Phrase**.

### 1) Noun Phrase

Noun Phrase is usually a phrase with a noun as its head. The general pattern of a noun phrase is: (determiner +) (premodifier +) noun (+ post modifier), e.g.

the People's **Republic** of China

his new **book** on phonology

the tall **boy** sitting in the corner

However, in the following examples, a noun forms a noun phrase:

*Milton* lived in the 17th century.

*Sugar* dissolves in water.

*Knowledge* is power.

In the above examples, *Milton*, *Sugar* and *Knowledge* are noun phrases; but they are only a proper noun, a material noun and an abstract noun respectively out of the context. All the phrases except **Prepositional Phrase** have the similar situation.

## 2) Verb Phrase

Verb Phrase is a phrase with a main verb as its head. A verb phrase can be ① simple or ② complex. In terms of grammatical form, a verb phrase can be ③ **finite** or ④ **non-finite**.

> finite verb
> 限定动词
> non-finite verb
> 非限定动词
> auxiliary
> 助动词

① A simple verb phrase is just a main verb or "modifier + main verb", e. g.

She **looks** pale.

They *fully appreciate* our problems.

② A complex verb phrase is a main verb preceded by an **auxiliary** (or auxiliaries) (+modifier), e. g.

She *ought to have told* him about it.

The children *might have been playing* in the garden.

③ A finite verb phrase is initiated by a finite form, that is, a verb form that changes according to tense or subject. Examples in ① and ② are the ones of finite verb phrases.

④ A non-finite verb phrase is a phrase initiated by a non-finite form, that is, a verb form that does not change according to to tense or subject. Non-finite verb phrases include infinitive phrase, -ing participle phrase and -en participle phrase.

Sam got up early *to catch* the train.

It's no use *crying* over spilt milk.

*Written* in simple English, the book is easy to read.

## 3) Adjective Phrase

The adjective phrase is a phrase with an adjective as its head. The general pattern of an adjective phrase is: (modifier + ) adjective ( + postmodifier/complementation).

That work is *too difficult for that boy*.

Rob lay on the ground, *unable to move*.

## 4) Adverb Phrase

The adverb phrase is a phrase with an adverb as its head. The general pattern of an adverb phrase is: (modifier + ) adverb ( + postmodifier).

*How often* do the buses run?

He spoke *loudly* and *clearly*.

She spoke *very clearly indeed*.

### 5) Prepositional Phrase

The prepositional phrase is a phrase with a preposition as its head. The general pattern of a prepositional phrase is: (modifier +) preposition + complementation.

We are *of a mind*.

What is there *on the desk*?

Food has been scarce *since before the war*.

**Task 4**

Discuss: What phrases are they and why?

(1) Now their footsteps could be heard *directly above my head*.
(2) The weather is *too hot to be enjoyable*.
(3) This is *a very interesting story*.
(4) *Honesty* is the best policy.
(5) We *study English every day*.
(6) I *have rarely received* a more dishonest book.
(7) We went there *to see a film*.
(8) She spoke *very clearly indeed*.
(9) *Not knowing what to say*, he kept silent.
(10) You are *not careful enough*.

## ◆ 1.4 Clauses

The clause is composed of one or more than one phrase. The clause is a sequence of phrases, a grammatical structure of "**Subject + Predicate**". Clauses can be various according to their different syntactic functions.

### 1) Independent and Dependent Clauses

In terms of grammatical function, a clause can be independent or dependent. An independent clause is a clause that can stand by itself and act as a complete utterance, as distinguished from a dependent clause which forms only part of another clause or of a phrase.

He knows everything about it. (Independent Clause)

I don't think *he knows everything about it*. (Dependent Clause)

His new book will soon come out. It is on grammar. (Independent Clause)

His new book *that will soon come out* is on grammar. (Dependent Clause)

*Make up your mind*, or *you'll miss the chance*. (Independent Clause)

## 2) Simple and Complex Clauses

Simple Clause consists of only one construction of "Subject + Predicate". An independent simple clause is at the same time a simple sentence. When a clause comprises another clause or other clauses as its element or elements, it is a complex clause. An independent complex clause is at the same time a complex sentence.

*It is not true*. (Independent Simple Clause/Simple Sentence)
*What you said is not true*. (Independent Complex Clause/Complex Sentence)
*He said that it was not true*. (Dependent Simple Clause)
*He complained that what you said was not true*. (Dependent Complex Clause)

## 3) Main and Subordinate Clauses

In a complex clause, the clause that takes another clause as its element is the main clause, while the clause that forms part of the main clause is a subordinate clause. According to their functions in the sentences, subordinate clauses can be divided into: **Subject Clause**, **Predicative Clause**, **Object Clause**, **Appositive Clause**, **Complement Clause**, **Attributive Clause**, **Adverbial Clause**, all of which are called **Noun Clause** because they function as noun in the sentence.

*He said that it was not true*. (Main Clause)
*This is the man who wanted to see you*. (Main Clause)
*What you said is not true*. (Subject Clause)
*The fact is that I was not there*. (Predicative Clause)
*Do you know who he is?* (Object Clause)
*There is no doubt that he is honest*. (Appositive Clause)
*Call me what you want*. (Complement Clause)
*One who works hard deserves to succeed*. (Attributive Clause)
*Strike while the iron is hot*. (Adverbial Clause)

## 4) Finite and Non-finite Clauses

A finite clause is one with a finite verb phrase as its predicate verb or predicator; a non-finite clause is a clause with a non-finite verb phrase as its predicator. The above examples are all finite clauses. Below are non-finite

---

subject + predicate
主语 + 谓语
语法结构
independent and dependent clauses
独立分句和从属分句
simple and complex clauses
简单分句和复杂分句
main and subordinate clauses
主句和从句
finite and non-finite clauses
限定分句和非限定分句
verbless clauses
无动词分句
subject clause
主语从句
predicative clause
表语从句
object clause
宾语从句
appositive clause
同位语从句
complement clause
补语从句
attributive clause
定语从句
adverbial clause
状语从句

clauses.

*Lucy went to the hospital **to see her friend**.*
*I have received your letter **dated May** 5.*
***Leaving the room**, he tripped over the mat.*

#### 5) Verbless Clauses

When a clause is marked by the absence of any form of verb element, it is a verbless clause. A verbless clause is just a construction of "Subject + Predicate" without any form of verb element.

***Hungry and exhausted**, the climbers returned.*
***Confident of the justice of their cause**, they agreed to put their case before the arbitration panel.*
***Christmas then only days away**, the family was pent up with excitement.*

So-called Verbless Clause in fact is the clause structure in which subject and predicate verb are omitted. Verbless Clause can also have its own subject as is shown in the last case, which is called **Nominative Absolute Construction** in the traditional grammar.

> nominative absolute construction 独立主格结构

**Task 5**

Discuss: What clauses are they and why?

(1) I signed the paper *to get the license*.
(2) *That hat does not fit*; you may try another.
(3) *If that hat does not fit*, try another.
(4) *Do you study English or French*?
(5) This is *where she was born*.
(6) This is *where she was born*.
(7) *The discussion completed*, the Chairman adjourned the meeting for half an hour.
(8) *One of the most popular tourist sites in Italy*, Pompeii was viewed by nearly two million visitors last year.

## ◆ 1.5   Sentences

The sentence is the highest rank of grammatical unit. Based on one or more than one clause, the sentence is also the basic linguistic unit of connected discourse; it can stand alone and perform a function in social communication. In terms of structure, sentences can be divided into two types: 1) **Complete**

Sentence and 2) **Incomplete Sentence**.

## 1) Complete Sentence

Complete Sentence, or Full Sentence, is a sentence with an expressed subject and predicate. This kind of sentence is mostly used in formal speech and writing. Complete Sentence can be further divided into ① **Simple Sentence** that comprises only one independent clause; ② **Compound Sentence** that comprises two or more than two coordinated independent clauses; ③ **Complex Sentence** that comprises one or more dependent clauses as its element(s); ④ **Compound-complex Sentence** that comprises two or more coordinated independent clauses with at least one complex clause, e. g.

simple sentence
简单句
compound sentence
并列句
complex sentence
复杂句
compound-complex sentence
并列复杂句
elliptical sentence
省略句
amorphous sentence
无定形句

*The boy can stay in the room only for a few minutes.* (Simple Sentence)
*Tom and Mary often help each other and learn from each other.* (Simple Sentence)
*Steve is a teacher **and** his wife is a doctor.* (Compound Sentence)
*The banker is not happy, **though he is rich**.* (Complex Sentence)
*I didn't understand **what he meant**.* (Complex Sentence)
*Sam said he would come; **but** he didn't, **because** his mother was ill.* (Compound-complex Sentence)

## 2) Incomplete Sentence

Incomplete Sentence, or Minor Sentence, is only a sentence fragment which in specific contexts and situations can stand by itself and perform a communicative function. Incomplete Sentence can be further divided into ① **Elliptical Sentence** and ② **Amorphous Sentence**.

### ① Elliptical Sentence

A: *Are you from London?*
B: *Yes, **I am**.*
A: *Where is Mary?*
B: ***In her room**.*

### ② Amorphous Sentences (so-called Ungrammatical Sentence)

*All aboard!*
*Easy come, easy go.*
*So far, so good.*
*How goes it?*
*Why not?*

*Thanks a lot.*

*Goodbye*!

*What*!

*Of course*!

*Nonsense*!

According to their usage, in addition, sentences can be divided into **Declarative Sentence**, **Interrogative Sentence**, **Imperative Sentence** and **Exclamatory Sentence** (see Chapter 5).

**Task 6**  Discuss: What sentences are they and why?

(1) Do you study English or French?
(2) Make up your mind, or you'll miss the chance.
(3) I believe he is honest.
(4) They watched television and enjoyed themselves immensely, but we couldn't see the program because our television was broken.
(5) Beg your pardon.
(6) You hungry?
(7) Sorry!
(8) This way, ladies.
(9) Like father, like son.
(10) Next!

# EXERCISES

Ⅰ. Please add prefix or suffix to each of the following words to form new words.

| 1. desire | 2. own | 3. moral | 4. attack | 5. estimate |
| --- | --- | --- | --- | --- |
| 6. pay | 7. president | 8. conscious | 9. power | 10. practice |
| 11. biography | 12. final | 13. red | 14. angle | 15. courage |
| 16. response | 17. burden | 18. harvest | 19. earth | 20. rely |

Ⅱ. Identify each of the words in the following sentences as (1) noun, (2) pronoun, (3) determiner, (4) adjective, (5) verb, (6) adverb, (7) preposition, (8) conjuction, (9) structure word or (10) interjection.

1. China is a great country.
2. My uncle works in a factory.
3. What is there on the table.
4. Oh, David, come here a moment!
5. It is not easy to learn it well.

6. I have something to tell you.

7. The sun is shining in all his splendid beauty.

8. He does not care whether he gets it or not.

9. Do you really have a good time at the party?

10. If you do that again, you will catch it.

**III. Identify the italicized phrases in the following sentences as (1) noun phrase, (2) finite verb phrase, (3) non-finite verb phrase/infinitive phrase, (4) non-finite verb phrase/-ing participle phrase, (5) non-finite verb phrase/-en participle phrase, (6) adjective phrase, (7) adverb phrase, (8) prepositional phrase.**

1. He is *a liar* ( ). You *can't believe anything he says* ( ).

2. They invited *all their relatives* ( ) to *stay at Christmas* ( ).

3. *A microswitch* ( ) *is a very small electric switch* ( ).

4. John wouldn't *be so careless* ( ) *as to forget his pen* ( ).

5. *Few people there* ( ) *speak English very fluently* ( ).

6. *Here and there* ( ) we *can find small stores* ( ) *specializing in such dairy products* ( ).

7. You're looking *very good* ( ) —*living in the country* ( ) *must suit you* ( ).

8. It is *very important* ( ) *for everyone* ( ) *to come to the meeting* ( ) *on time* ( ).

9. There have been *many great discoveries* ( ) *made by scientists* ( ) *in the 20th century* ( ).

10. Mark *passed the practical exam* ( ) but *the teacher* ( ) failed him *in the written paper* ( ).

**IV. Identify the italicized clauses in the following sentences as (1) subject clause, (2) predicative clause, (3) object clause, (4) appositive clause, (5) complement clause, (6) attributive clause, (7) adverbial clause.**

1. I wonder *what really happened*.

2. Mike is the man *who told me the news*.

3. All the things are difficult *before they are easy*.

4. It is certain *that prices will go up*.

5. I'm very glad *that you have all come*.

6. You may make it *what you like it to be*.

7. That's not *what I mean*.

8. Who is responsible for *what has happened*?

9. I have a feeling *that our team is going to win*.

10. *As you were out*, I left a message.

**V. Identify the sentences as (1) simple sentence, (2) compound sentence, (3) complex sentence, (4) compound-complex sentence, (5) elliptical sentence, (6) amorphous sentence.**

1. The sun is rising in the east.
2. Anyone who will go to the supermarket with me?
3. When speaking English, we should pay attention to our intonation.
4. John painted the door white.
5. Well begun is half done.
6. Paul told me he was an engineer, but he wasn't.
7. What a good idea!
8. When to start?
9. Mr. John and his son once lived and worked in Beijing.
10. I'd like to go with you, however I am very busy now.

# Part One

# The Structure of English Sentences

# 2. Sentence Components

## Aims of the Unit

> In this unit we will discuss some general matters about Sentence Components. We will mainly talk about the following:
> - What main components are there in the sentence?
> - What are their functions respectively in the sentence?
> - What is subject? What can be a subject? What is predicate? How important are subject and predicate in the sentence?
> - What is object? What can be used as an object? What verbs usually take both a direct object and an indirect object?

Those that possess different grammatical functions are called Sentence Components which mainly include the **subject**, the **predicate verb**, the **object**, the **adverbial**, the **complement**, the **attribute**, the **appositive** and the **independent element**. Complete sentences in English are composed of two parts: the subject and the predicate. In most sentences, subject (S for short), predicate verb (V for short), object (O for short), complement (C for short) and adverbial (A for short) are essential, while the rest three are not.

---
subject 主语
predicate verb 谓语动词
object 宾语
adverbial 状语
complement 补语
attribute 定语
appositive 同位语
independent element 独立成分
---

**Activity 1**    Read the following statements about subject, predicate, object. When you have finished, compare your results with your partner. Try to give reasons for your decisions.

| | Agree/Disagree |
|---|---|
| (1) All the sentences must explicitly or implicitly contain the subject and the predicate. | |
| (2) The subject complement is another name for the predicative. | |
| (3) Not all adverbials in a sentence are grammatically obligatory. | |
| (4) Components like the object and the adverbial can be arbitrarily moved within the sentence. | |
| (5) All English sentences begin with the subject. | |
| (6) Theoretically, the subject of an English sentence can be infinitely complex in form. | |
| (7) If the subject of an English sentence is singular, the precidate verb must be singular, too. | |
| (8) All English sentences have an object. | |
| (9) Not all noun phrases following the main verbs are objects. | |
| (10) The position of the object is filled by a nominal expression. | |

## ◇ 2.1    Subject and Predicate

In this section, we'll discuss the relationship between subject and predicate, subject forms and predicate forms.

**Table 1**

| Subject | Predicate |
|---|---|
| (1) All the men | have done their best. |
| (2) Somebody | wants you. |
| (3) Mary's | is the largest house. |
| (4) The English | drink a lot of beer. |
| (5) Smoking cigarettes | causes trouble in the lungs. |
| (6) To read | is easier than to write. |
| (7) Whoever knows him | respects him. |
| (8) It | is raining. |
| (9) It | was known by everyone that he had traveled the world. |
| (10) | Take out the trash! |

From Table 1, we can see that the subject is the topic or theme of sentence, which tells of what the sentence is about. The predicate says something about the subject and bears the new information which the speaker or writer wants to transmit to the listener or reader. The subject is generally realized by a noun phrase or an equivalent of noun phrase, while the construction of the predicate, which is more complicated, generally consists of a verb phrase with or without

## 2. Sentence Components

complementation (such as object, complement, or adverbial). We can see that the subject can be realized by a noun phrase or a pronoun as in (1) and (2), genitive noun as in (3), and nominal adjective as in (4), non-finite verbs as in (5) and (6), a relative clause as in (7), non-referring "it" as in (8) and (9), zero (but implied) subject as in (10) (see Section 5.3). The subject is nominal in the sense that it describes some person, place, action, event, fact, etc. A sentence may not always begin with the subject as in the case in Section 2.5.

At the time, we can see that the predicate must contain a finite verb, which is generally called the predicate verb. And a predicate must not have more than one finite verb, unless they are co-ordinated ones:

*He wrote a letter, (and) sealed it, and took it to the post.*
*He came here but didn't stay long.*

### ◇ 2.2 Object

In this section, we'll discuss the relationship between predicate verb and object, the forms of object, direct object and indirect object.

First of all, when the predicate verb is **transitive** or used as a transitive verb, it must take an object. Compare the two groups of sentences in the following:

| TRANSITIVE | INTRANSITIVE |
|---|---|
| He plays the violin. | He plays very well. |
| He left London. | He left yesterday. |
| He borrows money. | I neither borrow nor lend. |
| He is painting a picture. | She does not paint. |

transitive verb
及物动词
intransitive verb
不及物动词

Then what can be an object? As objects we find in Table 2:

Table 2

| | |
|---|---|
| (1) Noun or noun phrases | Nobody answered *the question.*<br>I want *a return ticket.* |
| (2) Pronoun or pronoun phrases | Did you see *any*?<br>I don't know *anything about it.* |
| (3) Infinitive phrases | I want *to take one.*<br>I was wondering *what to do next.* |
| (4) -ing particle phrases | I hate *lying.*<br>The ballerina enjoys *going to parties.* |
| (5) Noun clauses | He said (*that*) *he was busy.*<br>I don't know *what he said at the meeting.* |
| (6) Complex structures | (6-1) I saw *him go out.*<br>(6-2) I feel *it* my duty *to help them.* |

Table 2 illustrates clearly the forms of object except (6) which really means the complex object of "Object + Object Complement" (see Section 2.3). When the object is an infinitive phrase, an -ing phrase or a clause, the formal object *it* is used and the real object is placed at the back as in (6-2).

Some verbs frequently or even regularly take two objects:

They gave **the boy** *a prize*.

We call **the boy** the **Indirect Object** (Oi for short) and *a prize* the **Direct Object** (Od for short). The direct object is more essential to the verb. We may leave out the indirect object and say "They gave a prize", but we cannot say "They gave the boy" without saying what they gave him.

The commonest verbs that can take both a direct object and an indirect object are *give*, *refuse*, *tell*, *teach*, *cause* and their synonyms.

> direct object
> 直接宾语
> indirect object
> 间接宾语

Give **me** *some*.

I sent **you** *those books* yesterday.

I'll buy **you** *one*.

I'll show **you** *the room*.

He paid **the man** *the money*.

Bring **me** *the book* next time you come.

Pour **me** *a cup of of tea*, will you?

He cannot refuse **you** *this little favour*.

The delay caused **us** *a great deal of trouble*.

Tell **me** *one of your stories*.

I shall write **him** *a letter*.

As is seen from these examples, the indirect object generally precedes the direct object and the indirect object nearly always denotes a person and is generally a personal pronoun. If the direct object is also a personal pronoun (*it* or *them*), it is placed immediately after the verb and the indirect object is generally introduced by *to* (or *for*):

Give **it** *to me*.

I sent **them** *to you* yesterday.

I'll buy **it** *for you*.

I'll get **them** *for you*.

Some speakers occasionally say:

Give **it** *me*.

Give **it** *them* back.

## 2.3 Complements

The complement is of two kinds: the subject complement (Cs for short) and the object complement (Co for short).

### 1) Subject Complement

There are two situations in the subject complement. In the first situation, the subject complement characterizes the referent of the subject as in ①, answering the question "What is/was X like?" or "How did X change/How has X changed?" **The linking/copular verbs** are: *be*; *seem* (*to be*), *appear* (*to be*), *look*, *prove* (*to be*); *become*, *get*, *grow*, *keep*, *remain*, *fall*, *turn*. The subject complement is an adjective phrase or indefinite noun phrase or adjective-equivalents. In the second situation, the subject complement identifies the subject referent as in ②, answering the question "Which one is/was X?" The **copular verb** is invariably *be*. The subject complement is a definite noun phrase. The two situations of the subject complement in traditional grammars were generally termed the **predicative**.

subject complement
主语补语
predicative
表语
linking/copular verbs
连系/系动词

① I've **been** a skinhead for eight years. Now I **am** a Klansman and a politician.
He'**s** American.
I had intended to **become** an Anglican priest but I saw more dark than light.
He **remained** anxious about the surgery and its outcome but felt that he understood what was happening to him.
② My headmistress **was** the president of the Shakespeare League.
The only reliable source of work **is** the water industry.
Meredith **is** the leader in providing multimedia packages.
Delaware Park **is** the city's showpiece.

There are two more notes about subject complement: ③ shows us Cs in passive constructions further explains what the subject is like or what happens to the subject; ④ illustrates that quite a number of verbs do not take a complement as a rule but take one occasionally.

③ Dan was made **secretary**. (We made Dan **secretary**.)
The mountain climber was found **badly injured**. (I found the mountain climber **badly injured**.)

Cathy is often heard *to sing upstairs*. (We often hear Cathy *sing upstairs*.)

Clearly, the above subject complements become object complements in the bracket sentences.

④ The natives go **naked** all the year round.

I'll go **mad** if you don't stop that noise.

I wish you had stood **firm**.

She turned **pale** at the name.

He fell **silent**.

We parted **the best of friends**.

I left home **young** and returned **old**.

**Task 1** Discuss in groups and decide what can be subject complement.

(1) It is *a cat*.
He became *the headmaster of the school*.
(2) That is *something you ought to know*.
It is *mine*, not *yours*.
(3) My plan is *to have a look at the place first*.
But that's *cheating*.
(4) He is no longer *what he used to be*.
That's *where you are mistaken*.
(5) You look *busy*.
Isn't it *amusing*?
(6) Sorry, I can't get *away*.
When will he be *back*?
(7) That letter is *from my brother*.
The show is *at the end*.

## 2) Object Complement

object complement
宾语补语
nominal-adjectival
complement
名词性-形容词
性宾语补足语
verbal complement
动词性宾语补
足语

By the **Object Complement** we mean that part of the sentence which stands in the same relation to the object as the predicate stands to the subject. Compare:

| PREDICATE | OBJECT COMPLEMENT |
| --- | --- |
| He was the captain. | We elected him captain. |
| He was angry. | You made him angry. |
| He laughed. | We heard him laugh. |

As there are two types of predicates, in one of which the most important word is a verb while in the other it is a noun or an adjective, we have accordingly two types of object complements, ① a **nominal-adjectival** one and ② a **verbal** one.

## 2. Sentence Components

① *They made him* **chairman**.

*We think this* **a great shame**.

*I found the room* **empty**.

*Make yourself* **comfortable**.

*Send him* **away**.

*They just put him* **out of the way**.

*She only wished the dinner* **at an end**.

② *I saw him* **enter the house**.

*I can't have* (=let) *you* **do all that**.

*Ask him* **to call on me some time next week**.

*They believe him* **to be innocent**.

*It's great fun to watch people* **coming and going**.

*Take care to keep the clock* **going**.

*He saw his face* **reflected in the water**.

*I must have my luggage* **sent to the station**.

Prepositional objects may also be followed by verbal complements:

*I hope I could count* **upon** *you* **not to interfere**.

*He was anxious* **for** *his sister* **to get married**.

*He wonders* **at** *me* **doing that**.

*They will be laughing* **at** *you and me* **falling out**.

**Task 2**     Discuss in groups and complete the following sentences with object complement.

> (1) We used to call it _____. (noun)
> (2) Don't you think it _____? (adj.)
> (3) Do you want your tea _____? (adj.)
> (4) What makes the picture so _____? (adj.)
> (5) I found the book _____. (adj.)
> (6) I found the book _____. (prep. phr.)
> (7) He kept the windows _____. (adj.)
> (8) He left the letter _____. (prep. phr.)

## 2.4　Attribute

**Activity 2**　Discuss in pairs and decide what can be the attribute.

(1) *a* book　　*the* office　　*your* sister　　*that* house
(2) a *good* book　　a *great* country　　a *very fine* day
　　a *long and tedious* story
(3) a *flower* garden　　a *wood* cottage　　the *physics* teacher
　　a *10-day* leave
(4) *two* miles　　the *second* lesson　　*one or two* days
　　the *first and second* lines
(5) Cathy has no one *to help her*.　　I have many books *to read*.
(6) a *swimming* pool　　the *reading* room
　　There is someone *knocking at the door*.
(7) a *broken* glass　　a *retired* worker
　　We bought a TV set *imported from Japan*.
(8) a cow *in milk*　　his days *in school*
　　travel *in China*　　a teacher *of English*
(9) a village *nearby*　　a *stay forward*
　　the *up/down* train　　the *upstairs* room
(10) Do you know the man *who is speaking*?
　　It's a good film *you should not miss*.

restrictive and non-restrictive attribute
限定性和非限定性定语
pre-attribute and post-attribute
前置和后置定语
determinative, descriptive, and classifying attribute
限定性定语、描绘性定语和分类性定语

The attribute is the component which modifies and restricts a noun phrase or a noun-equivalent. In terms of its relation with the noun or pronoun, the attribute can be divided into ① **restrictive attribute** and **non-restrictive attribute**. According to its position in a noun phrase, the attribute may be classified into ② **pre-attribute** and **post-attribute**. In semantics, there may be ③ **determinative**, **descriptive**, and **classifying attribute**.

### 1) Restrictive and Non-restrictive Attribute

Generally speaking, a restrictive attribute is concerned with the inherent qualities of the noun phrase. Its absence often results in defectiveness in the structure of the noun phrase. A non-restrictive attribute, however, only adds some explanation, without which the noun phrase still refers to the same person or thing.

*his* two young sisters (restrictive)
his *two young* sisters (non-restrictive)

*a well-known* **Catholic** *priest* (restrictive)

*a* **well-known** *Catholic priest* (non-restrictive)

*The great fire* ***of 1666*** *started in* ***the*** *house* ***of a baker***. (restrictive)

*The* ***great*** *fire of 1666 started in the house of a baker.* (non-restrictive)

## 2) Pre-attribute and Post-attribute

A pre-attribute occurs before the noun it modifies, while a post-attribute appears after the noun it modifies.

***a yellow sports*** *shirt* (pre-attribute)

***the dirty old brown*** *coat* (pre-attribute)

*The visitor is a man* ***in his thirties***. (post-attribute)

*I have something* ***important to tell you***. (post-attribute)

A pre-attribute usually has a permanent feature or attribute while post-attribute illustrates a temporary feature or action. Please compare:

   a. *This is a* ***singing*** *bird* (= *a bird that can sing*).

      *The girl* ***singing*** (= *who is singing*) *is his sister.*

   b. *This is a* ***used*** (= *second-hand*) *car.*

      *This car* ***used*** (= *which is being used*) *is mine.*

## 3) Determinative, Descriptive, and Classifying Attribute

A determinative attribute restricts the person or the thing that the modified noun refers to.

*a* ***large*** *vegetable garden*

***some*** *young college students*

***the first two*** *chapters*

A descriptive attribute describes the quality or feature of the modified noun.

*a* ***large*** *vegetable garden*

*some* ***young*** *college students*

*The mountain,* ***whose peak was barely discernible***, *was an impressive sight.*

A classifying attribute illustrates the categories of the modified noun or pronoun.

*a large* ***vegetable*** *garden*

*some young* ***college*** *students*

*David resists anyone* ***who tries to help him.***

## 2.5 Adverbial

In terms of their functions, adverbials fall into four categories: 1) **descriptive adverbial**, 2) **complementary adverbial**, 3) **conjunctive adverbial** and 4) **commentary adverbial**. Strictly speaking, it is only **complementary adverbial** that can be rightly labelled an adverbial, which is treated as one of the five essential elements of a sentence.

### 1) Descriptive Adverbial

A descriptive adverbial (or adjunct) modifies the verb, the adjective, the adverb, the sentence, etc. Descriptive adverbials are normally realized by adverb phrases, prepositional phrases, nouns, as well as by finite, non-finite and verbless clauses. Semantically, descriptive adverbials may denote time, place, manner, purpose, cause, result, condition, concession, and accompanying circumstances, e.g.

> The headmaster walked *up and down* in his office.
> I'll come back *in a few days*.
> The wall is *13 feet* high.
> *To look at him*, you could hardly help laughing.
> *Aroused by the crash*, he leapt to his feet.
> Stay *where you are*.

Descriptive adverbials can often be cancelled without affecting the meaning, e.g.

> Susan works (*very*) hard.
> You are (*quite*) right.
> Miss Liu speaks English (*fluently*).

### 2) Complementary Adverbial

A complementary adverbial or an obligatory adverbial, an essential element of the verb phrase, complements the meaning of the verb phrase, e.g.

> Larry sat *at his desk*.

---

descriptive adverbial
修饰性状语
complementary adverbial
补足性状语
conjunctive adverbial
连接性状语
commentary adverbial
评注性状语

*Perry treated his wife **vilely**.*

*The secretary showed me **into the office**.*

*She placed the baby **on a blanket in the living room**.*

*Put a note **on my door**.*

The adverbial in the SVA, SVOA patterns (see Section 4.1) most typically expresses location. Unlike adverbials in general, it cannot normally be moved.

### 3) Conjunctive Adverbial

Conjunctive adverbials (or conjuncts) differ from descriptive adverbials in that they do not modify anything but function as connectives between phrases, clauses or sentences, such as *first(ly)*, *second(ly)*, …; *for one thing … for another (thing)*; *namely, for example*; *consequently, therefore, so*; *equally, likewise, then, rather, instead, on the contrary*; *anyhow, nevertheless, after all*; *meanwhile, in the meantime*; *by the way, (all) in all, in short, to sum up*. Please compare:

*This dress is **too** small for me.* (descriptive adverbial)

*Jonathan is going. I'm going **too**.* (conjunctive adverbial)

*Zoe hasn't done much **yet**.* (descriptive adverbial)

*Ted worked hard, **yet** he failed.* (conjunctive adverbial)

A conjunctive adverbial differs from a coordinator in that it sometimes be **preceded by a coordinator**, e.g.

*This car is smaller **and therefore** cheaper.*

It also differs from a subordinator because what is introduced by a conjunctive adverbial is not a subordinate clause. Compare:

***Though** they knew the war was lost, they continued fighting.*

*They knew the war was lost. They continued fighting, **though**.*

> preceded by a coordinator
> 并列连词前置

### 4) Commentary Adverbial

A commentary adverbial (or disjunct) does not modify the predicate verb but expresses an evaluation or comment on what is being said. Commentary adverbials, often positioning at the beginning of the sentence and detached from the clause structure with a comma, are mostly realized by adverb phrases, e.g.

*I don't think he will come **personally**.* (descriptive adverbial)

***Personally**, I don't think he will come.* (commentary adverbial)

*Alan began to talk **seriously** to her.* (descriptive adverbial)

***Seriously**, you ought to take more care of yourself.* (commentary adverbial)

The adverbs that are commonly used as commentary adverbials include:

| admittedly | naturally | surprisingly |
| certainly | officially | perhaps |
| educationally | possibly | luckly |
| practically | frankly | unfortunately |
| probably | really | surely |

Commentary adverbials can also be realized by prepositional phrases, non-finite clauses, verbless clauses, and occasionally by finite clauses such as *what's more important*, etc. (see more details in Section 12.4)

## ◆ 2.6  Appositive

The appositive is a special element in the sentence, which further explains, modifies and describes its antecedent. In this section we'll discuss the forms of appositives and the indicators of appositives.

### 1) Forms of Appositives

An appositive to a noun phrase may be another noun phrase, and it may also be a reflexive pronoun, an indefinite pronoun, a demonstrative pronoun, a non-finite clause or a nominal clause, e.g.

*Your brother, **a proud and unbending man**, refused all help that was offered him.*

*My father will go and see it **himself**.*

*My friends **all** understand me.*

*Air, food, water and heat—**these** are four requirements of all living things.*

*She likes her job, **teaching English**.*

*The question **who should preside over the meeting** has not been settled.*

### 2) Indicators of Appositives

Appositives are sometimes introduced by indicators which help to express different semantic relationships between the items in apposition. Some indicators denote "equation", including *namely* (*viz*), *that is* (*i.e.*), *that is to say*, *in other words*, *or*, *for short*, etc.

## 2. Sentence Components

*A pronoun is a pronoun*, **i.e.** *a form used to refer to a person or a thing.*

*He studies linguistics*, **or** *the science of language.*

*He is a culter*—**that is to say**, *a man who sells knives and sharp tools.*

Other indicators denote "exemplification", including *for example*, *for instance*, *such as*, *say*, *including*, etc.

*Some animals,* **for example** *the fox and squirrel, have their bushy tails.*

*Besides English he knows other foreign languages,* **such as** *French and German.*

*Any dictionary,* **say** *Hornby's Advanced Learner's Dictionary, will serve my purpose for the time being.*

Still others denote "focalization": *especially*, *particularly*, *chiefly*, *mostly*, etc.

*Most students in our class,* **particularly** *David and Chris, are fond of music.*

*I want very much to read these new novels,* **especially** *the one you mentioned.*

Sometimes the preposition *of* can be used to introduce an apposition, for example, *the city* **of** *London, the month* **of** *May.*

**Task 3**   Discuss in groups and decide what can carry appositives besides noun or noun phrases.

(1) **They** are **both** in trouble now.
(2) Jane is **homely**, that is to say, **plain**.
(3) **When** shall we leave, **today or tomorrow**?
(4) He always wrote **so**—**childishly but legibly**.
(5) They **summoned help**—**called the police and the fire brigade**.
(6) **Playing football, his only interest in life,** has brought him many friends.
(7) **The leaves are falling from the trees, an indication that the summer is over.**

## 2.7 Independent Element

**Activity 2**  Discuss in pairs to see the difference between A and B in each pair.

(1) A: Everybody, stand up!
    B: Everybody stands up.
(2) A: This, I think, is the best one.
    B: I think this is the best one.

> vocative 呼语
> parenthesis 插入语

The Independent Element is the element which is not related grammatically but semantically to the other elements, and can only exist in the sentence context. There are three kinds of independent elements: **vocative**, **interjection**, **parenthesis**.

### 1) Vocative

Vocative is used to address the other or to call his/her attention. Vocative is usually a noun or a nominal phrase and put at the beginning, in the middle or at the end of a sentence.

*John*, let's go.

Oh, *John*, please don't.

May I ask you a question, *Mr. Blake*?

### 2) Interjection

An interjection is a word or phrase that expresses a strong feeling. It can be put at the beginning, in the middle or at the end of a sentence.

*Wow*! That is lovely.

His father, *alas*, is no better today.

You are joking, *eh*?

### 3) Parenthesis

A parenthesis is a word or a clause that is inserted in a sentence to express the speaker's attitude or explanation, which can be put at the beginning, in the middle or at the end of a sentence.

*Honestly*, that's all the money I have.

*To speak frankly*, I don't like the idea.

They are, **in my opinion**, very wise.

You're not complaining, **I hope**.

# EXERCISES

**I. Complete the following sentences.**

1. He seems to be _____. (noun)
2. He seems to be _____. (adj.)
3. He seems to _____. (inf.)
4. Shall we let him go _____? (adj.)
5. The house proved to be _____. (adj.)
6. Shall I ask her to _____? (inf.)
7. You mustn't let him _____. (inf.)
8. He does not allow anybody to _____. (inf.)
9. What made you _____? (inf.)
10. The pilot had to keep the plane _____. (part.)
11. I must have the letter _____ before six. (part.)
12. I have to have my teeth _____. (part.)

**II. Correct the mistakes in the following sentences.**

1. Dick admired Tom great.
2. She was born in 1950 in Chongqing.
3. I don't understand you simple.
4. Quickly he didn't answer the question.
5. They watch television hardly ever.
6. These days I eat desserts rarely.
7. We have lectures every day all the morning this week.
8. Denny left cowardly, sneaking out the back way.
9. Tim went to the hospital alone to see his friend yesterday afternoon.
10. Lucy lives in USA, Pennsylvania, at 125 Bower Hill Road, Mt Lebanon.

**III. Complete the following sentences with descriptive adverbials in brackets inserted in the right place.**

1. I go (in summer, usually, to Paris).
2. We meet (on Sunday afternoon, in the park, always).
3. I saw John (about an hour ago, just, in the office).
4. I have a cup of tea (in bed, always, before I get up).

5. I get up (on Sunday, seldom, early).

6. He plays (in an important game, always, well).

7. We eat (usually, when we go to the theatre, out).

8. He spoke (last night, at the debate, every well).

9. He arrived (at eight o'clock, at the meeting, punctually).

10. We are going to meet (tomorrow, at John's house, at nine o'clock).

## IV. Supply a suitable conjunctive adverbial in each blank to connect the sentence concerned.

1. I don't want to buy the house. The price is too high. And _____ the house isn't in a suitable position.

2. He is being a fool. _____, he is behaving foolishly.

3. This food is very good and it's probably something that people wouldn't get at home. _____, it's not difficult to cook and it's quick to prepare.

4. You say you took the book without his permission. _____, you stole it.

5. He says he wants to marry Susan. _____, he shouldn't be quarrelling with her all the time.

6. The term papers were very brief. _____, they were better than I expected.

7. He has been in office only a few months. He has, _____, achieved more than any of his predecessors.

8. Officially, he is in charge. _____, his secretary does all the work.

9. They don't often use their car over the weekend. _____, you can borrow it if you want to.

10. The news may be unexpected. _____, it is true.

## V. Rewrite the following sentences, using proper commentary adverbials.

1. It is natural that I will have to answer her letter.

2. I will say frankly that I was rather impressed by his manner.

3. It is clear that there has been a mistake.

4. It is sure enough that a solution will be worked out to the satisfaction of all the parties concerned.

5. It is odd enough that he did not raise any objection to the plan.

6. It is even more important that we ought to put this on the agenda.

7. I am sure to have met him before.

8. It is hoped that the two sides may come to an agreement on this issue.
9. It is quite obvious that he does not want to go with us.
10. It is lucky that someone managed to find me.

# 3. Subject-verb Concord

## Aims of the Unit

> In this unit we will discuss some general matters about subject-verb concord. We will mainly talk about the following:
> - What does subject-verb concord mean?
> - What principles are there guiding subject-verb concord?
> - Are all the subject nouns ending in-s treated as plural?
> - How do you understand collective nouns? How do you deal with concord with collective nouns as subject?
> - Is coordination by "and" or "both ... and" usually treated as plural?
> - What are the problems of concord with the expressions of quantity as subject?

**Task 1**    Discuss in pairs and then fill in the blank in each sentence.

(1) Many a man _____ (have, has) done his duty.
(2) The *New York Times* _____ (is, are) published daily.
(3) This pair of trousers _____ (costs, cost) fifty dollars.
(4) Every girl _____ (come, comes) on time.
(5) Either my father or my brothers _____ (is, are) coming.
(6) There _____ (is, are) a pen, two pencils on the table.

## ◇ 3.1 Person and Number Forms

The predicate verb, if in the **indicative mood** (present tense), must agree with its subject in person and number. Except in the case of *be*, all the verbs use original verb forms to indicate the present tense only different in using the -s form for the third person singular and -ed to indicate past tense.

I/We/You/They **like** the picture very much. He/She **likes** the picture very much.

---
person 人称
number 数
indicative mood
陈述语气

# 3. Subject-verb Concord

*I/We/You/They/He/She **liked** the picture very much.*

The verb *be* has different forms for the three persons either in indicating present tense or past tense.

**Table 1**

| Tense \ Person \ Number | Singular | | | Plural | | |
|---|---|---|---|---|---|---|
| | First | Second | Third | First | Second | Third |
| Present | am | are | is | are | | |
| Past | was | were | was | were | | |

However, modal auxiliary has no change in person or number.

## ❖ 3.2   Three Guiding Principles

By subject-verb concord is meant agreement between subject and predicate verb in number. There are three principles guiding subject-verb concord: **grammatical concord**, **notional concord** and **proximity**.

### 1) Grammatical Concord

The principle of grammatical concord refers to the rule that the verb must match its subject in number. If the subject is plural, the verb should take the plural form; if, on the other hand, the subject is singular or is a mass noun, the verb should take the singular form, e.g.

*Both boys **have** their own merits.*   *Each girl **comes** on time.*
*Much effort **is** wasted.*   *More than one school **has** closed.*
*Many a ship **has** been wrecked on the rock.*

Difficulties arise when this principle comes into conflict with the other two principles: principles of notional concord and principle of proximity.

### 2) Notional Concord

The principle of notional concord refers to the rule that the verb can sometimes agree with the subject according to the notion rather than to the actual presence of the grammatical marker for that notion, e.g.

*Fifteen miles **seems** like a long walk to me.*
*Fifty-six dollars **was** stolen from the cash register.*
*My family **are** all early risers.* (*cp. My family **is** a large one.*)

---

grammatical marker
语法标记
grammatical concord
语法一致
notional concord
意义一致
principle of proximity
就近原则：谓语动词的单复数形式决定于最靠近它的词语（名词短语中心词）的单复数形式，这种一致关系所依据的原则叫作"就近原则"。

Our class *are* going to the cinema. ( cp. Our class *is* an advanced collective.)

### 3) Proximity

The principle of proximity denotes agreement of the verb with a closely preceding noun phrase in preference to agreement with the head of the noun phrase that functions as subject, e. g.

*No one except his own supporters **agree** with him.*
*Neither Julia nor I **am** going.*
*Either your eyesight or your brakes **are** at fault.*
*Either your brakes or your eyesight **is** at fault.*

Note that grammatical concord is the basic principle, but when the subject is realized by a collective noun, a coordinate form or an expression of quantity, the other two principles will have to be considered.

## ◆ 3.3  Concord with Nouns Ending in -s

**Task 2**  Discuss in pairs and then fill in the blank in each sentence.

(1) He suffers from diabetes, which _____ (is, are) a kind of chronic disease.
(2) What _____ (is, are) his politics?
(3) Politics _____ (is, are) the art or science of government.
(4) The United Nations _____ (was, were) formed in San Francisco in 1945.
(5) _____ (Has, Have) skittles been a popular game in England?
(6) The remains of Shakespeare _____ (is, are) buried on Stratford-on-Avon.
(7) Mumps _____ (is, are) a kind of infectious disease.
(8) The Himalayas _____ (has, have) a magnificent variety of plant and animal life.

There are quite a few nouns that end in -s but which are not countable. Some of these nouns are treated as singular, some as plural, and some either as singular or as plural. All this can be dealt with under the following headings.

### 1) Disease and Game Names Ending in -s

Names of diseases ending in -s ( such as *arthritis*, *bronchitis*, *rickets*, *mumps*, *diabetes*, etc.) are mostly treated as singular, but there are a few such names ( as *measles* and *rickets*) which can be used either as singular or as plural. Game names ending in -s are generally used as singular with the

---

arthritis 关节炎
bronchitis 支气管炎
rickets 软骨病
mumps 腮腺炎
diabetes 糖尿病
measles 麻疹
cards 纸牌

exception of *card* which is usually treated as plural, e. g.

> *Arthritis* **is** *a disease causing pain and swelling in the joints of the body.*
>
> *Measles* **is/are** *contagious.*
>
> *Rickets* **is/are** *caused by malnutrition.*
>
> *Cards* **are** *not allowed here.*

### 2) Subject Names Ending in -ics

Names of subjects ending in -ics (such as *physics*, *mathematics*, *mechanics*, *acoustics*, *politics*, *statistics*, *economics*, *linguistics*, etc.) are generally singular nouns, but some such nouns are treated as plural when used in other senses than subject names. Compare:

> *Acoustics* **is** *the science of sound.*
>
> *The acoustics in the new concert hall* **are** *faultless.*
>
> *Economics* **is** *a required course for all the students.*
>
> *The economics of the project* **are** *still being considered.*
>
> *Mathematics* **is** *the study of numbers.*
>
> *My mathematics* **is/are** *rather shaky.*

physics 物理学
mathematics 数学
mechanics 机械学
acoustics 声学
politics 政治学
statistics 统计学
economics 经济学
linguistics 语言学

### 3) Geographical Names Ending in -s

Geographical names such as the names of archipelagos, mountain ranges, straits and falls are generally used as plural, except for a few treated as singular when used as country names, e. g.

> *The West Indies, apart from the Bahamas,* **are** *commonly divided into two parts.*
>
> *The Straits of Gibraltar* **have** *not lost their strategic importance.*
>
> *The Niagara Falls* **are** *perhaps the most famous waterfall in the world.*

archipelagos 群岛
mountain ranges 山脉
straits 海峡
falls 瀑布
The West Indies 西印度群岛
the Bahamas 巴哈马群岛
The Straits of Gibraltar 直布罗陀海峡
The Niagara Falls 尼亚加拉大瀑布

### 4) Other Nouns Ending in -s

Names for things made of two parts such as *scissors*, *pincers*, *glasses*, *shorts*, *trousers*, *jeans*, *pajamas/pyjamas*, etc. are usually used as plural. But when they are preceded by such unit noun as *a pair of* and *two pairs of*, the number form of the following verb is generally determined by the number marker of the unit noun.

> *Where* **are** *my trousers?*
>
> *How much* **are** *these pajamas?*
>
> *One pair of scissors* **is** *not enough.*

scissors 剪子
pincers 钳子
glasses 眼镜
shorts 短裤
trousers 裤子
jeans 牛仔裤
pajamas/pyjamas 睡衣

*Two pairs of pincers, one large and one small, **are** missing from my tool box.*

Nouns usually taking plural ending such as *archives, arms, contents, eaves, fireworks, goods, minutes, remains, stairs, suburbs, thanks, wages,* etc. are generally used as plural with exception of *whereabouts, dramatics,* etc. which may be treated either as plural or as singular.

*The archives of this society **are** kept in the basement.*

*The contents of this book **are** most fascinating.*

*High wages often **result** in high prices.*

*His thanks **were** most profuse.*

*His whereabouts **were/was** known only to his personal staff.*

*The dramatics of the performance **were/was** marve.*

Nouns ending in -ings such as *clippings, diggings, earnings, surroundings, sweepings,* etc. are generally used as plural with the exception of *tidings* which can be used both ways.

*The clippings of the hedges **are** usually burnt.*

*Her earnings **are** higher this year.*

*The surroundings **are** not good for the child.*

*Sad tidings **have/has** come at last.*

There are also nouns such as *barracks, headquarters, means, series, species, works,* etc. whose singular and plural number shares the same form. These nouns are treated as plural when used in the plural sense, or vice versa.

*A headquarters **was** set up to direct the operation.*

*Their headquarters **are** in Paris.*

*The only means to achieve success **is** to appeal to arms.*

*All means **have** been tried out to increase agricultural production.*

*A series of pre-recorded tapes **has** been prepared for language lab use.*

*There **are** two series of readers: one for beginners and one for advanced students.*

---

archives 档案
eaves 屋檐
fireworks 烟火
minutes 记录
remains 遗体
suburbs 郊区
whereabouts 行踪
dramatics 舞台艺术
clippings 剪下来的东西
diggings 掘出的东西
earnings 收入
surroundings 环境
sweepings 扫拢的垃圾

barracks 营房
headquarters 总部
means 方法,手段
series 系列
species 种类
works 工厂

## 3.4 Concord with Collective Nouns as Subject

**Task 3** Discuss in pairs and then fill in the blank in each sentence.

(1) Domestic cattle _____ (provide, provides) us with milk, beef and hides.
(2) His poetry _____ (is, are) of a very high order.
(3) The football team _____ (is, are) being organized.
(4) The football team _____ (is, are) having baths and _____ (is, are) then coming back here for tea.

When a collective noun is used as subject of the sentence, the choice between grammatical and notional concord is mostly dictated by usage. There are three situations in subject-verb concord.

### 1) Collective Nouns Usually Used as Plural

Collective nouns are singular in form but plural in meaning. The principle of notional concord is always applied. These collective nouns include *people*, *folk*, *police*, *cattle*, *militia*, *poultry*, *vermin*, etc.

The Chinese people **are** a great people.
Such vermin as bugs and rats **are** hard to get rid of.
The police **have** caught him.

> collective nouns 集体名词
> militia 民兵
> poultry 家禽
> vermin 害虫
> foliage 叶子
> merchandise 商品
> stationery 文具
> crew 全体船员或机组人员
> flock 群,羊群
> jury 陪审团

### 2) Collective Nouns Usually Used as Singular

The principle of grammatical concord is always applied. These include *foliage*, *machinery*, *equipment*, *furniture*, *merchandise*, *poetry*, *stationery*, etc.

The foliage of the tree **is** very beautiful.
The merchandise **has** arrived undamaged.
How much machinery **has** been installed.

### 3) Collective Nouns Used Either as Plural or as Singular

There are collective nouns that can be used either as plural or as singular, such as *audience*, *band*, *board*, *class*, *committee*, *company*, *crew*, *crown*, *enemy*, *family*, *flock*, *government*, *group*, *jury*, *party*, *public*, *staff*, *team*, *youth*, etc. The choice of the verb form following such norms depends on the exact meaning of the noun in a specific context. When the noun is used in the sense of a collective as a whole, the verb takes the singular form. If, on the other hand, the noun is used in the sense of the individuals that make the collective, the verb takes the plural form.

The anti-crime committee **is** to make its report tomorrow.

The committee **are** divided in opinion about this problem.

That group of soldiers **is** a top-notch fighting unit.

That group of soldiers **have** the best ratings of individual performance.

The audience **was** enormous.

The audience **were** enjoying every minute of it.

Note that all these nouns behave like ordinary countable nouns, i.e. the verb takes the plural form when such nouns as subject are plural.

The audiences **were** enormous.

Specifically the committees **have** the following functions.

Two companies of travelers **are** expected to arrive soon.

## ◈ 3.5  Concord with Coordinate Subject

| Task 4 | Discuss in pairs and then fill in the blank in each sentence.

(1) War and peace _____ (is, are) a constant theme in history.
(2) War and peace _____ (is, are) alternatives between which men must constantly choose.
(3) Law and order _____ (means, mean) different things to people with different political opinions.
(4) Fish and chips _____ (is, are) getting very expensive.
(5) The vessel, with its entire crew and cargo, _____ (was, were) lost.
(6) Every flower and every bush _____ (is, are) to be cut down.
(7) Not only one, but all, of us _____ (is, are) hoping to be there.

In the case of a coordinate subject, the principle of notional concord is applied. In detail, the following rules are to be observed.

### 1) Coordination with *and* or *both ... and*

Coordination by *and* or *both ... and* is usually treated as plural when it refers to two or more than two persons/things, but it is treated as singular when it refers to only one person or thing. Compare:

Tom and Mary **are** playing together.

*Tom and Mary at the same bridge table **is** unthinkable.*

*Whisky and soda **are** kept in different places.*

*Whisky and soda (whisky mixed with soda) **is** my favorite drink.*

*The 10th and last chapter **is** well written.*

*The 10th and the last chapter **are** well written.*

*Indian (tea) and Chinese tea **smell** totally different.*

Coordination by *both ... and* is usually treated as plural because it always refers to two persons/things, so the verb takes the plural form.

*Both brother and sister **are** in the army.*

*Both her calmness and her confidence **are** astonishing.*

When such determiners as *each*, *every*, *no*, *many a*, etc. occur in front of the coordination, the following verb takes the singular form.

*Each boy and each girl in this class **studies** very hard.*

*No bus and no taxi **is** available here at small hours.*

*Many a man and women in this community **finds** himself or herself in need.*

## 2) Coordination with *or/either ... or*, *nor/neither ... nor*, *not only ... but also*

Here the problem of concord is generally dealt with according to the principle of proximity. But in informal style, items coordinated by *neither ... nor*, *not only ... but also* can sometimes be regarded as plural, e.g.

*My sister or my brother **is** likely to be at home.*

*Either my father or my brothers **are** coming.*

*Neither the players nor the coach **was**/(**were**) overconfident.*

*Not only the switches but also the old wiring **has**/(**have**) been changed.*

## 3) Subject + *as much as*, etc.

When such subordinate structures as *as much as*, *rather than*, *more than*, *no less than*, etc. occur behind the subject, the following verb form depends on the meaning of the subject, either singular or plural, e.g.

***Some of the workers** as much as the manager **were** responsible for the loss.*

***His brother** rather than his parents **is** to blame.*

***My wife**, more than anyone else in the family, **is** anxious to go there again.*

***Man**, no less than the lower forms of life, **is** the product of the evolutionary process.*

## 4) Subject + *as well as*, etc.

When such phrases as *as well as, in addition to, with, together with, except*, etc. occur behind the subject, the following verb form depends on the form of the subject itself, e.g.

*The manager* with someworkers *was* working during the holidays.
*The father*, as well as his sons, *is* going to enroll.
*The truck* along with all its contents *was* destroyed.
*The barn*, in addition to the house, *was* burned.
*No one* except two girls *was* late for dinner.

Note that in informal style, the above examples can be treated according to the principle of notional concord or proximity, e.g.

*Alice as well as Jane were there.*
*The captain together with half a dozen sailors were taken prinsoners.*

## ◆ 3.6 Concord with Expressions of Quantity as Subject

**Task 5** Discuss in pairs and then fill in the blank in each sentence.

(1) Only 25 per cent of the capital _____ (is, are) American-owned.
(2) Two more dollars _____ (is, are) missing from the till this morning.
(3) Nearly 50% of the doctors _____ (is, are) women.
(4) All of the fruit _____ (looks, look) ripe.
(5) All _____ (is, are) eager to leave now.
(6) More than one student _____ (has, have) failed the exam.
(7) A majority of the town's younger men _____ (is, are) moving to the city.
(8) A majority of three votes to one _____ (was, were) recorded.

Quantitative expressions fall into two categories: definite (such as three months, five kilos, six quarts, etc.) and indefinite (such as all of..., some of..., none of..., enough of..., etc.).

### 1) Concord with Expression of Definite Quantity as Subject

> expression of definite quantity as subject
> 确定数量的名词词组作主语

When a definite quantity is regarded as a single unit, the verb takes the singular form and when used in the sense of the individuals that constitute the quantity, the verb takes the plural form. Compare:

He thought that 65 dollars **was** not too much to ask.

There **were** 6 silver dollars in each of the stockings.

If the subject is "a fraction/percentage + of-phrase", the form of the verb is determined by the noun in the of-phrase. A plural noun in the of-phrase requires a plural verb; a singular or a mass noun in the of-phrase is to be followed by a singular verb, e. g.

Over 60% of the city **was** destroyed in the war.

Two-thirds of the swampland **has** been reclaimed for farming.

Nearly 50% of the doctors **are** women.

If the subject is an expression of "A plus/and B" or "A multiplied by B", the verb can either take the singular or the plural form. If, on the other hand, the subject is one of "A minus B" or "A divided by B", the verb can only be singular, e. g.

Seven plus/and five (7 +5) **makes/make** twelve.

Forty minus fifteen (40 −50) **leaves** twenty-five.

Five times eight (5 ×8) **is/are** 40.

Forty divided by eight (40 ÷8) **is** five.

If the subject is a noun phrase composed of "one in/out of + plus noun", the verb takes the singular form in formal style, but in informal style it can be plural, following the principle of proximity, e. g.

One in ten students **has/have** failed the exam.

One out of twenty **was/were** badly damaged.

## 2) Concord with Expression of Indefinite Quantity as Subject

When the subject is a noun phrase composed of *all of …, some of …, none of …, half of …, most of …,* etc., the number of the verb is determined by the noun in the of-phrase. This is also true of *lots of, heaps of, loads of, scads of, plenty of* +noun, e. g.

expression of indefinite quantity as subject
非确定数量的名词词组作主语

All of the cargo **was** lost.

All of the crew **were** saved.

Lots of food **is** going to waste.

Lots of people **are** waiting outside.

There **are** lots/heaps/loads/scads of apples on scale.

There **is** lots/heaps/loads/scads of equipment lying about.

When the subject is a noun preceded by *a portion of, a series of, a pile of, a panel of*, the verb invariably takes the singular form, whatever the forms of the noun. Likewise, when the subject is a noun, singular or plural, preceded by *a kind/sort/type of* or by *this kind/sort/type of*, the verb takes the singular form. If *kind/sort/type of* is preceded by *these/those* and followed by a plural noun, the verb should be plural, e. g.

A substantial portion of the report **is** missing.

A series of accidents **has** been reported.

This kind of man **annoys** me.

That type of car **is** old-fashioned.

These sort of machines **are** up to date.

If the subject is a plural noun preceded by *an average of/a majority of*, the verb form is determined by the notion of the noun phrase: if the noun head is the word *average/majority*, the verb should be singular; if the head is the plural noun, the verb should be plural. Compare:

An average of 25 persons **apply** each month.

An average of 25 applications a month **is** not unusual.

A majority of the town's younger men **are** moving to the city.

A majority of three votes to one **was** recorded.

## ◆ 3.7  Other Problems of Subject-verb Concord

**Task 6**  How do you deal with a nominal clause or other structures as subject?

(1) Playing tennis _____ (is, are) very good exercise.
(2) To know merely the main facts _____ (is, are) not enough.
(3) Why he entered the house and how he managed to get out of it without being seen by people _____ (remains, remain) a mystery to us all.
(4) What was real to him _____ (was, were) the details of his life.
(5) That is one of the remarks that _____ (is, are) intended to start arguments.
(6) She's the only one of these women who _____ (plays, play) bridge well.
(7) It's me that _____ (am, is) responsible for the organization.
(8) It's I who _____ (am, is) to leave at once.
(9) There _____ (is, are) a time to be silent and a time to speak, a time for study and a time for resignation or action.

a nominal clause as subject
名词性分句作主语
a non-finite clause as subject
非限定分句作主语

### 1) Problems of Concord with a Nominal Clause as Subject

When the subject is a nominal clause introduced by *what*, *who*, *which*, *how*, *why*, *whether*, etc, the verb usually takes the singular form. But when two or more such clauses are coordinated by *and* or *both ... and*, a plural verb is required, e. g.

> *What caused the accident **is** a complete mystery.*
>
> *What caused the accident and who was responsible for it **remain** a mystery to us.*

In SVC constructions with a what-clause as subject, the verb usually takes the singular form. But when the subject complement is plural, or when the what-clause is plural in meaning, the verb of the main clause can be plural, e. g.

> *What was real to him **were** the details of his life.*
>
> *What are often regarded as poisonous fungi **are** sometimes safely edible.*

## 2) Subject-verb Concord with a Non-finite Clause as Subject

When the subject is a non-finite clause, the verb of the main clause usually takes the singular form. But when two or more such clauses are coordinated by *and*, the principle of notional concord is used. The verb of the main clause takes the singular form when the subject refers to one thing, and the plural form when the subject refers to separate things, e. g.

> *To climb mountains **requires** courage.*
>
> *Early to bed and early to rise **makes** one happy and wise.*
>
> *Drinking goat's milk and getting plenty of exercises **are** responsible for his physique.*
>
> *What I say or what I do **is** no business of yours.*

## 3) Subject-verb Concord in Relative Clauses

In the construction of "*one of* + plural noun + relative clause", the principle of grammatical concord is generally observed. Sometimes, especially in British English, in order to lay emphasis on *one*, the verb can also take the singular form. When *one* is preceded by *any*, *the* or *the only*, the verb can only be singular. Compare:

> *She is one of **the girls** who **play/plays** bridge well.*
>
> *This is one of **the best books** that **have/has** ever appeared.*
>
> *Selfishness is **the one** of her many faults which **defeats** itself.*
>
> *Is there **any one** of you who **wants** to go with me?*
>
> *She is **the only one** of the girls who **plays** beidge well.*

When the antecedent is one part of the main sentence or the main sentence itself, the verb takes the singular form, e. g.

> ***The decision was postponed**, which **was** exactly what he wanted.*

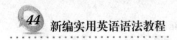

*Pam said **that he had never seen me before**, which **was** not true.*

### 4) Subject-verb Concord in Cleft-sentences

In cleft-sentences, subject-verb concord in that-/who-clause is generally determined by the number of the focal element functioning as subject in the clause. There is one point that should be noted: when the focal element is *I*, the verb *to be* in the following who-/that-clause usually agrees with *I* in both person and number; if, on the other hand, the focal element is *me* instead of *I*, the verb *to be* in the following who-/that-clause should take the third person singular number, e. g.

*It is I who **am** to blame.*
*It is me that **is** to blame.*

### 5) Subject-verb Concord in Existential Sentences

In existential sentences, subject-verb concord is generally determined by the number of the "notional subject", but in informal style, especially in spoken language, the verb often agrees with the "formal subject" and takes the singular form, even though the notional subject is plural. When the notional subject is a coordinate construction, the verb form goes with the first coordinate element of the notional subject, singular or plural, e. g.

*There **are** three routes you can take.*
*There **is** a man and a couple of boys there.*
***There's** some parents in the waiting room.*

## EXERCISES

**I. Fill in the blanks with the verbs in proper forms.**

1. There _____ (be) little change in the patient's condition since he was sent to the intensive care center.
2. The aged _____ (be) well taken care of in their country.
3. What has happened _____ (prove) that our policy is right.
4. Every change of season and every change of weather _____ (make) some changes in the wonderful colors and shapes of these mountains.
5. Most of the buildings on our campus _____ (be) gray-brick constructions.
6. An expert, together with some assistants _____ (send) to help them with the project.

### 3. Subject-verb Concord

7. More than one person _____ (have) been infected with this kind of disease.
8. All the information _____ (be) true.
9. Now that the stress on examination and interviews _____ (be) over, we can all relax for a while.
10. Neither Mike nor his brother _____ (be) able to wake up early enough to catch the morning train.
11. Only about one of twelve of the young men and women of this country _____ (receive) a college education.
12. At present a large number of people _____ (think) the worst danger from automobile is accidents not pollution.
13. The committee _____ (argue) among themselves for four hours.
14. The secretary and accountant of the company _____ (be) absent at the meeting yesterday.
15. Writing essays and reading novels _____ (be) different assignment.

Ⅱ. **Choose a correct answer to complete each of the following sentences.**

1. Neither the girls nor the teacher _____ going to visit Nanjing this Sunday.
   A. are        B. is        C. were        D. was
2. All but one worker _____ here just now.
   A. is        B. was        C. has been        D. were
3. Anyway, it is you who _____ the right to decide.
   A. have        B. is        C. has        D. are
4. Mr. Brown, together with his wife and children, _____ photos on the Great Wall.
   A. was seen take        B. were seen take
   C. was seen taking        D. were seen taking
5. The population of China _____ faster and faster.
   A. become        B. has become
   C. is becoming        D. are becoming
6. To get up early in the morning _____ a lot of good for one's health.
   A. do        B. will do        C. did        D. does
7. The police _____ a thief all around the building.
   A. is searching        B. are searching
   C. searches        D. has been searching

8. AIDS _____ a very complicated disease for a doctor to research.
   A. are      B. is      C. has      D. have

9. This is one of the bridges that _____ in this city.
   A. has been built      B. have been built
   C. were built           D. was built

10. The office staff _____ gathered to have a public meeting.
    A. will have   B. has   C. is   D. are

11. One and half months _____ not enough for us to finish that job.
    A. are   B. were   C. have   D. is

12. Linguistics _____ the subject of linguistics.
    A. belong to           B. belonged to
    C. belongs to          D. has belonged to

13. Not only the teacher but also all the students _____ good progress.
    A. was made            B. were made
    C. has made            D. have made

14. The peasants in this village are much richer than _____ in that one.
    A. one   B. those   C. that   D. it

15. What _____ used as chief building materials today _____ steel and contrete.
    A. have been, are      B. is, are
    C. are, are            D. are, is

Ⅲ. Correct the mistakes in the following sentences.

1. The government are doing its best to boost production.
2. The militia was called out to guard the borderland.
3. There are heaps of fun in the story.
4. The majority of the damage are easy to repair.
5. Every teacher and every student are asked to contribute.
6. A total of 1,500 students was enrolled last year.
7. His courage and endurance were tried to the utmost.
8. The secretary and director are in the next room.
9. Red and white cabbage is useful ingredients for a salad.
10. Law and order have been established.
11. Tom, not me, am to be blamed.
12. Not only my friends but also my brother were there.
13. A writer, or sometimes a scientist, are invited to address the students.

14. My shoes are white, and his is black.
15. The total of the unemployed are believed to exceed 10,000.
16. What are left behind is empty bottles.
17. Diabetes are generally regarded as a chronic disease.
18. The audience was fascinated by her performance.
19. Jim is the only one of the students who are interested in reading.
20. The public hasn't realized the urgency of the matter.

# 4. Sentence Constructions and Analysis

## Aims of the Unit

In this unit we will discuss some general matters about sentence structure. We are going to discuss seven questions in particular:

- What is sentence pattern?
- What are the three main means to expand the basic sentence?
- What are the basic clause types?
- What are the differences between coordination and subordination?
- What is a special type of sentence structure that denotes the existence of something?
- What can be used as a predicator in the existential sentence?
- How do you distinguish existential "there" from locative "there"?

**Task 1**

Do you think the following two sentences have the same pattern? If yes, can you point out the sentence pattern? If no, what are their patterns?

(1) Susam sent her boyfriend *a birthday card*.
   We consider her *the best candidate for the job*.

(2) The porter called me *a taxi*.
   The porter called me *a blackguard*.

(3) Lesley sounds *an interest girl*.
   Lesley knows *an interest girl*.

(4) He found his secretary *a reliable typewriter*.
   He found his secretary *a reliable typist*.

(5) The pleasant summer lasted *well into March*.
   The patient lasted *the attack*.

(6) He studies *at school*.
   He is studying *law at school*.

---

sentence pattern
句型
basic patterns
基本句型
underlying patterns
基础句型
noun 名词
pronoun 代词
adjective 形容词
verb 动词
adverb 副词
conjunction 连词
preposition 介词
interjection 感叹词
SVC 主-动-补结构
SV 主-动结构
SVA 主-动-状结构
SVO 主-动-宾结构
SVOA
主-动-宾-状结构
SVOC
主-动-宾-补结构
SvoO
主-动-宾-宾结构

## 4.1 Sentence Patterns

Sentence patterns can be understood as the way sentences are usually structured. It is important to learn the most common sentence patterns in English, because most of the sentences you hear and write will follow these **basic patterns**. There are a number of common sentence patterns used to write most sentences in English. The basic sentence patterns presented in this part will help you understand the **underlying patterns** in even the most complex English sentences. In English, parts of speech are put together to create sentence patterns. There are about eight parts of speech often used: **noun**, **pronoun**, **adjective**, **verb**, **adverb**, **conjunction**, **preposition**, and **interjection**.

In terms of the different combinations of clause elements, English clauses can be classified into seven basic types. The **seven basic clause types** are **SVC**, **SV**, **SVA**, **SVO**, **SVOA**, **SVOC**, **SVoO**. These seven combinations of clause elements are wholly or largely determined by the main verb in the clause.

**Task 2**  Are there any differences among the verbs in the seven basic sentence patterns?

**Table 1**

| Clause Type | Example |
|---|---|
| SV (Intransitive Verb) | Sara teaches. |
| SVO (Monotransitive Verb) | Sara teaches adults. |
| SVA (Intransitive Verb) | Sara lives in Manchester. |
| SVC (Linking Verb) | Sara is a teacher. |
| SVoO (Ditransitive Verb) | Sara teaches adults English. |
| SVOC (Complex Transitive Verb) | The teacher made Sara course leader. |
| SVOA (Monotransitive Verb) | Sara put the book on the table. |

### 1) SV

SV pattern is formed by a noun followed by a verb. It's important to remember that only verbs that do not require objects are used in this sentence pattern, namely, verbs are **intransitive verbs**.

*People work.*

*Frank eats.*

intransitive verb
不及物动词
monotransitive verb
单宾语及物动词
linking verb
连系动词
ditransitive verb
双宾语及物动词
complex verb
复杂宾语及物动词

This basic sentence pattern can be modified by adding a noun phrase, possessive adjective, as well as other elements. This is true for all the sentence patterns that follow.

*Our employees work.*

*My dog Frank eats.*

Intransitive verbs show an action but there is no specific object on which the action is being done. To recognize these verbs, we ask the question "What is the subject verb + ing?" or "What did the subject -verb-?" If there is no answer present, then the verb in the sentence is an intransitive verb.

*Rose is painting right now.*

Here, if we ask the question "What is Rose painting?" There is no answer, which means that in this sentence *painting* is an intransitive verb.

### 2) SVO

In SVO pattern, verbs are **monotransitive verbs**, that is to say, there is only object that can be used to follow the verb.

These action verbs have a definite object on which or for which the action is being performed. That means that the action has a definite recipient or object. To identify them we can ask the question "What is the subject verb + ing?" or "What did the subjece -verb-?" If there is a definite recipient or object after the verb, it means that the verb is a transitive verb.

*Rose is painting the kitchen walls.*

Here the verb is "painting" and the subject is "Rose". If we form the question "What is Rose painting?" The answer is "The kitchen walls". Thus, we see that there is a specific object on which the action of painting is being done.

*John plays softball.*

*The boys are watching TV.*

### 3) SVA

In SVA pattern, verbs are also intransitive verbs. The difference between SV pattern and SVA pattern is that in SVA pattern, after the **intransitive verb**, an **adverbial** must be followed to describe how an action is done. The removal of the adverbial in SVA pattern or SVOA pattern would result in ungrammaticality or meaninglessness.

*I live in Beijing.*

*Jack weighed 200 pounds.*

*The film lasted two hours.*

### 4) SVC

In SVC pattern, verbs are **linking verbs** which must be followed by a subject complement. Linking verbs are also known as equating verbs—verbs which **equate** one thing with another such as *be*, *become*, *seem*, etc. These verbs are unlike other verbs as they do not tell anything about a subject themselves, instead linking verbs connect the subject to a complement that is acted by a noun or an adjective to help in describing or providing additional information about the subject. That is the reason why those nouns or adjectives are called the **subject complements**.

> equate 等同

*Jack is a student.*
*This seed will become an apple.*
*I am tired.*
*He feels sleepy.*
*Lisa is fussy about food.*
*They are stubborn children.*

The best way to recognize linking words in a sentence is to see whether the verb can be replaced by certain form of the verb *be*, such as *is*, *am* or *are*. If the sentence still sounds logical after substitution, you know you have a linking verb.

*The students felt relieved.* → *The students are (were) relieved.*

### 5) SVoO

In SVoO pattern, verbs are **ditransitive verbs**, which means that this sentence pattern is formed by verbs that take both direct and indirect objects. A ditransitive verb is a type of verb that requires both a direct object and an indirect object in the sentence with it in order to make the meaning of the sentence to be complete. This type of verb is typically used when something is being given or exchanged between two or more parties, as something is the direct object and the receiver is the indirect object.

*I bought Katherine a gift.*
*Jennifer showed Peter her car.*
*The man gave the cat a fish.*

## 6) SVOC

> **Task 3**
> 
> Would you please underline the complement of the following sentences? And could you speak out what can be used as a complement?
> 
> I depend on you to do it.
> 
> You'd better keep the door open.
> 
> His action made him respected.
> 
> I found him out just now.

In SVOC pattern, the verb is a **complex transitive verb**. The verb should be followed by an object, and then a complement is attached to identify a quality or an attribute pertaining to the direct object. Many phrases can be used to act as a complement, such as infinitive, to infinitive, adjective, noun, present participle, past participle, adverb, etc.

I asked him not to be so silly.

I consider him to be the best student.

They believed him to be innocent.

I think it wrong to tell a lie.

They called them cowards.

They chose Mr. Smith chairman.

He saw her enter the room.

We watched the children play games.

He kept me waiting.

Can you smell something burning?

I heard the song sung in English.

Please lead the man in.

## 7) SVOA

In SVOA pattern, the verbs are **monotransitive verbs**. In such pattern structure, adverbials are often functioned by the adverbial of place and manners. Without those adverbials, the sentences will become incomplete.

I put the material evidence in front of him.

He treated her vilely.

## 4.2 Sentence Transformation and Expansion

Basic sentence patterns are affirmative statements with active voice, which can be transformed into negatives, or questions, or statements with passive voice by using some **transformational-generative rules** to expand the meaning.

*Lucy eats green apples.*
→Does *Lucy eat green apples*?
→*Green apples* were eaten *by Lucy.*
→*Lucy* never *eats green apples.*

English sentences are built upon the foundation of an independent basic clause consisting of two parts, a subject and a predicate. **Coordination**, **subordination** and **adding modifiers** are three main means to expand the basic sentence.

### 1) Coordination

The basic clause types can be expanded by coordination. Coordination places elements on an **equal footing** position. The most often used **coordinators** are *and*, *or*, *but*. Besides these, *yet*, *so*, *nor*, *both ... and*, *not only ... but also*, *not ... nor*, *neither ... nor*, *either ... or*, etc. can all be regarded as coordinators; and *as well as*, *as much as*, *rather than*, *more than*, etc. are called "quasi-coordinators".

*Jack types letters.*
*Jack and Lucy type letters.*
*Jack and Lucy type letters and memos.*
*Jack and Lucy type letters and memos but write out short notes and signatures.*
*Jack types letters but Lucy types memos.*

### 2) Subordination

The basic clause types can also be expanded by subordination. Subordination ranks one element as more important than the other. Subordinate clauses are generally introduced by **subordinators**, like *after*, *although*, *because*, *for*, *if*, *since*, *until*, *unless*, *except that*, *in order that*, *provided that*, *providing that*, *as far as*, *as long as*, *even if*, *if only*, *just as*, etc.

*It was already 6 o'clock.* → ***When*** *he got up this morning, it was already 6 o'clock.*
*They don't die.* → ***Although*** *these trees lose their leaves every winter, they don't die.*
*The recently thawed river was icy cold.* → ***Although*** *the recently thawed river was icy cold,*

---

sentence transformation and expansion
基本句型的转换与扩大
transformational-generative rules
转换生成规则

coordination
并列关系
subordination
从属关系
adding modifiers
增加修饰词
equal footing
同等位置
coordinators
并列连词
subordinators
从属连词

*we dove right in.*

### 3) Adding Modifiers

Adding a modifier comes to be the easiest and most common way to develop the basic clause pattern. A modifier is a word or word group that changes the meaning of another word or word group that is more basic to the sentence. The modifier can be placed before the subject, verb, even the complement. Notice how the basic pattern remains even after several modifiers have been added.

*Lucy eats apples.*
→ *Lucy eats green apples.*
→*Little Lucy eats green apples.*
→*Little Lucy never eats green apples.*

## 4.3 Coordinate Constructions

<small>coordinate construction
并列结构
subordinate construction
从属结构</small>

Coordinate constructions are formed by the use of **coordinating conjunctions** (also known as **coordinators**) such as *and*, *or*, *but*. These join linguistic units which are equivalent of the same rank. For example:

*It rained, but I went for a walk anyway.*
*Shall we go home or go to a movie?*

Coordinate constructions may be on different ranks in grammatical hierarchy. They may be a sequence of coordinated words, phrases, clauses, and sentences. In addition, comma is also functioned as a coordinator.

*Forgive **and** forget.*
*East **or** west, home is best.*
*To be **or** not to be, it is a question.*
*Prosperity makes friends, adversity tries them.*

## 4.4 Subordinate Constructions

Subordinate constructions are formed by the use of **subordinating conjunctions** (also known as **subordinators**) such as *because*, *when*, *unless*, *that*. These subordinators help to join an independent clause and a dependent clause. For example:

*I knew **that** he was lying.*

***Unless** it rains, we'll play tennis at 4.*

A subordinate clause cannot stand alone as a sentence because it does not provide a complete thought. The reader is left wondering, "So what happened?" A word group that begins with a capital letter and ends with a period must contain at least one main clause. Otherwise, you will have written a fragment, a major error.

**Task 4**

Which of the following sentences is right and why?

A. Even though the broccoli was covered in cheddar cheese, Emily refused to eat it.

B. Even though the broccoli was covered in cheddar cheese Emily refused to eat it.

C. Emily refused to eat it even though the broccoli was covered in cheddar cheese.

D. Emily refused to eat it, even though the broccoli was covered in cheddar cheese.

When you attach a subordinate clause **in front of a main clause**, use a **comma**, like this: Subordinate Clause + , + Main Clause.

*Unless Christine finishes her calculus homework, she will have to suffer Mr. Nguyen's wrath in class tomorrow.*

*While Bailey slept on the sofa in front of the television, Samson, the family dog, gnawed on the leg of the coffee table.*

When you attach a subordinate clause **at the end of a main clause**, you will generally use **no punctuation**, like this: Main Clause + Ø + Subordinate Clause.

*Diane decided to plant tomatoes in the back of the yard where the sun blazed the longest during the day.*

*Tanya did poorly on her history exam because her best friend Giselle insisted on gossiping during their study session the night before.*

## ◇ 4.5 Existential Sentences

The existential sentence is a special type of sentence structure that denotes the existence of something.

- There + be + NP + locative/temporal adverbial

*There is a tree in my garden.*

- Introductory *there*: unstressed, meaningless

*There is no bus now.*

- A fronted adverb *there*: stressed, acts as an adverb of place

*There is our bus.*

**Task 5**   Would you fill in the appropriate form of the verb *be* in the blanks?
(1) There _____ a train due to arrive.
(2) There _____ a lot of rain last year.
(3) There _____ an English lecture at three this afternoon.
(4) There _____ much talk about it.
(5) The predicators in the existential sentence are often in the following four types.

The predicators in the existential sentence are often in the following four types.

(1) The predicator of an existential sentence is commonly a form of the verb *be*, simple present, simple past, present perfective or past perfective, etc., just as the sentences in Task 5.

(2) The predicator may also be realized by "modal + be/have been", e.g.

There **must be** no more money wasted.

**Mustn't** there **be** another reason for his behavior?

There **can/can't be** very little doubt about his guilt.

There **can't have been** much traffic so late at night.

(3) The predicator may also be realized by "semi-auxiliary + be".

There **is going to be** a storm.

There **seems to be** something wrong.

There **is to be** an investigation.

There **appears to be** no doubt about it.

There **used to be** a church round the corner.

(4) Apart from the above mentioned three types, there are at least three classes of semantically-related verbs that can act as predicator.

- Verbs of existence and position, such as exist, live, stand, lie.
- Verbs of motion, such as come, go, walk.

# 4. Sentence Constructions and Analysis

- Verbs of emergence or development, such as appear, arise, emerge, develop, happen, occur, etc.

There **stands** a post office on the corner of the street.

There **lived** an old fisherman in a village by the sea.

There **happened** to be no people in the hall.

**Existential** *there* has a unique syntactic role; there is no other word in English which behaves in the same way. It is often described as **an anticipatory subject.**

There were **people** on the floor.

There wre **roses** in the garden.

There were **20 to 30 people** standing there shocked and bewildered.

**Existential** *there* should be distinguished from **locative** *there* which is used as an adverb. The two types frequently co-occur in the same clause, as in the following example (existential *there* in bold; locative *there* marked by [ ]):

"But it's empty, **there's** no one [there]," the child said.

"**There is** real value [there]," says Cant.

## EXERCISES

I. **Read the following sentences, analyze them, and then decide which patterns they belong to.**

1. I met many old classmates at the new senior high school yesterday.
2. We all felt very happy at Mary's birthday party last Tuesday.
3. John and his friends were doing tons of homework at this time yesterday.
4. My first day at the new school made me a laughing stock of the classroom.
5. Buses and cars are moving up and down the street.
6. Mr. Black was bitterly punished for his selfishness that day.
7. Most adults think of play as the opposite of work.
8. We found it difficult to climb down the mountain in the fog.
9. People all over the world want their own native language to be the international language.
10. We were told that he would be just fine in a day or two.

II. **Find out the basic sentence style of the following sentences.**

1. Horse kicks.
2. Tom kicked the wall.
3. Tom kicked the ball into the yard.

4. Tom kicked Bill blue and black.

5. Tom kicked his way out of the classroom.

6. Tom kicked the ball to Bill.

7. The African people have long been our close friends.

8. The African people have long been our close friends in fighting against power politics.

9. The girl likes reading.

10. The girl with blonde hair likes reading.

### Ⅲ. Transform the sentences based on the requirements.

1. She gave him the book. (an affirmative → a negative)

2. She gave him the book. (a statement → a question)

3. She gave him a book. (an active clause → a passive)

### Ⅳ. Analyze the following sentences

1. <u>The janitor</u> <u>staggered down the stairway</u>, <u>stunned by the bizarre noise</u>.
       A              B                        C

2. <u>The janitor</u> <u>staggered down the stairway</u>, <u>stunned by the bizarre noise</u> <u>he heard</u>.
       A              B                        C        D

3. <u>The janitor</u>, <u>who had been working there for twenty years</u>,
       A                           B

   <u>staggered down the stairway</u>, <u>stunned by the bizarre noise</u> <u>he heard</u>.
               C                      D             E

4. <u>The janitor</u>, <u>who was one-eyed</u>, <u>staggered down the stairway</u>,
       A           B                C

   <u>stunned by the bizarre noise</u> <u>which he heard in the attic</u>, <u>and shouted for help</u>,
           D                    E                    F

   and as a result, <u>the whole village were woken up in the midnight</u>.
                               G

### Ⅴ. Turn the following sentences into existential sentences.

1. Something must be wrong.

2. A storm is approaching.

3. Someone is knocking on the door.

4. Some people were playing basketball.

5. A girl is dancing over there.

6. Something is causing her distress.

7. A whole box of jewelry has been stolen.

8. No traces of the burglar were to be found.

9. A lot of people are in the street.

10. An old man once lived in this village.

# 5. Uses of Sentences

## Aims of the Unit

> In this unit we will discuss some general matters about uses of sentences. We are going to discuss seven questions in particular:
> - What is Declarative Sentence?
> - What is Interrogative Sentence?
> - What is Imperative Sentence?
> - What is Exclamatory Sentence?
> - What are the purposes of these four types of sentences?
> - What are the differences of these four types of sentences?
> - How do you transform from one sentence type to a different sentence type?

**Task 1**

> Can you change each sentence into the kind named in parentheses, and write a new sentence?
> (1) Grandpa likes telling stories. (Interrogative)
> (2) Are his stories always true? (Declarative)

A sentence is a group of words that expresses a complete thought or idea. All sentences begin with a capital letter and end with a punctuation mark. Different types of sentences have different purposes. Based on the purposes of sentence use, they are divided into four types of sentences as **declarative sentences, interrogative sentences, imperative sentences and exclamatory sentences.**

declarative sentences
陈述句
interrogative sentences
疑问句
imperative sentences
祈使句
exclamatory sentences
感叹句

## 5.1 Declarative Sentences

Declarative sentences are the most common sentence type in English, and they are used when you want to make an assertion or a statement. The primary purpose of declarative sentences is to give information. But some declarative sentences do more than just give information. In a declarative sentence, the subject normally precedes the verb, and it always ends with a simple period.

There are many different uses of declarative sentences. Here are some examples:

- Expressing approval: *You're doing a good job.*
- Expressing sympathy: *It was bad luck you didn't pass TEM-4 exam.*
- Expressing thanks: *I am very grateful.*
- Asking for information: *I need to know your plans.*
- Giving orders: *I want you to try harder.*

In certain situations, a declarative sentence is not the only way to ask for information. A different type of sentences can also be used to meet this purpose. Compare the following three types of sentences:

*I need to know your plans.*

*What are your plans?*

*Please tell me about your plans.*

The first sentence is a declarative sentence, the second one is an interrogative sentence, while the third one is an imperative sentence. All of these types of sentences can ask for information.

**Task 2** Change each sentence into its negative one.
(1) The balloon is red.
(2) The baby is crying.
(3) The man has a horse.
(4) The television is broken.
(5) The children are happy.

Declarative sentences can be affirmative or negative. Declarative sentences that have an affirmative meaning are called **affirmative sentences**. Declarative sentences that have a negative meaning are called **negative sentences**. A negative declarative sentence is to inform someone that what they might think or expect is not so. Negative sentences are usually the opposite of affirmative sentences.

> affirmative sentences 肯定句
> negative sentences 否定句
> operator 操作词

### 1) *Not* with an Operator

In the most basic kind of negative declarative sentences, *not* or *n't* comes after the operator. Sometimes the operator and *n't* together are written as one word.

Some people have **not** read the book.

The monster **wasn't** called Frankenstein.

That might or might **not** have given the author the idea for the name.

East London is **not** on most tourist maps.

These shoes **aren't** very comfortable.

### 2) *Not* in Other Positions

*Not* can come before a word or phrase when the speaker is correcting the previous one.

I ordered tea, **not** coffee.

—That's a nice green. —It's blue, **not** green.

—Is there a meeting today? —**Not** today. —It is tomorrow.

### 3) Words with Negative Meanings

There are some words besides *not* which have a negative meaning.

| | |
|---|---|
| no | There's no change. |
| | The patient is no better. |
| none | We wanted tickets, but there were none left. |
| no one | I saw no one acting strangely. |
| nothing | I saw nothing suspicious. |
| nowhere | There is nowhere to park. |
| few/little | Few people were interested |
| | There was little enthusiasm. |
| never | He was never a doctor. |
| seldom/rarely | We seldom/rarely eat out. |
| no longer | He no longer lives in this apartment. |
| hardly/scarcely | We haven't finished. In fact, we've hardly/scarcely started. |
| neither/nor | —I didn't go to cinema yesterday. —Neither/Nor did I. |

#### 4) Double Negatives

<u>double negatives</u>
双重否定

A double negative is one of the typical declarative sentences. It is usually produced by combining the negative form of verb with a negative pronoun, a negative adverb or a negative conjunction. A double negative usually provides the sentence with a strong positive sense.

He **didn't** see **nothing**. (He saw something.)
She is **not unattractive**. (She is attractive.)
We are **not unprepared** for the worst. (We are prepared for the worst.)
It **wasn't uninteresting**. (It was interesting.)
I **hardly** have **none**. (I have some.)
I **don't** want **nothing**. (I want something.)

**Task 3**  Rewrite each of the following sentences as a question, and compare your new interrogative sentences with declarative sentences.

(1) Jack is leaving today.
(2) Robert ate the last doughnut.
(3) You can understand why I am upset.
(4) There's a physician in the house.
(5) We have received a pay raise this year.
(6) Laura knows how to serve her customers effectively and efficiently.
(7) The doctor told us to add cereal to the baby's formula.
(8) The repairs to the TV set cost more than the TV set was worth.
(9) All of your friends try to cheer you up when you are sad.

## 5.2 Interrogative Sentences

Interrogative sentences are used to raise a question. An interrogative sentence ends with a question mark. The most basic use of an interrogative sentence is to ask for information, e.g. —*Where are you now?* —*In the downtown.* But interrogative sentences can also have other uses such as requesting, e.g. *Could you come over here, please?*

There are two types of interrogative sentences. In one kind, the

## 5. Uses of Sentences

interrogative sentence is named as yes/no interrogative sentence. It is constructed by varying the subject and predication of a declarative sentence. Such interrogative sentences usually will be answered with *Yes* or *No*. In most of the first type of interrogative sentences there is inversion of subject and operator. The second kind of interrogative sentences is named as wh- interrogative sentences. It is constructed by using an interrogative word, and it begins with a question word, e.g. *where, what, who,* etc.

**Task 4**

Complete each sentence, using *what, where, when, who* or *why*.
(1) _____ is the time please?
(2) _____ did I just say?
(3) _____ do you think you are?
(4) _____ is my coat?
(5) _____ do you want to leave? This evening?
(6) _____ didn't you go to college this morning?
(7) _____ was the Battle of Hastings?
(8) _____ are you looking for?
(9) _____ is the front door open?
(10) _____ didn't you call me last night?

Wh- questions are frequently used in the interrogative sentences to ask certain types of questions. *What* questions are used to ask for information, *where* for location, *when* for time, *who* for people and *why* for reasons.

For the wh-question structure, a wh-question is formed by inserting a wh-word into a sentence in the place of missing information. A wh-question focuses on particular parts of sentence, while not on the whole sentence like the way that *yes/no* questions do. If wh-questions focus on the subject of a sentence, just insert *who* or *what* and keep the same word order. If wh-questions focus on anything in the predicate, insert a wh-word and then manipulate the word order by moving that wh-word to the beginning and moving the operator in front of the subject. If there is no operator in the verb phrase, then one has to be added. Like *yes/no* questions and negatives with *not* in the verb phrase, wh-questions also need to add an operator like *do/does/did*.

## 5.3 Imperative Sentences

Imperative sentences are used to state a command, request, or direction. The subject is always *you* in the sentence, even it may not be expressed directly. The imperative form is the base form of the verb and it is a second-person form. When someone says "*Come in*", he or she means that you should come in. The negative is "*do not/don't* + base" form, and for emphasis it is suggested to use "*do* + base" form.

positive 肯定的
negative 否定的
emphatic 强调的

| | |
|---|---|
| Positive: | Look at the blackboard. |
| | Read the instructions carefully. |
| Negative: | Do not remove this book from the table. |
| | Don't make so much fuss. |
| Emphatic: | Do be careful. |

Imperative sentences are used to give orders, state warnings, give advice or make a request. Here are examples:

| | |
|---|---|
| Giving orders: | Sit down now! |
| | Come in, please! |
| Warning: | Watch out! |
| | Don't cross! |
| | Keep away! |
| Giving advice: | Don't drink too much alcohol! |
| | Don't eat high calorie food! |
| Requests: | Please take a rest. |
| | Please wait here. |
| | Please don't smoke here. |

Except for the second person imperatives, there are also the first person imperative and the third person imperative. In the first person imperative, it is constructed with "let + me" or "let + us". For the first person negative imperative, "not" is put before the imperative, e.g. *Let us not be worried.* In the third person imperative, it is constructed with "let + him/her/it/them + verb", and the infinitive goes without "to". Here are examples:

| | |
|---|---|
| The first person imperative: | *Let me do it for you.* |
| | *Let me see.* |
| | *Let's do some exercises.* |
| The third person imperative: | *Let him go.* |
| | *Let it be.* |
| | *Let them try it.* |
| Negative imperatives | *Let's not do it so soon.* |

Imperative sentences are often used to emphasize the requests with "do". It is common in polite requests to introduce "do" in the imperative sentences, e.g. *Do be quiet. Do be responsible.* A polite request is also made if "shall we" or "will you" are put at the end of the imperative sentence, e.g. *Let's get started, shall we? Be careful, will you?*

## ◆ 5.4 Exclamatory Sentences

Exclamatory sentences are used to express a strong feeling or emotion such as surprise, pain or joy. They are usually followed by an exclamation point. Exclamatory sentences are rarely used in expository writing. Spoken exclamations are often a single word or an incomplete sentence. A formal exclamatory sentence usually begins with the word *what* or with the word *how*.

Compare the following two patterns.

| | |
|---|---|
| Interrogative: | *How warm is the water?* |
| Exclamatory: | *How warm the water is!* |

Both of the above two sentences start with the word *how*. The exclamatory sentence indicates that the water is very warm. It expresses the speaker's feeling about the degree of warmth. The interrogative sentence raises a question, and the speaker wants to know the degree of warmth of water.

**Task 5**  Complete the following sentences with *how* or *what* to make exclamations.

(1) _____ cold it is!
(2) _____ beautifully you sing!
(3) _____ a rude guy!
(4) _____ a pleasant surprise!
(5) _____ lovely weather!
(6) _____ a fool you are!
(7) _____ foolish she is!
(8) _____ you have grown!

There is usually an adjective or adverb after *how* if it is used as an exclamatory sentence, e.g. *How lucky you are!* In the exclamatory sentence, *how* can also be used to modify a verb, e.g. *How we laughed!* In the exclamatory sentences, *what* is usually put before a noun phrase with *a/an* or zero article, e.g. *What a journey we had!* An exclamation can also be just a phrase with *how* or *what*, e.g. *What a journey!*

There are also other types of exclamatory sentences without *how* or *what*. Any phrase or short sentence can be an exclamation, e.g. *You idiot! Stupid!* In these exclamations, there is usually a greater rise or fall of the voice than in other types of sentences. An exclamatory point is used at the end.

Some exclamatory sentences have the form of a negative question. The voice rises and then falls, e.g. *Aren't you lucky!*

## EXERCISES

**I. Classify the following sentences based on its uses.**

1. I wish I could go to Mississippi this winter.
2. Please set the table for dinner.
3. The vice-president will visit Egypt next week.
4. Don't you ever get tired of watching television.
5. We bought our car in April, 1975.
6. Didn't I meet you at Crystal Lake last summer?
7. Have you ever roasted a turkey?
8. Ouch! I burned my figure!
9. Turn left at the second stop sign.

## 5. Uses of Sentences

10. Russia is the largest country in the world.
11. Initial the top right-hand corner of each sheet of paper.
12. Robert's short stories have appeared in many magazines.
13. Have you ever read *Reading Critically Writing Well*?
14. You can't be serious!
15. Meet me at seven o'clock in front of our lab.
16. Why are you so worried about the English test?
17. Don't close your mind to the other side of the question.
18. Maria wants to be a nurse.
19. I can't believe it's all over.
20. Do you attend concerts given by the Chicago Symphony Orchestra?

**II. Write four types of sentences including a declarative sentence, an interrogative sentence, an imperative sentence and an exclamatory sentence with the subjects given. Be sure to use the proper ending punctuation.**

1. backpack    2. friend    3. school    4. pet    5. hobby
6. dress    7. homework    8. movie    9. computer    10. car
11. love    12. rose    13. gift    14. job    15. activity

**III. Decide if there is an error in the underlined part of each sentence, and choose the correct answer based on the types of sentences.**

1. <u>You do like</u> to see movies about knights and castles?
   A. you do like    B. Do you like    C. correct as is
2. Please hand me that mystery book about <u>the Middle Ages?</u>
   A. the Middle Ages!    B. the Middle Ages.    C. correct as is
3. Grandfather described life in the early part <u>of the century.</u>
   A. of the century?    B. of the century!    C. correct as is
4. Why don't you write about <u>your life!</u>
   A. your life?    B. your life.    C. correct as is
5. <u>Begin by describing</u> your very first memory.
   A. begin by describing    B. By describing    C. correct as is
6. I had such fun swimming <u>in the ocean?</u>
   A. in the ocean.    B. in the ocean!    C. correct as is
7. What do you remember about your first day <u>in school?</u>
   A. in school!    B. in school.    C. correct as is
8. <u>another story</u> about our relatives in Mexico.
   A. Tell me another story    B. Another story    C. correct as is

9. The fish looked so colorful swimming in the Caribbean Sea

    A. the Caribbean Sea!    B. the Caribbean Sea?    C. correct as is

10. He told us about his trip?

    A. his trip    B. his trip.    C. correct as is

## Ⅳ. Match the two columns to make instructions.

1. Feed              A. have a drink
2. wash              B. put on your jacket. It's hot.
3. Don't             C. your bedroom.
4. Do                D. go to class. It's five o'clock.
5. Let's              E. the dishes
6. Tidy              F. your homework.
7. Don't             G. the bird.
8. Let's              H. leave the door open.

## Ⅴ. Correctly punctuate the following sentences with a period, question mark, or exclamation point where needed.

1. Did you know there are more than half a million snowflakes in each cubic foot of snow

2. Is there anything you'd give your life for

3. The track meet was supposed to start at 2:00 pm, but it began at 2:45 pm.

4. If you take this action, where will it lead

5. Wow What an absolutely fantastic idea

6. They're going to the theater tonight, aren't they

7. Will you meet me at 2:00 pm tomorrow

8. There are only two lasting things we can give our children—roots and wings

9. They discussed colors, fabrics, styles, etc. but came to no decision

10. fantastic Did you see that stunt

# Part Two

# Predicate and Related Grammatical Categories

# 6. Tense and Aspect Systems

**Aims of the Unit**

> In this unit we will discuss some general matters about the tense and aspect systems. We are going to discuss seven questions in particular:
> - What is the tense of the predicate?
> - What is the aspect of the predicate?
> - What is the present tense?
> - What is the past tenses?
> - What is the future time?
> - What are the differences among these two types of tenses?
> - How do you transform from one tense of the predicate to a different tense?

## ◆ 6.1 The Tense of Predicate

The predicate is the part that modifies the subject in some way in a sentence. Usually the subject is a person, place or thing that a sentence is about (usually the subject is what a sentence is talking about), so the predicate contains a verb explaining what the subject does. The tense of the predicate is a grammatical form related to verbs that tell of the distinctions of time. Time has three divisions grammatically in English: past time, present time and future time and time is usually expressed by means of tense. English predicate has two tenses: one is the present tense and the other is the past tense. There is no obvious future tense but there is a variety of strategies to indicate the future time.

## 6.2 The Aspect of Predicate

The aspect indicates whether an action or state is considered to be complete or incomplete at a given time in the English grammatical system. The predicate has two different kinds of aspects: the progressive aspect and the perfective aspect. A combined use of tenses and aspects can make a larger variety of grammatical forms (with the main verb *do* as an example).

| | |
|---|---|
| Simple Present | does |
| Present Progressive | am/is/are doing |
| Present Perfective | has done |
| Present Perfective Progressive | has been doing |
| Simple Past | did |
| Past Progressive | was/were doing |
| Past Perfective | had done |
| Past Perfective Progressive | had been doing |

## 6.3 Present Tense

**1) Simple Present**

The Simple Present is used to describe an action that is regular, true or normal. It is also used to express habits, repeated actions, unchanging situations, and emotions and wishes. The structure of the Simple Present is as follows:

Subject + Main Verb

The Simple Present is often used to indicate repeated or regular actions in the present time period as in the following examples:

I ***usually go*** to school on foot.

The train to Shanghai ***leaves every 40 minutes***.

I ***often get up*** at 6 am on Friday.

It is also used to indicate a fact. For example, *The dog has four legs.* Sometimes it expresses habits. For example, *Carol brushes her teeth twice a day.* It is also used to indicate things that are generally true. For example, *It* rains a lot in winter here.

In addition, the Simple Present has some special uses such as referring to the future and the past (historical present). Here are some examples:

The plane **arrives** at 6:00 am tomorrow.

Tanya **has** a yoga class tomorrow afternoon.

The train **leaves** in ten minutes.

The war criminal **escapes** from courtroom.

1945: the war in Europe **comes** to an end.

**Task 1**  Complete each sentence using the words in parentheses with an appropriate tense form.

(1) I usually _____ (work) as secretary at the Bank of China, but this spring I _____ (study) French at a language school in Shanghai. That is why I am in Shanghai now.

(2) Don't forget to take your umbrella. It _____ (rain).

(3) I hate living in Seattle because it _____ (rain, always).

(4) I'm sorry I can't hear what you _____ (say) because everybody _____ (talk) so loudly.

(5) Every weekend, Sarah _____ (drive) her kids to tennis practice.

## 2) Present Progressive

The Present Progressive is mainly used to express the idea that something is happening at the moment of speaking. It is also used to describe activities in progress (not at the moment). Sometimes it is used to indicate temporary actions or future plans. The structure of the Present Progressive is as follows:

Subject + Auxiliary Verb *be* + Main Verb (Present Participle)

The Present Progressive is often used for actions happening exactly now or around now. Here are some examples:

The candle **is burning**.

It **is snowing** outside.

I **am learning** to drive.

I **am living** with my sister until I find an apartment.

The baby **is sleeping**.

The Present Progressive is also used to indicate the future, especially the future when a plan has been made to do something before speaking.

When *are* you *starting* your new job?

We're *not going* anywhere tomorrow.

He's *flying back* to his hometown in October.

They can play tennis with you tomorrow. They *are not working*.

### 3) Present Perfective

The Present Perfective is most used when an action that happened in the past continues to have a strong connection with the present. It indicates a connection between the past events and the present. It is also used with the words or expressions of unfinished time. The unfinished time started in the past, and continues into the present. The structure of the Present Perfective is as follows:

Subject + Auxiliary Verb *have/has* + Main Verb (Past Participle)

Here are examples:

I *have lost* my dictionary.

He *has fixed* my second-hand car.

*Have* you *seen* my calculator?

I've *played* tennis three times already this week, and it's only Thursday.

She's *been* back to America twice already this year, and she's going again next week.

I *haven't seen* my brother for two months.

**Task 2** Complete each sentence using the words in parentheses with the Present Perfective or the Present Perfective Progressive.

(1) Linda _____ (not, be) to France.

(2) It has _____ (be) snowing a lot this week.

(3) The children _____ (find) the lost puppy.

(4) I am tired because I have been _____ (work) out.

(5) Have your brother and sister been _____ (get) along well?

(6) I haven't _____ (work) since last December.

### 4) Present Perfective Progressive

The Present Perfective Progressive is used to indicate actions that started in the past and continued until recently or that continue into the future. It often goes with *since*, *for*, *lately*, *recently*, *over the last few months*, etc. The structure of the Present Perfective Progressive is as follows:

Subject + Auxiliary Verb *have/has* + *been* + Main Verb (Present Participle)

There is usually a connection with the present. The function of the Present Perfective Progressive is used for an action that has just stopped or recently stopped. Here are some examples:

*I am tired because I have been running.*

*You don't really understand because you haven't been listening.*

*Why is the grass wet? Has it been raining?*

It is also used for an action continuing up to now as in the following examples.

*We have been studying since 9 o'clock.*

*How long have you been learning English?*

*We have not been smoking.*

## 6.4　Past Tense

**Task 3**　　Put the verbs into the correct tense form (Simple Past or Present Perfective)

(1) Tom _____ (move) to his hometown in 2011.

(2) I can't take any pictures because I _____ (not/buy) a new camera yet.

(3) Mary _____ (already, write) five letters.

(4) _____ (they, spend) their holidays in Paris last summer?

(5) Last night, Paul _____ (go) to the cinema.

(6) I _____ (already, travel) to New Orleans a couple of times.

### 1) Simple Past

The Simple Past is used for finished actions or situations that began and ended before now. Verbs are action words in the Simple Past, and they have two forms: regular and irregular. For regular verbs, they are just added with "ed". For irregular verbs, they are used with the past forms. The structure of the Simple Past is as follows:

Subject + Main Verb (Past)

The function of the Simple Past is to indicate an action, an event or a situation in the past. In general, the Simple Past is used to indicate the past time or the place of the event no matter how long ago the event was. The action can be a few seconds or minutes in the past or a very long time in the past. Here are some examples for short events:

*The car exploded at 9 pm last Friday.*
*I didn't hear the telephone.*
*Did you see that car?*

The Simple Past also can be used to indicate long events as follows:

*I lived in that house when I was young.*
*He didn't like that movie.*
*We didn't sing at the concert.*

| Task 4 | Complete each sentence using the words in parentheses with an appropriate tense form. |

(1) My brother _____ (see) a bear an hour ago.
(2) My brother and sister _____ (play) tennis at 11 am yesterday.
(3) Snowing _____ (fall) lightly. Suddenly a reindeer appeared.
(4) I _____ (go) to the shopping mall after school.
(5) I _____ (read) a detective story when I heard a noise.
(6) What _____ (do) you eat for lunch yesterday?

## 2) Past Progressive

The Past Progressive describes actions or events at a particular moment in the past. The actions started before that moment but had not finished at that moment. The structure of the Past Progressive is as follows:

Subject + Auxiliary Verb *be* + Main Verb (Present Participle)

Here are some examples:

*I was working at 10 pm last night.*
*What were you doing at 11 am the day before yesterday?*
*We were having dinner when it started to rain.*
*Lisa went back home early because it was snowing.*
*She was cooking when I telephoned her.*

## 6. Tense and Aspect Systems

### 3) Past Perfective

The Past Perfective is often used for actions that happened before a past event, and it indicates "past in the past". The structure of the Past Perfective is as follows:

Subject + Auxiliary Verb *had* + Main Verb (Past Participle)

The basic function of the Past Perfective is to indicate an action that happened before a past event. Here are some examples:

*When I got home yesterday, my father had already cooked dinner.*

*I was very tired as I hadn't slept well for several days.*

*As soon as she had done her homework, she went to bed.*

*I arrived very late at the party. All my friends had already gone home.*

The Past Perfective is used in reported speech. It is common when reporting people's words or thoughts as in the following examples:

*John said that he had never eaten Sushi before.*

*She wondered why he had been so unkind to her.*

*I thought I had sent her a birthday card, but I was wrong.*

The Past Perfective is also used in unreal or hypothetical situations as in the following sentences:

*If I had known you were in Shanghai, I would have called you.*

*I wish I had studied for my final exams.*

*I would have been in big trouble if you hadn't helped me.*

**Task 5** Complete each sentence using the words in parentheses with an appropriate tense form.

(1) My dad _____ (smoke) in the garage.

(2) We _____ (have not, finish) eating our dinner.

(3) The CD player _____ (be) working well.

(4) Nobody explained why the project _____ (have not, complete) on time.

(5) We were shocked to see her. We _____ (not expect) her.

(6) Sarah thought she _____ (be) to that zoon before.

### 4) Past Perfective Progressive

The Past Perfective Progressive indicates a continuous action that was completed at some point in the past. It is often used to express an action that started in the past and continued until sometime in the past. The structure of the Past Perfective Progressive is as follows:

Subject + Auxiliary Verbs *had been* + Main Verb (Present Participle)

Here are examples:

*Had the pilot been drinking before the crash?*
*Suddenly my car broke down. I was not surprised. It had not been running well for a long time.*
*I have been living in America since 2010.*
*It had been raining for three days.*
*Had she been waiting for me for one hour?*

**Task 6**  Complete each sentence with an appropriate auxiliary verb *will* or *be going to*.

(1) A: Do you think the Republicans or the Democrats _____ (win) the next election?
    B: I think the Republicans _____ (win) the next election.
    A: No way! The Democrats _____ (win).

(2) A: I _____ (buy) a new car this weekend, but I'm a little worried because I don't really know much about cars. I'm afraid the salesman _____ (try) to make advantage of me when he sees how little I know.
    B: I used to work for a mechanic in high school and I know a lot about cars. I _____ (go) with you to make sure you are not cheated.

## 6.5  Future Time

Future time means that action will happen in the future, and in other words, sometime after this moment. English verbs have two tenses: the present tense and the past tense. There is no obvious future tense corresponding to the time/tense parallel for present and past. Instead there are a number of possibilities of denoting future time: **modal auxiliaries**, **semi-auxiliaries**, the **simple present** and **present progressive** forms.

---

modal auxiliaries
情态助动词
semi-auxiliaries
半助动词
the simple present
一般现在时
the present progressive
现在进行体

## 6. Tense and Aspect Systems

### 1) Will/Shall + Infinitive

In the *will/shall* future time, *will* is now the standard choice for expressing future plans and expectations. However, in first person questions *shall* is often used to express politeness, and in legal statements, *shall* is used with a third person subject for stating requirements. *Shall* is becoming less common than *will* in the future time. *Shall* is not normally used in American English.

You **will** feel better after taking this medicine.
I'm sure I **shan't** lose my way in the woods.
I promise to pay him back in time, but he **won't** lend it to me.
I **won't** tell anyone your secret.

The future meanings expressed by these auxiliaries are very often colored by modal meanings from promises, offers, decisions, prediction to intention and willingness.

> prediction
> 预见
> intention
> 意图
> willingness
> 意愿

**Task 7**  Complete the following blanks with appropriate future times.
(1) I'll try my best to spot you. What _____ (you, wear)?
(2) Don't forget your snowpants. It _____ (snow) by the time you get to school.
(3) At noon tomorrow, I _____ (relax) on a beach somewhere.
(4) Sorry, I can't. I _____ (take) my daughter to work at that time.

### 2) Will/Shall + Progressive/Perfect Infinitive

**Will/Shall** + **Progressive Infinitive** expresses a colorless, pure future. This construction usually implies an action which will occur in the normal course of events without any human involvement, ie without being colored by volition or intention.

The train **will be arriving** at two o'clock.
I **shall be writing** to you soon.
**Will** you **be going** home next week-end?

This construction can also be used to denote an action that is still going on at a given future time:

I'll **be working** in Geneva during May.
They **won't be watching** TV at 9 pm on weekends.

She **will be sleeping** when you telephone her.

Please take your umbrella. It **will be raining** when you return.

**Will/Shall** + **Perfective Infinitive** refers to a completed action in the future, and it indicates that an action will have been finished at some point in the future:

You can call me at work at 8:30 am. I **will have arrived** at the office by that time.

By this time next week, I **will have worked** on this project for 25 days.

How long **will** it **have been since** we were together?

Before he sees his publisher, He **will have finished** four chapters in his new novel.

If an action has extended for a special length of time before a given future moment and possibly continues at that moment, we can use the construction of **Will/Shall** + **Perfective Progressive Infinitive**:

He'll be tired when he gets here. He **'ll have been travelling** all day.

Next Monday we **will have been living** here for exactly five years.

In July next year, you **will have been playing** basketballs for 20 years.

> **Task 8**   Complete the following blanks with appropriate future times.
> (1) Lee: Jack, why are you carrying that shotgun?
>   Jack: I _____ (kill) mosquitoes.
> (2) A: Why are you taking down all the pictures?
>   B: I _____ (repaper) the room.
>   A: What a terrible heavy box!
>   B: I _____ (help) you to carry it.

### 3) Be Going to + Infinitive

**Be Going to** + **Infinitive** is used to express two meanings: intention and prediction. In its first use, *be going to* form implies an intention of doing something in the near future. The doer of the intended action is generally the subject of the sentence.

On my next vacation, I **am going to stay** in a better hotel in Paris.

They **are going to share** an apartment when they move to Los Angeles next month.

She **is going to meet** us at the airport at 9:00 pm.

Both *will* and *be going to* can denote intention, but the chief difference is that the *be going to* form always implies a **premeditated intention**, while the *will* form implies intention alone, and this intention is usually, though not necessarily, **unpremeditated**:

A: *Why are you taking down all the pictures?*
B: *I'm going to repaper the room.*
A: *What a terrible heavy box!*
B: *I'll help you to carry it.*

In its second use, *be going to* can express the speaker's feeling of certainty. The time is usually not mentioned, but the action is expected to happen in the near or immediate future, especially there are explicit/implicit signs:

*Good heavens! I must hurry. I'm going to be late.*
*Look at these black clouds—there's going to be a storm.*

The difference between **Will + Infinitive** and **Be Going to + Infinitive** in expressing prediction lies in the fact that the *be going to* form implies that there are signs that something will happen, while the *will* form implies what the speaker thinks or believes will happen.

### 4) Present Progressive

**The present progressive** can refer to a future happening anticipated at the present. Its basic meaning is an action that will happen in the near future according to a present arrangement, plan, or programme. When it comes to the verbs like *go, come, leave, start, arrive, visit*, etc. we generally use the present progressive instead of the *be going to* form:

*We are visiting some friends in Scotland next week.*
*I am leaving for Shanghai tomorrow.*
*My uncle is arriving next weekend.*
*We are going to a concert tonight.*

Since both the *be going to* form and the present progressive can be used to refer to a future happening arising from the present decision, these two forms are sometimes interchangeable for future reference.

*She is getting/is going to get married this spring.*
*We are having/are going to have fish for dinner.*

> premeditated intention
> 事先经过考虑的意图
> unpremeditated intention
> 临时想到的意图

## 5) Be to + Infinitive / Simple Present

**Be to + Infinitive** can denote a future happening based on a present plan or arrangement which sounds very formal.

You *are to destroy* this message now:

When you arrive, you *are to meet* our agent who will give you further information.

This construction is very much used in newspapers, and in headlines with the verb *be* often omitted to save space, indicating official decisions.

The Queen *is to visit* Japan next year.

Another use of this construction is to convey orders, instructions, or prohibitions or destiny.

You *are to stand* here. Do you understand?

Tell her she's *not to be* back late.

The dictionary *is not to be* had here.

The future use of the simple present is more frequent in dependent, especially conditional and temporal, clauses than in main clauses.

If she *comes*, I'll tell her all about it.

It won't be long before the rain *stops*.

In main clauses, the simple present refers to an immutable future event predetermined by a timetable or a schedule which is very definite and unalterable.

Hurry up! The bus *departs* in 10 minutes.

When *does* the conference begin?

She *retires* next month.

Tomorrow *is* Saturday.

Next Christmas *falls* on a Thursday.

For future reference, the simple present, like the present progressive, usually goes with **transitional verbs** ( *come*, *go*, *leave*, *arrive*, etc. ) with the implication of a plan or programme already made, but the plan implied by the simple present is more impersonal than that by the present progressive, and, therefore, more fixed and unalterable.

## 6) Means of Expressing Past Future

If the speaker refers to a future event from a viewpoint in the past, that is past future. There are five ways to express past future: would + infinitive, was/were going to + infinitive, was/were to + infinitive, was/were about to +

---

transitional verbs
位置转移动词
unalterable
不可变易的

infinitive, past progressive and simple past.

- *He said he **would** come back the next day.*

For past future reference, the modal auxiliary construction with *would* is usually accompanied by an adverbial denoting future time in the past. This construction is commonly used in dependent clauses.

- *He never imagined that some day he **would be living** away from his motherland.*

If an action still continues at a given future time in the past, we can use *would* + progressive infinitive.

- *He said he **would have finished** his thesis by the end of next month.*

If an action has finished before a given future time in the past, we can use *would* + perfective infinitive.

- *She said that by the end of May she **would have been studying** medicine for three years.*

If an action has extended for a specific length of time up to a given future time in the past and possibly continues at that time, we can use *would* + perfective progressive infinitive.

- *I had a feeling that the vacation **was going to** be a disaster.*
- *He said that we **were to leave** at six.*
- *We **were to have left** at six but it rained.*
- *They said goodbye, little knowing that they **were never to meet** again.*

*was/were going to* + infinitive is commonly used with past future reference clearly indicated in the context; *was/were going to* + infinitive usually occurs in dependent clauses, and in main clauses often denotes an unfulfilled intention. Was/Were to + infinitive is commonly used in formal style to denote a future action based on a past plan or arrangement. If the plan or arrangement is cancelled or unfulfilled, we will have to use *was/were to* + perfective infinitive; *was/were to* + infinitive can also be used in the sense of *was destined to*, in denoting a past destiny.

- *He said they **were going** on Tuesday.*

The past progressive can express an arrangement predetermind in the past.

- *He said he would tell her all about it if he **met** her.*
- *She told me that she would come to see me when she **visited** China again.*

For past future reference, the simple past is commonly found in adverbial clauses of condition and in those of time.

## EXERCISES

**I. Fill in the blanks with the correct forms of the verbs.**

| Base Form | Simple Present | Simple Past | Present Perfective |
|---|---|---|---|
| clean | | | |
| play | | | |
| sit | | | |
| teach | | | |
| buy | | | |
| live | | | |
| write | | | |
| eat | | | |
| give | | | |
| have | | | |
| travel | | | |
| say | | | |
| take | | | |
| bring | | | |
| make | | | |

**II. Fill in each blank with *will* or *be going to*.**

1. A: Why are you holding a piece of paper?
   B: I _____ (write) a letter to my friends back home in Shanghai.
2. A: I'm about to fall asleep. I need to wake up!
   B: I _____ (get) you a cup of coffee. That will wake you up.
3. A: I can't hear the television.
   B: I _____ (turn) it up so you can hear it.
4. We are so excited about our trip next month to Yellow Stone National Park.
   We _____ (visit) the world's greatest concentration of geysers.
5. Jack _____ (come) to the party.
   Sarah _____ (be) there as well.
6. A: It's so hot in here!
   B: I _____ (turn) the air-conditioning on.

7. I think he _____ (be) the next chairperson of Committee.
8. After I graduate, I _____ (attend) medical school and become a doctor.
9. A: Exercise me, I need to talk to someone about our hotel room. I am afraid it is simply too small for four people.

   B: That man at the service counter _____ (help) you.
10. As soon as the weather clears up, we _____ (walk) down to the beach and go swimming.

### III. Find the correct forms of tense and aspect to the actions.

A. Simple Present      B. Simple Past      C. Present Perfective

D. Present Progressive    E. Past Progressive    F. be going to—future time

G. will—future time

1. things in general
2. actions began and finished in the past
3. actions happening at the moment of speaking
4. actions happened in the past—the results of them are important in the present
5. actions in the present—one follows the other
6. actions in the past—one followed the other
7. actions started in the past and continue up to the present
8. this action was in progress when a new action interrupted it
9. repeated actions in the present
10. predictions in the future
11. actions express plans in the future
12. fixed plans in the near future
13. fixed arrangements (timetable)

### IV. Put the verbs into the correct tense.

1. Look! Sarah _____ (go) to the movies.
2. Linda usually _____ (put) on black shoes but now she _____ (wear) white trainers.
3. When she _____ (start) learning English she _____ (already, learn) French.
4. Before that day we _____ (never, think) of traveling to Japan.
5. My friend _____ (be) in America two years ago.
6. _____ (you, ever, see) a whale?
7. The receptionist _____ (welcome) the guests and _____ (ask) them to fill in the form.

8. While one group _____ (prepare) dinner the others _____ (collect) wood for the campfire.
9. I _____ (finish) it by the end of this month.
10. Tomorrow I think I _____ (start) my new project.

# 7. Voice System

## Aims of the Unit

> In this unit we will discuss some general matters about voice. Five questions will be discussed in particular:
> - What is voice? What are the two voices in English?
> - How is an active sentence transformed into a passive one?
> - What are the constraints on the transformation?
> - What are the uses of the passive voice?
> - Is there always an absolute division of work between an active and a be + v-ed construction in expressing the meaning of voice?

### ◇ 7.1  Active Sentence and Passive Sentence

Voice is the form of a verb that designates its relationship with the subject in a sentence. There are two types of voice in English, the active voice and the passive voice. The active voice shows that the action of the verb is performed by the subject. When the subject is the recipient of the action, the verb takes the form of passive voice. In this book, the subject indicating the person or thing that performs the action is thus called a **performer**, and the one receiving the action a **receiver**. A sentence/clause whose predicator (predicate verb) is active is called an active sentence and a sentence/clause whose predicator (predicate verb) is passive is called a passive sentence.

performer
执行者
receiver
接受者

**Task 1**  Analyze the following sentences and fill in the table below them. The first sentence is analyzed with the results filled in for you.

(1) The bird built a nest.
(2) A nest was built by the bird.
(3) Tom cleaned the blackboard.
(4) The blackboard was cleaned by Tom.
(5) Many people heard the explosion.
(6) The match was won by our team.
(7) The shoemaker made the shoes.
(8) The ball was caught by Mary.

| No. | Subject | Performer/Receiver | Voice of Verb |
| --- | --- | --- | --- |
| (1) | The bird | performer | active |
| (2) |  |  |  |
| (3) |  |  |  |
| (4) |  |  |  |
| (5) |  |  |  |
| (6) |  |  |  |
| (7) |  |  |  |
| (8) |  |  |  |

## 7.2 Transformation of Active Voice into Passive Voice

Most clauses with a transitive verb in the predicate can be put into the passive. The transformation, in general, consists of four steps: a) to move O to the initial position of the sentence, so that now it becomes S, thus taking on the subjective case form if it is a pronoun; b) to change the active verb into the passive construction; c) to add a preposition *by* after the passive construction; d) to move S after the preposition, forming a by-phrase. Now this S, if it is also a pronoun, takes on the objective case. There are three patterns of English clauses that contain the object: the SVO, SVoO and SVOC pattern. Details of transformation as arising from the differences of the three patterns will be discussed below.

### 1) SVO Pattern

It seems to be a simple process to transform the SVO construction, according to what was stated above.

*Tom cleaned the room.* → *The room was cleaned by Tom.*

If, however, the sentence is complex, with O being an objective clause, its passive counterpart must contain a formal subject. The way to do it is to make the main clause passive by using *it* to represent O, and putting it in the subject position, thus leaving the objective clause in place. The main verb, of course, must then be transformed into the passive form. Now the pronoun *it* acts as the formal subject of the sentence, while the subordinate clause the real subject.

*They think **that he will come.***

→ *It is thought **that he will come.***

*People said **that a hospital would be built in the town.***

→ *It was said **that a hospital would be built in the town.***

## 2) SVoO Pattern

The SVoO pattern is transformed with either the direct or the indirect object moved to the subject position. Contrast:

*They gave each of the boys an apple.*

→ ***Each of the boys*** *was given an apple*

→ ***An apple*** *was given each of the boys.*

*The Prime Minister offered him a post in the Cabinet.*

→ ***He*** *was offered a post in the Cabinet.*

→ ***A post*** *in the Cabinet was offered him.*

Of the two passives in each example, the first form is more common. The second form is usually replaced by the corresponding pattern with a prepositional phrase.

*An apple was given **to each of the boys.***

*A post in the Cabinet was offered **to him.***

Other prepositions may take the place of *to*, depending on the property of the verb used in the sentence.

*They built him a house.*

→ *A house was built **for him.***

## 3) SVOC Pattern

The SVOC pattern is transformed with the object moved to the initial position of the sentence, now acting as subject, and the object complement remaining in place, but now acting as subject complement.

*I **heard him** singing in the classroom.*

→ *He **was heard** singing in the classroom.*

*A **woman picking blackberries found the puma** dead.*

→ *The **puma was found** dead **by a woman picking blackberries**.*

*People **took him** for my brother.*

→ *He **was taken** for my brother.*

*We **found all our seats** occupied.*

→ *All our seats **were found** occupied.*

While the active sentence allows the complex object to include a bare infinitive as object complement, the passive requires a to-infinitive as subject complement.

*People never heard her **sing so well before**.*

→ *She was never heard **to sing so well before**.*

**Task 2**  You are given four sentences. Complete the four steps of transforming each into the passive voice. You may decide whether to leave off the agent in the transformation. The first step of the transformation of the first sentence is done for you, in the relevant box below the sentences. Also notice that Sentence (2) can be transformed into two passive forms, with o and O moved respectively into the subject position.

(1) She recognized me at once.

(2) I bought him a gift.

(3) They saw a man standing in front of the house.

(4) John wanted her to go the office at once.

---

She recognized me at once.

→ *I* She recognized at once

→

→

→

## ◆ 7.3  Constraints on Transformation

Every verb has an -ed form, but it does not follow that every active sentence can be transformed into a passive one. Constraints are various. On the other hand, there are also verbs that normally occur in passive constructions, which means the sentence using such a verb as predicate does not have an active counterpart.

**1) Constrains on the Transformation of Active Sentence into Passive Sentence**

① **Property of the verb as constraint**: Generally, **static verbs**, such as *have*, *hold*, *lack* and *resemble*, can not be transformed into the passive voice. Transformations like these, therefore, are not allowed.

> The quiet little room **becomes** me perfectly.
> → * I *was quite* become by the quiet little room perfectly.
> The color of the dress **doesn**'t suit her.
> → * She *isn*'t suited by the color of her dress.

There are exceptions; the verb *own*, for example, which is static in nature, can still be used in the passive construction.

> Bob **owned** a house in the city.
> → The house **was owned** by Bob.

Some verbs, which are polysemous and which can be either static or dynamic, may be used in the passive with a meaning that is dynamic.

> The book may **be had** ( = obtained) at any bookstall.

Set phrases of the V + N construction, a special type of **phrasal verb**, can not be treated as a **free verb phrase**, which means the N can not be moved to the subject position of the sentence, where the set phrase occurs, to make it passive. Transformations like these, therefore, are not allowed.

> The medicine soon **took effect**.
> → * *Effect was* soon **taken** by the medicine.

An exception to this rule concerns the V + N + Prep construction, which may either be treated as a phrasal verb, or as a free verbal phrase.

> He **took good care of** his books.

---

constraint
限制性
property of the verb as constraint
动词属性的限制性
dynamic verbs
动态动词
static verbs
静态动词

---

phrasal verb
词组动词"动词+名词"相当于一个不及物动词。词组动词中的任何构成成分一般都不可替换,如 take place,没有被动语态。
free verb phrase
自由动词词组,即词组中的非中心成分可根据上下文和表达的需要而替换,如 look after the children,从而有被动态。

→ *His books were taken good care of.*

→ *Great care was taken of his books.*

② **Property of object as constraint**: Sentences with a **reflexive** or **reciprocal pronoun** as object can not be turned into the passive.

*He hurt himself when he fell from the ladder.*

→ \* *Himself was hurt when he fell from the ladder.*

*We should help each other.*

→ \* *Each other should be helped by us.*

Sentences with a **gerund** or an **infinitive verb** as object can not be turned into the passive.

*John enjoyed seeing her.*

→ \* *Seeing her was enjoyed by John.*

*John hoped to go with her.*

→ \* *To go with her was hoped by John.*

There is an exception to this rule concerning the sentence with a to-infinitive verb as object. A few verbs, such as *desire*, *decide*, *agree* and *feel*, when followed by an infinitive, can be changed into the passive construction by using an anticipatory as the **formal subject**, which now represents the infinitive as the real subject, in the passive sentence so transformed.

*We desired to have the report delivered here.*

→ *It was desired to have the report delivered here.*

*My family decided to go abroad.*

→ *It was decided (by my family) to go abroad.*

Sentences with a **cognate object** can not be turned into the passive.

*We are living a happy life.*

→ \* *A happy life is being lived.*

*She dreamed a sweet dream.*

→ \* *A sweet dream was dreamed by her.*

Some nouns are only suitable for use as object in the active sentence, such as (A) abstract nouns and (B) names of the body parts, thus disallowing transformations like these.

(A) *No one but Barry showed much **interest** in the proposal.* (abstract noun)

→ \* *Much interest was shown in the proposal by no one by Barry.*

(B) *He shook his **head** as if to say no.* (noun for a body part)

→ \* *His head was shaken as if to say no.*

## 2) Passive-only Verbs

For various reasons, some verbs are always used in the passive construction to express a certain meaning, and this means the sentence in which such a verb occurs does not have an active counterpart.

(A) Shakespeare was **born** in 1564.

(B) She is **reputed** to be the best singer in Europe.

(A) contains *born*, the base form of which, *bear*, is rarely used in an active sentence to express the meaning intended here—brought into existence. The alternative expression that may replace it is the phrasal verb *give birth to*.

(C) Belinda Whiting gave birth to Sophie, a baby with Down's syndrome, 18 months ago.

This is also the case with (B), where *repute* is normally not used in active form either. Similarly the sentence can be altered by using *reputation*, the noun form of *repute*:

(D) She has a reputation of being the best singer in Europe.

**Task 3** Read each of these statements carefully and decide whether it is true or false. Write T for true or F for false in the bracket after each statement.

(1) All active sentences can be changed into passives.

(2) Every passive sentence has an active counterpart.

(3) A sentence with a static verb as predicate can be changed into the passive.

(4) Whether transformation is allowed may, in some sentences, depend on the form of the object.

## ◈ 7.4　Voice of Phrasal Verbs

Phrasal verbs, which fall into three basic types, ie. v + adv, v + prep and v + adv + prep, can occur in passive constructions like these:

| Passive Forms | Examples |
| --- | --- |
| be + v-ed + adv | be set up |
| be + v-ed + prep | be looked at |
| be + v-ed + adv + prep | be done away with |

It is actually the head word that occurs in passive construction, followed by adv, prep, or adv+prep, particles that join them to form a phrase.

### 1) Passive Constructions of Non-finite Verbs

*passive non-finite verb 非限定动词的被动式*

Non-finite verbs are not used as predicate verbs, thus do not make a sentence passive, but they may have passive forms themselves. Because a passive construction is composed of a v-ed preceded by an auxiliary, relevant to the discussion here are other two forms, the infinitive and the -ing form, the latter functioning either as present participle or as gerund. Their passives are as follows:

| | |
|---|---|
| to be done | the passive infinitive |
| being done | the passive -ing form |

Non-finite verbs do not vary for tense, but for aspect, and as always the change occurs with the auxiliary be. To analyze:

| Forms | Analyses |
|---|---|
| to *be* done | passive infinitive |
| to *have been* done | passive perfect infinitive |
| *being* done | passive present participle or passive gerund |
| *having been* done | passive present perfect participle or passive perfect gerund |

### 2) Sentences with Passive Non-finite Verbs

A sentence is active in voice with its predicate verb active, but it may contain a non-finite verb in passive construction. Just as an active non-finite verb plays various functions other than that of predicate, so does a passive construction of non-finite verb. To analyze:

**Functions of passive infinitive construction:**

| Examples | Functions |
|---|---|
| It's an honor for me *to be asked to speak here.* | subject |
| The survey is expected *to be completed by late 1998.* | subject complement |
| I asked *to be relived of my job.* | object |
| I want this letter *to be opened* now! | object complement |
| There are a lot of things *to be done.* | attribute |
| The kids went to the hospital *to be inoculated.* | adverbial |
| My wish is *to be given permission to try this new method.* | subject complement |

## 7. Voice System

**Functions of passive gerund contruction:**

| Examples | Functions |
|---|---|
| So *being killed* by sharks was a common occurrence. | subject |
| She doesn't like *being kept* waiting. | object |
| She is far from *being pleased*; she's very angry. | prepositional object |

**Functions of passive present participle contruction:**

| Examples | Functions |
|---|---|
| The building *being renovated* is an ancient temple. | attribute |
| *Being given* a chance, she immediately jumped at it. | adverbial |
| He often came to watch the boats *being loaded and unloaded*. | object complement |

**Task 4**   Point out the tense and aspect of the passive construction in each of the following sentences. Where the verb is non-finite, you are also required to name its syntactic function in the sentence.

(1) The small temple is visited by tourists from all parts of the country.
(2) The meeting was put off till next Monday.
(3) A Korean acetic acid plant will be completed on time.
(4) The dogs were being looked after by a warm-hearted neighbor.
(5) Your cosmetics will have been chosen from the vast range that only Pia can offer.
(6) The last years of his life seem to have been largely given over to this task.
(7) He had been mayor of Cologne before being expelled by the Nazis.
(8) There is a distinction to be drawn here between simplifications and assumptions.

### ◈ 7.5   Uses of Passive Voice

Notice that there is not always a one-to-one relationship between a sentence and a specific use. A sentence removed from the context may be analyzed as having a few potential uses. The exact use in a certain context is normally determined by any of the various factors: speaker's intension, the demand of cohesion and the register.

### 1) Speaker-related Use of Passive Voice

Basically, whether to use the passive voice depends on the intention of the speaker. There are cases where the speaker intends to

① show courtesy or politeness by omitting the mention of the performer, as in making a demand, request, or an invitation:

*You are asked to be punctual.*

*It's hoped that you'll join us in the activity.*

② be tactful, as in offering an explanation for a state of affairs, or an excuse for an action:

*This proposal was generally considered as not very practical.*

*I'm not supposed to disclose the details of the plan.*

③ avoid an unnecessary mention of the performer:

*We respected him.*

*He was respected.*

Or of the performer that is understood in the context:

*Jack fought Michael in the men's singles and was beaten.*

*You'll be asked many questions at the press conference.*

④ keep who the performer is as a secret:

*Tom: The cup's broken, Mom.*

*Mom: I know it is broken, but who broke it?*

*Tom: I don't know who. I only know it's broken.*

It is actually Tom who broke the cup himself, but concerned about the possibility of getting punished, he uses a passive sentence to describe only the present status of the cup, excluding the mention of himself as the performer.

⑤ describe an action whose performer is unknown:

*My bike was stolen yesterday.*

*The book had been mysteriously moved from its customary place.*

### 2) Cohesion-related Use of Passive Voice

**Cohesion** can be roughly defined as the quality that holds together the linguistic elements in a text to make it meaningful. This quality sometimes demands the use of passive voice.

① Cohesion within a Clause

This may happen to a pair of verbs sharing one subject, the first verb taking the subject as performer, and the second receiver. Though the two verbs are in different semantic relations with the subject, the whole sentence reads compact and smooth, due to the passive form the second verb takes on. Contrast the two sentences, of which (A) is preferable.

(A) *Jack fought Michael in the men's singles* **and was beaten.**

(B) *Jack fought Michael in the men's singles* **and his rival beat him.**

② Cohesion between Clauses

This may happen to a complex sentence where the subjects of the two clauses refer to the same person. Semantically, however, the main clause subject is the performer, hence an active verb in this clause, while the subordinate clause subject the receiver, hence a passive construction. Though the two clauses are different in voice, they read smooth, as both share the same point of view. Contrast the two sentences, of which (A) is preferable:

(A) *He arrived at London where* **he was met by his friend.**

(B) *He arrived at London where* **his friend met him.**

It may also happen to a clause with a by-phrase to mention the performer at its end, so that the attributive clause modifying the performer noun may come just close, a principle of sentence making that facilitates cohesion. Contrast the two sentences, of which (A) is preferable:

(A) *The picture was painted by* **a very good friend of mine whom I'd like you to meet sometime.**

(B) **A very good friend of mine** *painted the picture* **whom I'd like you to meet sometime.**

③ Cohesion between Sentences

This may happen to a sentence where the receiver to be mentioned is the same person or thing as the one that has just been mentioned in the preceding sentence. Thus it would be desirable that the receiver in this second sentence be mentioned as subject, so as to be in the position closest to the preceding sentence, where the same noun occurred. Distance in the linier order is an importance means of cohesion. Contrast the two sentences, of which (A) is preferable:

(A) *He visited* **China's northeastern provinces** *in 1935.* ***Those provinces*** *were being overrun by the Japanese invaders.*

(B) *He visited* **China's northeastern provinces** *in 1935.* ***The Japanese invaders*** *overran those provinces.*

## 3) Register-related Use of Passive Voice

**register** 语域

**Register** is a form of a language used for a particular purpose or in a particular social setting. There are registers where passive voice is used more frequently.

① In Public Notices (Sometimes with *Be* Omitted)

Road **blocked**.

Cameras **forbidden**.

② In Announcements

Passengers **are requested** to remain seated until the aircraft comes to a complete stop.

You **are required** to give a talk to the members of your group on a topic of your choice.

③ In News Reports

The search for the bank robbers continues. Meanwhile many people **have been questioned** and the owner of the stolen getaway car **has been traced**.

④ In News Headlines (Usually with *Be* Omitted)

Kennedy **assassinated**!

Trade Agreement **Broken**!

⑤ In Business Letters

Your letter **has been received**.

If additional work, or special items such as gold taps **are requested** by you, then you **will be expected** to pay for these.

⑥ In Articles of Science and Technology

Today, spaceships **are being launched** regularly. The space shuttle **is being perfected**. Satellites **are being sent into** orbit to beam radio, television and telephone signals worldwide. Space stations **are being designed**. And lasers, powerful rays of directed light, **are being used** in all areas of high technology.

**Task 5**

Fill in the blanks with appropriate adjectives according to what you have learned about the uses of passive voice.

Passive voice may be used when it is (1) _____ to mention the performer that can be understood from either the linguistic or situational context, (2) _____ to mention the performer, which may cause unwelcome consequences, or (3) _____ to mention the performer who is still unknown even to the speaker himself.

## 7.6 Passivity—Form and Meaning

Actually, not all passive meanings are expressed by passive verbs—some active constructions may express passive meanings. On the other hand, not all "be+v-ed" constructions are passive; some may serve as the predicate in the sentence of SVC pattern. In addition, **active non-finite verbs** may also express passive meanings in certain constructions.

### 1) Active Sentences with Passive Meanings

There are certain verbs that are transitive, but they can be used intransitively, without an object following. To understand such a sentence, one will have to look for the receiver of the action described by the verb in the same sentence, only to find the subject qualifies in terms of meaning, hence the emergence of the passive relation between the verb and the subject. The verb may be in simple present tense, modified by an adverb of degree, such as *easily* and *well*.

> active non-finite verbs
> 非限定动词的主动式

The books **sell** well.

The box **doesn't close** properly.

Or it may occur with a negative modal auxiliary:

The belt **won't buckle**.

This material **won't wear**.

Or it may simply be in the progressive aspect:

The house **is building**.

The book **is printing**.

An active sentence with a passive meaning draws attention to the receiver itself, with the verb describing the condition about it, condition in connection with the inherent quality of the product or goods being talked about in business communication, which is the subject or receiver in the sentence. Also notice that the last two sentences represent a style of the past and are found in some professional jargons of some special fields today.

### 2) "*Be+v-ed*" as Predicate in SVC Pattern

Not all "be+v-ed" constructions are passive forms; some may serve as the predicates in the sentence of SVC pattern, with *be* acting as linking verb and v-ed as subject complement or predicative, the typical role of an adjective.

He is *easily drunk*.

He is *more interested* in chess *than* in ball games.

In meaning the complement indicates a state, mostly a **mental state**, differing from a passive construction, which mostly indicates an action. One guideline is that of modification. The v-ed form, if it is subject complement and therefore describes a state, may be modified by an adverb, such as *very* and *terribly*, or may take on a comparative form—typical features of an adjective. The examples above show the two v-eds, *drunk* and *interested*, as having such features.

> mental state
> 精神状态

Another guideline is that an **adjective v-ed** may be followed by a prepositional phrase as modification, rather than by a by-phrase mentioning the receiver, which is the case with a passive construction. Contrast:

> adjective v-ed
> 由-ed 分词转化来的形容词

① (A) He is more *interested in chess* than *in ball games*. (SVC)

  (B) He was *interested by what you told him*. (passive voice)

② (A) I am very *surprised at your behaviour*. (SVC)

  (B) I was *surprised by a knock at the door*. (passive voice)

③ (A) The ground is *covered with snow*. (SVC)

  (B) The ground is *covered by snow*. (passive voice)

Still another guideline has something to do with *be* as not being the only linking verb in English; there are other ones like *seem*, *look*, *become*, etc. One may choose a proper one depending on what one intends to say. This is different from the case of a passive construction, which admits only *be*, or occasionally *get*, as its auxiliary. Contrast:

He *is/looks/seems/feels tired*. (SVC)

They *are bogged down in all sorts of problems*. (passive voice)

They *are getting bogged down in all sorts of problems*. (passive voice)

### 3) Active Non-finite Verbs with a Passive Meaning

① Active Infinitives

• Active infinitives as post-attributes

I have a lot of clothes *to wash*.

With so many exercises *to do*, I can't go to the cinema.

There is no time *to lose*.

He is an impossible person *to work with*.

> active infinitiv
> as post attribu
> 作为后置定
> 的主动不定з
> active infinitiv
> as adverbials
> 作为状语的
> 动不定式

- Active infinitives as adverbials

*The question is difficult **to answer**.* ( *cf. The question is difficult **for me to answer**.* )

*The box is too heavy **to carry**.*

*The house is big enough **to live in**.*

*We found the text difficult **to learn**.*

- Active infinitives after an interrogative word

Such infinitives may serve as subject complement, or as object.

*The question is what **to do** next.*

*I don't know what **to do**.*

- Active infinitives *to let* and *to blame* acting as subject complements

*Tom is **to blame**.*

*The house is **to let**.*

The use of the active non-finite verbs discussed above does not mean that their corresponding passive forms are never used. In many cases the choice of a voice is a matter of intention and style. Generally, if the speaker intends to focus on the receiver and the circumstances around it, he will use an active infinitive; if, however, the focus is on the action and performer, a passive infinitive will be used. Where the performer is mentioned in a by-phase, the infinitive will invariably be passive.

*I have a lot of clothes **to be washed**.*

*Since your price is too high **to be accepted**, we have no choice but to place our order elsewhere.*

*To be washed* is used probably because the speaker intends to emphasize the action of washing, and yet definitely because he intends the performer to be someone else not mentioned in the sentence, rather than the one expressed by subject.

*To be accepted* is used to show politeness, a matter of style. As discussed above, the "too + adj. + to + do" construction would be understood as one with the performer omitted. In this sentence the performer to be understood is *us*, the party that refuses to accept the offer from the other party, an unpleasant action to notify. The use of the passive infinitive, which saves the mention of the performer that performs the unpleasant action, helps avoid being overdirect and abrupt.

Sometimes the choice of a voice makes a difference in implication. Contrast:

(A) There's nothing to do.

(B) There's nothing to be done.

By (A), the speaker implies he does not have anything to do at the time of speaking and therefore feels bored; by (B), however, he implies he does not find anything possible to do at present, not able to change the current state of affairs.

> Active Gerund
> 主动动名词

② Active Gerunds with a Passive Meaning May Be Used

• After a verb that expresses a meaning about need

Your room is really a mess! It **needs cleaning**.

The plants **want watering** every day.

• After a word that expresses a meaning about deserving

I don't think his article **deserves reading**.

They **merit praising**.

• After the preposition worth:

I don't think that film is **worth seeing**.

• After a preposition with a meaning about exceeding

The problem is **past understanding**.

Such hardships are **beyond bearing**.

**Task 6** The table below contains four types of sentence regarding voice, ① active both in form and meaning, ② passive both in form and meaning, ③ active in form but passive in meaning and ④ be + v-ed as predicate in SVC pattern. Decide the type of each and fill proper space in the table.

| Analysis \ Sentences | Form | Meaning |
|---|---|---|
| (1) The ship was moving. | active | |
| (2) Susan was so amused! | | |
| (3) The surface cleans easily. | | |
| (4) He was born in China. | | |
| (5) His leaves some questions to be answered. | | |
| (6) The guy does not know what to say or do. | | |
| (7) The problem is beyond my understanding. | | |
| (8) This question left Rei with nothing to say. | | |

# EXERCISES

I. **Make sentences with the following groups of words and expressions, one group for a sentence. You must decide whether to mention the agent or instrument, and to use *be* or *get*, *with* or *by* for each group, so as to render the sentence proper.**

1. punished, criminal
2. the senators, signed, the bill
3. the work, should, do, at once
4. they, must, have finished, their work
5. be likely, let down, you
6. beginners, be apt to, make such mistakes
7. he, never, punish enough
8. the boy, hurt, on his way home from work
9. ground, covered, snow
10. such work, must, handle, great care

II. **Correct the mistakes in the following sentences.**

1. I feel greatly honored to welcome into their society.
2. He hurried to the booking office only to tell that all the tickets had been sold out.
3. At the beginning of the class, the noise of the desks to open and close could be heard outside the classroom.
4. After he became conscious, he remembered to attack and hit on the head with a rod.
5. I hear they've promoted Tom, but he didn't mention promoting when we talked on the phone.
6. Having shown around the Water Cube, we were then taken to see the Bird's Nest for the 2008 Olympic Games.
7. The library renovated at present used to be a museum.
8. We are very worried about the blind man leading to a dangerous river bank.
9. All of them expected the family picture to keep on the wall of the hall.
10. What surprised the students most was their not allowed to visit the museum.

Ⅲ. **Transform the following sentences into the passive voice.**

1. Shakespeare wrote *Hamlet*.
2. We have to put off the sports meet.
3. People say he is a smart boy.
4. His friend lent him some money.
5. He disclosed to them the secret of his invention.
6. He sold the young man the wrong book.
7. They asked him to make a speech.
8. The boss made him work all day long.
9. They elected Tom monitor of the class.
10. My father was watching the boys playing basketball.

Ⅳ. **The following are the sentences that normally can not be transformed into the passive voice. Study each carefully, and figure out why it can not be so.**

1. The steward introduced himself as Peter.
2. They esteemed each other and made allowances for each other.
3. She will have been caring for her sick sister for a total of three years by the end of next month.
4. We slept a comfortable sleep last night.
5. She washed her face and hands.
6. I made faces to have the baby laugh.
7. This plan sounds a good one.
8. Mr. Smith wanted to have a try.
9. I enjoy listening to pop music.
10. The woolen coat fits her well.

Ⅴ. **Study the following sentences and explain the reason for the use of the passive voice in each.**

1. Most of the Earth's surface is covered by water.
2. The music was followed by a short interval.
3. You are cordially invited to this ceremony.
4. Visitors are requested not to touch the exhibits.
5. It's agreed that we all stand behind him.
6. Mr. Thompson is going to sell his pub because it is haunted.
7. It's alleged that goods were brought into the country illegally.
8. The strike is expected to end soon.

9. The original painting has been destroyed.

10. Goods of every conceivable kind are sold at the bazaar.

**VI. Fill in the blanks with appropriate expressions. You are to choose one from the pair of expressions supplied after each sentence.**

1. These engines used to be started by hand. _____.

    A. Now we start them by electricity

    B. Now they are started by electricity

2. The next morning he found that the doors had been blocked by chairs, and that _____.

    A. someone had moved the furniture

    B. the furniture had been moved

3. Tom: What is happening to the car?

    Jim: _____.

    A. It is being cleaned

    B. Albert is washing it

4. We are looking forward to the Olympic Games because _____ before in this country.

    A. they have never been held

    B. we have never held them

5. _____, who is a young artist from the States.

    A. The lecture will be made by Joe Smith

    B. Joe Smith will make the lecture

6. At 5:05 pm on Saturday 19th July, there was an accident at the junction of the Main Street and Panda Road when _____.

    A. a delivery van knocked a boy down off his bicycle

    B. a boy was knocked down off his bicycle by a delivery van

7. The boy was sent to St. Maria Hospital where _____.

    A. he was treated for shock and a broken arm

    B. the doctors treated him for shock and a broken arm

8. Compare clothes _____ with clothes washed by any other laundry.

    A. which we have washed

    B. which have been washed by us

9. _____ with a hail of insults as she arrived at the students' union.

   A. The crowds greeted the Prime Minister

   B. The Prime Minister was greeted

10. Another seeking a management post in Saudi Arabia knocked 10 years off his age but _____ when he had to hand in his passport.

    A. was caught out

    B. the officer caught him out

## VII. Translate the following into English.

1. 找女工。
2. 本室严禁吸烟。
3. 书籍不得携出室外。
4. 参观人士请勿触摸展品。
5. 请旅客们不要把头伸到窗外面去。
6. 五岁男童遭绑架!
7. 你的投诉正在调查之中。(in business letters)
8. 新厂建立时,通常为某工业链的一部分,因而总定位于该工业链中其他厂家之附近。
9. 将球茎置于玻璃瓶颈中,以保持干燥。
10. 对银行劫匪的搜寻仍在继续。许多人受到盘问,劫匪逃逸所用赃车的主人也受到了追查。

## VIII. Identify the construction of the underlined part in each of the following sentences.

1. The library is usually closed at 6.
2. The library is now closed.
3. The hill was covered with snow.
4. She was lost in the forest.
5. He was surprised at the news.
6. He was surprised by noise.
7. He'll be surprised when he meets me.
8. Liu Mei is gone.
9. The report is well written.
10. The report was written with great care.

## 7. Voice System

**IX. Multiple choice.**

1. I'm going to the supermarket this afternoon. Do you have anything _____ ?
   A. to be buying  B. to buy
   C. for buying    D. bought

2. I like getting up very early in summer. The morning air is so good _____ .
   A. to be breathed  B. to breathe
   C. breathing       D. being breathed

3. There is a new problem involved in the popularity of private cars _____ road conditions need _____ .
   A. that, to be improved   B. which, to be improved
   C. where, improving       D. when, improving

4. He will show you the room _____ as the meeting-room.
   A. to use      B. for use
   C. to be used  D. being used

5. Apart from some dark patches on the wall that he hadn't noticed before, there was nothing _____ .
   A. to see     B. to be seen
   C. being seen D. seeing

6. Well, you see, I think it's such a masterpiece in itself _____ there's just nothing _____ .
   A. that, to do        B. and, to do
   C. that, to be done   D. and, to be done

7. As one mother described, "I've seen me going three or four days without anything _____ ."
   A. to be eaten  B. to eat
   C. for eating   D. being eaten

8. You can usually work out who is to _____ and what you can do about it.
   A. blame    B. blamed
   C. blaming  D. to blame

9. They're to _____, not pitied.
   A. blame     B. blamed
   C. be blamed D. be blaming

10. There was nothing worth _____ on television, so he went back into the kitchen.
    A. to watch              B. to be watched
    C. watching              D. being watched
11. At last, exasperated beyond _____, I switched on the light again.
    A. bear                  B. bearing
    C. being born            D. be bearing
12. A properly constructed system, in good repair, does not normally require _____.
    A. cleaning              B. being cleaned
    C. clean                 D. to clean
13. Precisely how the disease process works is still a mystery, and a great deal remains _____ it.
    A. to be learned about   B. to be learned
    C. learn about           D. learn
14. It must be simple enough to _____ efficiently by non-planning professionals, but detailed enough to _____ meaningful results.
    A. be used, produce      B. use, produce
    C. use, produced         D. use, be produced
15. Dinah has done nothing to _____ _____ her career ended in such a way.
    A. deserve, have
    B. deserve, having
    C. be deserved, to have
    D. be deserved, having
16. In very dry weather, the light soil will want _____, not just a watering-canful, but a prolonged sprinkling with a spray attachment from a hose for about half an hour.
    A. water                 B. to water
    C. to be watered         D. watering
17. It was an agreeable house to _____, but the atmosphere was not conducive to study.
    A. live                  B. be lived
    C. live in               D. be lived in

18. He had been shut in a virtual cupboard all day without anything to _____ just because of his haircut.
    A. be eaten            B. be eating
    C. eating              D. eat
19. Anne had given her the parcel to _____ two days before and she had completely forgotten all about it.
    A. be posted           B. be posing
    C. posting             D. post
20. I am too clever and too hard to _____.
    A. manage              B. be managed
    C. managing            D. be managing

# 8. Mood System

## Aims of the Unit

> In this unit we will discuss some general matters about mood. Five questions will be discussed in particular:
> - What is mood?
> - What are the three types of mood in modern English?
> - What is be-subjunctive?
> - What is were-subjunctive?
> - What other forms are there in modern English expressing hypothetical meaning?

Mood is the form of a verb which expresses the speaker's attitude towards the action or state denoted by the verb used in a clause or sentence. The speaker may consider the action or state, for instance, as real, unreal or uncertain. The English language uses different forms of verbs to indicate such different attitudes.

**Task 1**  Study these sentences and decide whether the expressions in bold denote an action or state that is real, unreal or uncertain.

(1) I *went* to the theatre last week.

(2) *Come* to my office at once!

(3) If I *were younger*, I would travel all over the world.

## ◈ 8.1　Types of Mood

There are three moods in modern English: **the indicative mood**, **the imperative mood** and **the subjunctive mood.**

### 1) Indicative Mood

The indicative mood shows that the speaker considers an action or a state denoted by the verb or the verb phrase as a real or actual fact, hence an alternative term fact mood. It is used in statements (both affirmative and negative), questions and exclamations of facts.

> Tom *is cleaning* the room. (affirmative statement)
> Tom *didn't go* to Beijing. (negative statement)
> Will you *come* to the party? (question)
> How hot it *is* today! (exclamation)

The verb in the indicative mood is required to vary in form according to certain set of rules for subject-verb concord. (See Section 3 for details about this)

indicative mood
陈述式（语气）
imperative mood
祈使式（语气）
subjunctive mood
虚拟式（语气）

### 2) Imperative Mood

The imperative mood conveys the speaker's will to urge someone to fulfill an action, hence an alternative name will-mood. It is used to give a command, request or warning:

> ① *Give* him what help you can.
> ② *Do not make* the same mistake again.

The form of the sentence with this mood is simple: the base form of the verb like *give* and *make* in ① and ②, followed by other elements if necessary, all with the subject, usually the second person pronoun, unmentioned. Variant forms are possible, such as an emphatic demand of request. (See Section 5.3 for details about this)

command 命令
request 要求
warning 警告

### 3) Subjunctive Mood

The subjunctive mood shows that the speaker considers the action or state being talked about as unreal or uncertain, hence an alternative name thought-mood. It can be used to express ① a suggestion, where the action or state is considered uncertain, ② a wish or impossible hope, where the action or state is considered unreal, and ③ a supposition, where the action or state is considered either unreal or uncertain, e.g.

> I suggest Tom *go* home. (action uncertain)
> I wish I *were* younger. (state unreal)
> If I *were* you, I would not take it. (state unreal)
> This, if the news *be* true, is a very serious matter. (state uncertain)

Notice that the forms of the verbs in these sentences are all subjunctives and, therefore, not subject to any subject-verb concord rules in the **syntax of indicative clauses**. There are only two categories of subjunctive mood in modern English: the **be-subjunctive** and **were-subjunctive**, which will be dealt with separately in Section 8.2 and 8.3.

> syntax of indicative clauses
> 陈述式分句句法
> be-subjunctive
> be-型虚拟式
> were-subjunctive
> were-型虚拟式

**Task 2**

Identify the type of mood adopted in each of the three sentences given in Task 1. The sentences are copied here, to facilitate your identification:
(1) I *went* to the theatre last week.
(2) *Come* to my office at once!
(3) If I *were* younger, I would travel all over the world.

## ◈ 8.2   Be-subjunctive

Be-subjunctive includes the **bare infinitive** or the **base form of a verb**, normally a notional verb, with no variation for concord and tense, e.g.

① We propose that somebody neutral **take** the chair.
② I suggested he **consider** teaching and urged him to come to Fayetteville for an interview.

To form the negative, a negative word is put before the subjunctive verb:

③ The travel agent recommended strongly that we **not travel** on Thanksgiving Day.

This subjunctive can be used in nominal clauses, adverbial clauses and formulaic expressions, to express different kinds of uncertain meaning, as is discussed below.

> bare infinitive
> 不带 to 不定式
> base form of a verb
> 动词原形

> nominal clauses
> 名词性分句
> adverbial clauses
> 状语分句
> formulaic expressions
> 公式化语句

## 8. Mood System

### 1) In Nominal Clauses

This can be a clause stating an event which is not certain to happen—which it is hoped will happen, or imagined might happen or is wanted to happen. It may be an objective clause after a verb such as *suggest*, *propose*, *demand*, *insist*, *advise*, etc. as shown by ①, ② and ③ above. More examples:

Experts **advise** that the government **take** the problem of pollution seriously.

We **propose** that somebody neutral **take** the chair.

The clause may also serve other functions, when subordinating to the words of other parts of speech in the main clause:

④ It is **advised** by experts that the government **take** the problem of pollution seriously.

⑤ It is **advisable** that the government **take** the problem of pollution seriously.

⑥ Experts give **advice** that the government **take** the problem of pollution seriously.

⑦ Experts' **advice** is that the government **take** the problem of pollution seriously.

The two clauses in ④ and ⑤ both serve as subjects, in ⑥ as appositive and in ⑦ as predicative.

### 2) In Adverbial Clauses, Indicating Predictability, Concession, Prevention, etc. introduced by *if*, *as/so long as*; *though*, *whatever*; *lest*, etc.

If he **be** found guilty, John shall have the right of appeal.

So long as a volume **hold** together, I am not disturbed as to its outer appearance.

Though everyone **desert** you, I will not.

Whether she **be** right or wrong, she will have my unswerving support.

Whatever **be** his defense, we cannot tolerate this disloyalty.

Quietly we sat on the river bank, lest the fish **swim** away.

She is now studying for fear that she **fail** in English.

### 3) In Some Formulaic Expressions That Should Be Treated as Wholes

God **bless** you!

Heaven **forbid**!

So **be** it.

He will remain here if need **be**.

Far **be** it from me to spoil the fun.

---

appositive
同位语
predicative
表语
predictability
推测
concession
让步
prevention
防备

*Home is home*, **be** *it ever so homely.*

***Suffice*** *it to say that ...*

***Long live*** *the People's Republic of China!*

**Task 3**  Fill in the blanks with what you choose from the words and expressions given before the passage:

| nominal | unreal | adverbial | formulaic | uncertain |
| attributive | subjunctive | base | notional | linking |

Be-subjunctive includes the ___(1)___ form of any ___(2)___ verb used to express an ___(3)___ action or state. It can be used in a(n) ___(4)___ or an adverbial ___(5)___ clause, and in some ___(6)___ expressions.

## 8.3  Were-subjunctive

Were-subjunctive has only one form *were*, which goes with subjects of all persons: I/you/he/she/it/we/you/they ***were***.

This form applies to cases where the speaker considers the action or state being talked about unreal, and it may be used

• **In the nominal clause** after a verb such as *wish*, *would rather*, *suppose* and *imagine*, to express an impossible hope or preference

*I wish I **were** younger.*

*I'd rather I **were not** at the site of the accident.*

• **In the predicative clause** introduced by *as if*, *as though*

*She looks as if she **were** ten years younger.*

*The sun rises in the east and sets in the west, so it seems as if the sun **were** circling round the earth.*

• **In the adverbial clause** introduced by *as if/as though*, *though*, *if*, *if only*, etc. to denote an unreal condition or concession

*He spoke to me as if I **were** deaf.*

*He behaves as though he **were** better than us.*

*Even if she **were** here, she could not solve all the problems.*

*If I **were** you, I should wait until next week.*

*If only he **were** here with us, my son, how joyful would be this reunion!*

---

nominal clause
名词性分句
predicative clause
表语分句
adverbial clause
状语分句

## 8. Mood System

The subject-verb construction can be inverted in this clause, with the conjunction if omitted:

*Were* he in your position, he'd do the same.

*Were* they here now, they could help us.

As has been discussed, be-subjunctive may also be used in the adverbial clause of condition, but that form is formal in style. Besides, that form brings out a real condition, though uncertain, while were-subjunctive an unreal condition. Contrast:

*If the rumor be true, everything is possible.*

*If the rumor were true, everything would possible.*

Notice that this form can be used with the present and the past references. Contrast:

*I wish I were younger.* (present reference)

*He loves you as if you were the only person on earth.* (present reference)

*But he wasn't there. I wished he were.* (past reference)

*She wished she were a bird.* (past reference)

It may also be used with future reference, when followed by a to-infinitive:

*Just imagine everyone were to give up smoking.*

*If I were to do it, I should rely on you.*

There can also be subject-operator inversion in this structure:

*Were I to do it, I should rely on you.*

> present reference
> 照应现在
> past reference
> 照应过去
> subject-operator inversion
> 主语与操作词倒装

**Task 4** Fill in the blanks with what you choose from the words and expressions given before the passage:

| adverbial | conditional | concession | uncertain | manner |
| objective | only | real | supposition | unreal |

Were-subjunctive includes the __(1)__ member in this category. It is mostly used to express a(n) __(2)__ action or state. It can be used in the __(3)__ clause after a verb about wish or __(4)__, an adverbial clause that expresses unreal condition, __(5)__ and manner, and a predicative clause about __(6)__.

## 8.4　Other Forms Expressing Hypothetical Meanings

In addition to be- and were-subjunctive, modern English has a number of devices for expressing hypothetical meanings. We can use the past tense forms of verbs called did-hypothetical and the past tense modals (*should*, *would*, *could*, etc.) called should-hypothetical for the same purpose.

### 1) Did-hypothetical

This form is used to express hypothesis in the following contexts:
- It is time (that) ...

It is time we **went** to bed.

It is about time you **made up** your mind.

It is high time you **lent** her a hand.

- If only ...

If only I **knew** her address.

If only I **had** more money, I could buy a car.

If only she **had listened to** my advice.

- ... as if/as though ...

She works hard as if she never **knew** fatigue.

I've loved you so much as if you **were** my son.

She looked as if she **had had** some bad news.

In this construction, the choice of the verb form depends on the speakers's semantic intention. Contrast:

You sound as if you **knew** everything.

You sound as if you **know** everything.

I feel as if I **were going to** faint.

I feel as if I **am going to** faint.

- I wish (that) ...

I wish I **had been able** to help.

I wish I **hadn't said** that.

I wish the sun **was shining** at this moment.

She wishes she **had never got** involved in the whole affair.

- I would rather (that) you/he ...

*I would rather you **came** tomorrow.*

*I'm sure he is keeping something back. I would rather he **told** me the truth.*

*She got drunk last night. I'd rather she **hadn't drunk** so much.*

## 2) Should-hypothetical

This form may be used to express hypothesis in the following contexts.

- In conditionals

*If I knew the answer to all your questions, **I'd be** a genius.*

*If she were trying harder, her parents **wouldn't be** so anxious.*

*If it rained tomorrow, we'**d stay** at home.*

*If anything had happened, he **would have let** her know.*

*We **would have dropped by** if we had had time.*

- In implied conditionals

*But for your help, I **couldn't** have achieved anything.*

*Anyone who **should** do that **would** be laughed at.*

*In different circumstances, I **might** have aggred.*

*This same thing happened in wartime **would** amount todisaster.*

- In other contexts

*That she **should** forget me so quickly was rather a shock.*

*We insist that a meeting **should** be held as soon as possible.*

*Was it necessary that my uncle **should** be informed?*

**Oh that** *I* **could** *see him again!*

**Would that** *she* **could** *see her son again!*

*To think that he **would** marry such a nasty woman!*

*To think that he **should** have deserted his wife and children!*

*Who **would** have thought that things **should** come to such a tragic end!*

*The door was pushed open; who **should** come in but the woman they were talking about.*

---

implied conditionals
隐含条件句

**Task 5** Fill in the blanks with what you choose from the words and expressions given before the passage:

| a similar | subordinate | were-subjunctive | main | unreal |
| past | future | uncertain | supposition | unwelcome |

Did-hypothetical play __(1)__ grammatical functions as __(2)__, except that it may be used in it *is/was time* ... construction. Should-hypothetical is mostly used in the __(3)__ clause of a conditional sentence to express an __(4)__ or uncertain result. When used in the subordinate clause of a conditional sentence, it either refers to the __(5)__ time or suggests that the condition being talked about is unexpected or __(6)__.

# EXERCISES

Ⅰ. **Group the following sentences in terms of mood (indicative, imperative and subjunctive).**

1. <u>Let</u> me help you.
2. The earth <u>moves</u> round the sun.
3. I <u>don't think</u> he understood me.
4. He suggested that the meeting <u>be postponed</u>.
5. If I <u>were</u> you, I would not take it.
6. Please <u>don't make</u> a noise.
7. I wish I <u>didn't have to</u> go to work today.
8. <u>Come</u> here and speak to me.
9. Did you <u>have</u> a good time?
10. If he <u>be</u> found guilty, John shall have the right of appeal.

Ⅱ. **Rewrite the following sentences using be-subjunctive and then translate each into Chinese.**

1. I insist on his innocence.
2. If you insist on doing something, do it every day.
3. It is imperative to relax and calm down, if you feel your nerves racing.
4. It is imperative for all small islanders to act to mitigate and adapt to climate change.
5. I think it advisable for a secretary to be appointed at once.
6. The ambassador will stay there if necessary.

7. It suffices to say that the open policy will remain unchanged.
8. We propose somebody neutral for the chair.
9. May our great motherland live long!
10. If it is not so, let Mr. Darcy contradict it.

**III. Put the verbs in brackets into the proper subjunctive form in the following sentences and then translate each sentence into Chinese.**

1. Far (be) _____ it from me to tell you what to do, sir. But don't you think you should apologize?
2. _____ (be) it to snow tomorrow, they would not go out.
3. If I (be) _____ to pick a song that got me into radiohead, this would be it.
4. Everything was perfectly still, as if he (be) _____ the only living creature in that country.
5. "No, the damned Customs took it," John said, and as he had a gulp of whisky he added, "Devil (take) _____ them!"
6. If only she (be) _____ here now, we should be able to discuss the issue together.
7. He tossed off a pint of beer as though it (be) _____ a spoonful.
8. If he (be) _____ to succeed, the sun would rise from the west.
9. Speak frankly, I pray you, (be) _____ it for life or death.
10. Worse still, we leave the entire process to chance—to the Fates, as it (be) _____.

**IV. Multiple choices.**

1. If he _____ tomorrow, I would tell him everything.
   A. should come          B. comes
   C. will come            D. would come
2. Look at the terrible situation I am in! If only I _____ your advice.
   A. follow     B. would follow     C. had followed     D. have
3. As usual, he put on a show as though his trip _____ a great success.
   A. had been   B. has been    C. were    D. was
4. John is so strongly built that he looks as if he _____ an elephant.
   A. lifts      B. is lifting  C. lifted  D. could lift
5. There is a real possibility that these animals could be frightened, _____ a sudden loud noise.
   A. being there           B. should there be
   C. there was             D. there having been

6. If I had seen the movie, I _____ you all about it now.
   A. would tell					B. will tell
   C. have told					D. would have told

7. Who _____ that Eastern Europe could ever become so fashionable?
   A. would have thought			B. would think
   C. will think					D. have thought

8. It's about time people _____ notice of what women did during the war.
   A. take						B. took
   C. have taken					D. will take

9. He's working hard for fear that he _____.
   A. should fall behind			B. fell behind
   C. may fall behind				D. would fall behind

10. Keep the window closed lest the rain _____ in.
    A. comes					B. will come
    C. is coming					D. come

Ⅴ. Complete the following to make each equivalent of the Chinese version given in the brackets.

1. To think that _____! (谁想到这种事竟发生在我身上!)
2. _____, there is no place like home. (不管家是多么简陋,家是世界上最好的地方。)
3. It was essential that _____. (在月底前我们就签好租约,这一点至关重要。)
4. It is time that _____. (是政府采取措施保护珍稀动物和鸟类的时候了。)
5. The sun rises in the east and sets in the west, so it seems _____. (太阳东升西落,好像太阳是围绕地球转的。)
6. Your advice that _____. (你劝她等到下周,这是有道理的。)
7. _____, he would have been our chairman now. (保罗要是在最后的一次选举中多得6张选票,现在就是我们的董事长了。)
8. _____, we would be all right. (要不是下雪的天气,我们就不会这么糟糕。)
9. John did not feel well yesterday; _____. (约翰昨天身体不好,要不然就会来给他的同学送行了。)
10. I'd rather _____. (我宁愿你暂时什么也别做。)

# Part Three

## Parts of Speech

# 9. Nouns

## Aims of the Unit

> In this unit we will discuss some general matters about nouns. Four questions will be discussed in particular:
> - How many kinds of nouns are there in English?
> - What syntactical functions do they play in a clause or sentence?
> - What are number forms of nouns? How are they formed?
> - What are the genitive forms of nouns? What specific meanings do they express?

A noun is the name of a person, place or thing, or some quality, state or action. Nouns can be classified according to various criteria, such as morphology, notion and grammatical property. They serve as different kinds of sentence elements, chiefly subject, object and complement. To be used in sentences, they vary in form in terms of number, such as the singular or the plural. And there are regular and irregular plural nouns. A noun can also be genitive, a form indicating its relation, such as the possessive, with another noun it modifies. Genitive nouns are of various types, with s-genitive and of-genitive as chief ones, differing to various degrees in meaning or implication.

**Task 1** Underline all the nouns in the following story, find out the form for each, such as singular, plural or possessive, and fill them in the proper grids in the table below. You are also required to fill in the grammatical functions they play in their sentences, such as subject or object and attribute.

> One day a man went into a chemist's shop and said, "Have you anything to cure a headache?" The chemist took a bottle from a shelf, held it under the gentleman's nose and took out the cork. The smell was so strong that tears came into the man's eyes and ran down his cheeks. "What did you do that for?" he said angrily, as soon as he could get back his breath. "But that medicine has cured your headache, hasn't it?" said the chemist. "You fool," said the man, "It's my wife that has the headache, not me!"

| Form / Function | | | |
|---|---|---|---|
| Singular | | | |
| Plural | | | |
| Genitive | | | |

## ◆ 9.1　Classification of Nouns

### 1) In Terms of Morphology

According to their components nouns can be classified into **simple noun**, **compound noun** and **derivative noun**.

A simple noun is composed of one free morpheme: *man*, *chair*, *land*.

A compound noun is composed of two or more than two free morphemes: *armchair*, *seaside*, *forget-me-not*.

A derivative noun is composed of a base form, known as root, and an affix added to it: *arrangement*, *greatness*, *ability*.

### 2) In Terms of Notion

According to the notions that they denote, nouns can be classified into **common noun** and **proper noun**.

---

morphology
形态学
simple noun
简单名词
compound noun
复合名词
derivative noun
派生名词
common noun
普通名词
proper noun
专有名词
individual noun
个体名词
collective noun
集体名词
material noun
物质名词
abstract noun
抽象名词

- Common Noun

A common noun is the name common to a class of things that it denotes. It refers to anything, animate or inanimate, concrete or abstract, as an example of what is in that class. Common nouns may be further divided into four types: **individual noun**, such as *boy*, *house*, *tiger*, etc.; **collective noun**, such as *family*, *team*, *police*, etc.; **material noun**, such as *iron*, *air*, *snow*, etc.; **abstract noun**, such as *glory*, *honesty*, *failure*, etc.

- Proper Noun

A proper noun is the name of a particular person, place or thing, and is always spelt with a capitalized initial letter, e.g. *Tom*, *China*, *British Airways*.

### 3) In Terms of Grammatical Form

According to the grammatical form, nouns in English can be classified into two classes: **count or countable noun** and **non-count or uncountable noun**. Count nouns denote the things that are countable, while non-count nouns uncountable.

Of the four types of common nouns, individual nouns denote the things that are countable, material and abstract nouns uncountable, and some of collective nouns denote things countable and some uncountable. See the following table:

grammatical form
语法形式
countable noun
可数名词
uncountable noun
不可数名词
animate
有生命的
inanimate
无生命的

| Countability \ Notion | Count Noun | Non-count Noun |
|---|---|---|
| Individual Noun | a book, two books | |
| Collective Noun | a family, two families | furniture |
| Material Noun | | air |
| Abstract Noun | | honesty |

Notice that that a noun does not always belong to the same kind. Whether a noun is countable or uncountable is often determined by the sense or usage. The word *fish*, for example, can be

- an individual noun, as in

I saw ***a fish*** in the bowl.

- or a collective, referring to a group of individuals, as in

There are ***many fish*** in the pool.

- or a collective, referring to a kind of things, as in

These pools swarm with ***a great variety of fishes***.

**Task 2**  You are given four words in the table below. Decide what type of words each belongs to in terms of morphology, notion and grammatical property, and then fill your answer in the proper box in the table.

| Words \ Criteria for Classification | Morphology | Notion | Grammatical Form |
|---|---|---|---|
| people | | | |
| horse | | | |
| management | | | |
| man-power | | | |

## ◆ 9.2  Function of Noun Phrases

A noun phrase can function as all the elements in a sentence except the predicate verb.

### 1) Subject

*Children* at play seldom remember what time it is.
*Every man* has his faults.

### 2) Subject Complement

Where the bees are, there is *honey*.
Why he did it remained *a mystery*.
Mozart is considered *a genius*.

### 3) Object

I like *children*. (direct object)
Please give *that man* some money. (indirect object)
She looked at the *children*. (prepositional object)

### 4) Object Complement

They elected him *chairman of the board*.
One might call it *a mistake in tactics*.

## 5) Appositive

Mr. Brown, **director of the coal mine**, should be responsible for the accident.
She has great concern for us **students**.

## 6) Attribute

She studies at an **evening** school.
Have you been to the **flower** show?

## 7) Adverbial

He returned **last night**.
The meeting lasted **an hour**.

## 8) Conjunction

A photo is taken **each time** the button is pushed.
Joe's hearing started declining almost **the moment** he was born.

---

**Task 3**  Decide on the grammatical functions of the underlined nouns in these two sentences:
(1) Monica, the class adviser, was in the library.
(2) Tom found the machine a wonderful substitute for the old one.

---

## ◆ 9.3  Number Forms of Nouns

Number is a grammatical category that marks quantity. The English language has two categories of number, the singular, which denotes "one", and the plural, which denotes "more than one". The forms of plural nouns fall into two types, the regular and the irregular.

### 1) Regular Type

**Regular nouns** pluralize in -s or -es, depending on what sound the base form ends in. The suffix -s is pronounced [s] or [z] and -es almost invariably [iz]. In some cases there is also variation with the letter or sound at the end of the base. See this table:

| Sounds or Letters Bases End with | Suffixes to Add | Examples | Remarks |
|---|---|---|---|
| ① Vowels<br>② Voiced consonants | -s, [z] | seas, days, dogs, fields | |
| voiceless consonants | -s, [s] | ducks, boats, lakes, maps | |
| ① fricatives [s], [z], [ʃ], [ʒ]<br>② affricates [tʃ], [dʒ] | -es, [iz] | boxes, buzzes, dishes, watches | |
| | -s, [iz] | roses, horses, garages, colleges | nouns ending in fricatives or affricates followed by a silent -e |
| | | houses ['hauziz] | with [s] in the base vocalized; exceptional |
| ① consonant + y<br>② semivowel + y | -es, [iz] | ladies, soliloquies | changing y into i and then adding -es |
| -o | consonant + o | -es, [z] | heroes, potatoes | mostly adding -es |
| | | -es or -s, both [z] | zeros, zeroes volcanos, volcanoes | |
| | consonant + or vowel + o | -s, [iz] | radios, pianos, kilos | loan words, small in number |
| | -oo | -s, [z] | bamboos, zoos | |
| [θ] | after a short vowel | -s, [s] | moths, months | |
| | after a long vowel | -s, [z] | youths ['ju:ðz] mouths ['mauðz] | with [θ] in the base vocalized |
| [f], spelt -f or -fe | | -s, [s] | beliefs, safes | mostly changing -f into -v and then adding -es, pronounced [vz] |
| | | -es, [z] | leaves [li:vz] | |
| | | -s, [s]; -es, [z] | hoofs, hooves[hu:vz] scarfs, scarves[ska:vz] | |

regular nouns
规则名词
vowels 元音
short vowel
短元音
long vowel
长元音
voiced
consonants
浊辅音
voiceless
consonants
清辅音
fricatives
擦音
affricates
塞擦音
with [s] in the base vocalized
原来发[s]音
loan words
外来词
silent -e
不发音的-e

This table is a summary of the plural making rules in connection with the forms of nouns. There are also problems with the application of these rules in connection with the types of nouns.

① Compound Nouns

Most compounds form the plural in **the last element**:

*film goer → film goers*

*gentleman → gentlemen*

*consul general → consul generals*

*good-for-nothing → good-for-nothings*

Some in **the primary element**:

the last element
最后一个成分
the primary element
最初(第一个)成分

*looker-on* → *lookers-on*

*poet laureate* → *poets laureate*

*bride-to-be* → *brides-to-be*

*coat-of-mail* → *coats-of-mail*

Some in either the last or the primary:

*consul general* → *consuls general*, or *consul generals*

*lying-in* → *lyings-in*, or *lying-ins*

If the primary element is a verb, however, it is only the last element that pluralizes:

*stand-by* → *stand-bys*

• Compounds with man or woman as a component form the plural in both the first and the last elements:

*man cook* → *men cooks*

*woman doctor* → *women doctors*

*gentleman farmer* → *gentlemen farmers*

• The subordinate component in a compound does not pluralize for its own sake:

*a two-story house*, *a five-year plan*

*8-hour night shift*, *a seven-judge body*

*three four-act plays*, *two three-room apartments*

② Proper Nouns

• To most of them add -s:

*Henry* → *Henrys*

*Philipino* → *Philipinos*

*Germany* → *Germanys*

*Kansas City* → *Kansas Citys*

• To a few of them that end in -y, add -es, with y changed into i:

*Rocky* → *Rockies*

*Sicily* → *Sicilies*

③ Letters, Numerals and Abbreviations

• To letters add the combination of an apostrophe and an -s or -es:

*a* → *a's*

*s* → *s'es*

• To other items add either the combination, or simply an -s or -es:

MP → MP's or MPs

---

letters 字母
numerals 数字
abbreviations 缩略词
apostrophe [表示所有格和复数] 撇号 (即 ')
mutation 元音变化

PH D → Ph D's or Ph Ds

4 → 4's or 4s

in the 2010 → in the 2010's or 2010s

### 2) Irregular Type

Irregular as they are, there can be a certain degree of regularity in the making of their plurals.

① Some Pluralize by Mutation or Vowel Change

foot → feet, goose → geese

mouse → mice, louse → lice

man → men, woman → women

② Some Pluralize by Adding -en as Suffix

child → children, ox → oxen

③ Some Remain Unchanged

deer → deer, sheep → sheep

means → means, series → series

Chinese → Chinese, Japanese → Japanese

craft → craft, spacecraft → spacecraft

④ Loan Words Pluralize Chiefly by Inflecting Their Endings

stratum → strata, alumnus → alumni

alumna → alumnae, basis → bases

criterion → criteria, tableau → tableaux

tempo → tempi, matrix → matrices

Each represents a minor rule for a small group of words. To summarize: -us → -i, -a → -ae, -um → -a, -is → -es, -on → -a, -eau → -eaux, -o → -i, -ex, -ix → -ices.

Notice that the plural forms of some loan words, such as *data*, *agenda*, have been increasingly used as singular, with a verb either singular or plural, e.g.

Data is/are being analyzed.

If there is no objection, the agenda is adopted.

Some loan nouns have two plurals, one with an inflected word ending, brought over from their **source language** and commonly used in technical English, and the other in a form **consistent with the English convention**, commonly used in daily speech:

*memorandum* → *memoranda*, *memorandums*

*forula* → *formulae*, *formulas*

*index* → *indices*, *indexes*

Words borrowed from Chinese do not pluralize:

*one jin* → *five jin*

*one yuan* → *ten yuan*

*one li* → *twenty-five thousand li*

There are also nouns with two plural forms with different meanings and uses. *Pennies*, for example, one plural form of *penny*, indicates two or more than two penny-coins, while *pence*, the other form, indicates the face value of such a coin, often combined with a cardinal number to form a compound word, as in *sixpence*, *tenpence*.

### 3) Number Forms of Collective, Material, Abstract and Proper Nouns

#### ① Collective Nouns

Some collective nouns are countable, but some are not. As we have discused in Section 3.4, there are three types of collective nouns: those that are used as plural, as singular, and as either plural or singular. An uncountable collective noun has no plural noun.

Where it is necessary to count, a unit noun may be used that is related semantically to the collective, as in *a piece of furniture*, *two articles of equipment*, or an individuall noun equivalent in sense to the uncountable collective noun.

collective noun
集体名词
material noun
物质名词
abstract noun
抽象名词
proper noun
专有名词

| Collective Nouns | Individual Nouns | Collective Nouns | Individual Nouns |
|---|---|---|---|
| poetry | poem | cutlery | knife |
| machinery | machine | police | policeman |
| clothing | garment, coat, etc. | furniture | table, chair, etc. |
| foliage | leaf | luggage | trunk, bag, etc. |
| clergy | clergyman | equipment | tool |

#### ② Material Nouns

Material nouns are generally uncountable, with no need for distinction in number forms. In many cases, however, a material noun may indicate something else that is related, in this or that way, with the material the same noun denotes, and when this happens, this same noun will act as an individual noun, countable in notion and variable in form. We discuss a few of them below.

A noun that names a class of materials, such as *food*, *liquid*, can be used in either singular or plural form, to indicate that the materials in this class are of different varieties. Contrast:

*Bring us a lot of **food**, and you can be our king.*

*Eating artichokes kills the taste of all other **foods**.*

*But what do these nutrition facts really tell us about the health value of **a food**?*

A material noun denoting meat dish, such as *chicken* and *lamb*, can be used to indicate the poultry or livestock raised for the supply of such meat. Contrast:

***Lambs** gamboled in the meadow.*

***Beef**, **lamb**, and **pork** should also have marbling throughout the meat.*

A material noun denoting vegetable dish, such as *onion*, *potato*, can be used to indicate the dish made of the vegetable. Contrast:

*I always fry potatoes in hot pan with a bit of **onion**.*

*When you slice **an onion**, it makes your eyes sting.*

*We must weed out the yellow flowers among the **onions** as soon as possible.*

A material noun denoting a liquid food or a beverage, such as *coffee*, can be used to indicate an amount of it put in a container for easy counting or handling. Contrast:

*She brewed some **coffee** for me.*

*Bring me **two coffees**, please.*

A material noun denoting a raw material, such as *rubber*, can be used to indicate the product made of the material. Contrast:

***Rubber** is an elastic material.*

*He sponged a wrong letter off with **a rubber**.*

*We wear **rubbers** on our feet when it rains.*

A material noun denoting natural a substance, such as *water* and *sand*, can be used in plural form to denote a large body or area of it. Contrast:

*Get me a glass of **water**.*

*The ship will remain outside Chinese territorial **waters**.*

*The parting of the **waters** can be understood through fluid dynamics.*

***Sands** are a large area of sand.*

*Every morning he runs on the **sands** to keep fit.*

③ Abstract Nouns

Like material nouns, abstract nouns are also uncountable, because abstract things, such as a quality or a state, normally cannot be counted in number. Again, as a material noun may act as an **individual noun** with a slight difference in meaning, so can an abstract noun. This occurs when such a noun is used to indicate something concrete, which has the quality or state denoted by the same noun. In this case, this same noun behaves exactly as an **individual noun**, countable in notion and variable in form. Contrast:

They underestimated the ***difficulty*** of the task.

Liang said there were ***two difficulties*** in locating a governmental centre in the old city.

I should not be in any danger here, but ***experience*** has taught me caution.

The teacher told us his ***experiences*** in England.

Her ***beauty*** captured him.

She is ***a beauty***.

Notice that some abstract nouns have a corresponding individual noun. Contrast:

| Abstract | laughter | work | correspondence | music | fun | homework |
|---|---|---|---|---|---|---|
| Individual | laugh | job | letter, note, etc. | song, tune | joy | exercise |

④ Proper Nouns

In general, proper nouns do not pluralize, except those that invariably end in a plural suffix as their referents require, such as *the United States*, *the Philippines*, and *the Netherlands*. But sometimes it is necessary that a proper noun be used as a common noun in plural form, to refer to, for example, the whole family of the person using that family name, or a number people sharing this same personal name.

Have you invited ***the Gambles***?

There are two ***Miss Smiths/Misses Smith*** in this class.

### 4) Unit Nouns

Unit nouns are used to talk about a number of individuals or an amount of something uncountable taken as a single unit, so as to facilitate counting. They appear in an of-phrase modifying a noun that indicates what is being talked about. The noun that is modified may either be countable in notion, thus plural in form, or uncountable. Unit nouns fall into the following categories:

① General Unit Nouns

This category includes those that indicate a part of the whole, such as *piece*, *bit*, *item* and *article*. Of this group *piece* and *bit* are especially powerful

---

individual noun
个体名词

unit nouns
单位名词是表示事物个体性的词语。

in collocation, and phrases formed of them are capable of use with an uncountable noun, e.g.

*a piece of* advice/armour/bacon/bread/cake/chalk/cloth/coal/evidence/folly/furniture/ice/information/land/meat/music/news/paper/research/sugar/work

*a bit of* advice/bread/grass/news/trouble/wood/Latin/frustration/fertilizer/time/beauty/happiness/consultancy/inconvenience/amazement/local flavour

② Unit Nouns Related to the Shape of Things

There are unit nouns that are semantically related to the shapes of things and whose power of collocation is, therefore, quite limited, e.g.

| | |
|---|---|
| a cake of soap | ten head of cattle/caggage |
| a bar of chololate | a bundle of keys |
| a drop of water | a loaf of bread |
| an ear of corn | a lump of sugar |
| a flight of stairs | a spiral of incense |
| a grain of sand | a slice of meat |

③ Unit Nouns Related to Volume

Most of these words, as they denote containers of daily use when serving as common nouns, are powerful in collocation, e.g.

| | |
|---|---|
| a bottle of ink | a cup of tea |
| a bowl of rice | a handful of clay |
| a pail of water | two spoonfuls of sugar |
| a bucket of milk | a truckload of steel |
| a lass of beer | four busloads of soldiers |

④ Unit Nouns Related to the State of Action

These are found in set expressions, such as

*a fit of anger/coughing/laughter/fever*

*a peal of applause/laughter/thunder*

*a flash of hope/light/lightning*

*a display of courage/force/power/skill/fireworks*

⑤ Unit Nouns Denoting Pairs, Groups, Flocks, etc.

The phrases formed of these modify countable nouns, most of them plural in form.

| | |
|---|---|
| a pair of shoes | a school of whales |
| a flock of birds | a group of students |

---

unit noun related to the shape of things
表示形状的单位词
unit noun related to volume
表示容积的单位词
unit noun related to the state of action
表示动作状态的单位词
unit words denoting pairs, groups, flocks
表示成双、成组、成群的单位词

*a herd of elephants*  *a bench of judges*
*a litter of kittens*  *a troupe of actors*
*a swarm of bees*  *a gang of hooligans*
*a shoal of fish*  *a pack of wolves*

**Task 4**  Fill in the blanks with the words you choose from the ones supplied in the box before the passage.

| sibilant | preceded | vowel | regular | change | consonant |
|----------|----------|-------|---------|--------|-----------|
| unchanged | followed | source | irregular | uncountable | singular |

Most regular nouns pluralize in -s, and most of those ending in a __(1)__ or in the letter -o preceded by a __(2)__ pluralize in -es. Those ending in -y __(3)__ by a consonant pluralize by changing -y into -i and then adding -es. __(4)__ as they are, there are still minor variations, depending on what sound the noun ends. Of __(5)__ nouns, some pluralize by mutation, some by adding -en, and still some by remaining __(6)__. Foreign words mostly bring over the rules from their __(7)__ languages, but Chinese words are not subject to __(8)__. Number as form do not always agree with number as notion. Some words that are considered primarily __(9)__ in notion, hence invariable in form, may become countable when they are used in a slightly different sense, hence taking on a __(10)__ singular or plural form.

## ◆ 9.4   Genitive Nouns

> Genitive Noun
> 名词属格（case）是一个语法范畴，它表示名词（或代词）与句中其他词语（主要是动词）之间的语法关系和语义关系。现代英语名词没有主格和宾格的标记，名词在句中处于主语或宾语地位全靠词序来决定。在现代英语中，名词虽无主格、宾格之分，却保留着古英语的一点格的残余，这就是"属格"（Genitive Case），又叫"所有格"（Possessive Case）。名词不带格的标记传统上叫作"通格"（Common Case）。

In English, the term "genitive" is the case or the inflectional form of a noun or a pronoun indicating its relation with other words in a sentence.

### 1) Ways to Form Genitive Nouns

① Simple Genitive Nouns

The general rule is to add -'s, with the sound of the genitive following the rule of the plural -s inflection, e. g.

*my mother's* [ˈmʌðəz] *arrival*, *women's* [ˈwiminz] *clothes*
*Milton's* [ˈmiltənz] *poems*, *Mike's* [maiks] *books*

This also applies to nouns ending in the sound [s] or [z], e. g.

*a middle class's* [ˈklɑːsiz] *aspirations*

*a left float box's* [ˈbɔksis] *right margin*

*this practice's* [ˈpræktisiz] *main advantage*

*exercise's* [ˈeksəsaiziz] *supporting role in weight*

To irregular plural nouns add -'s, and to regular ones already having an -s ending, add only an apostrophe. Contrast:

*the children's books    the boys' books*

To personal names ending in the sound [s], add -'s, e.g.

*Marx's* [ˈmɑːksiz]    *Ross's* [ˈrɔsiz]

Those ending in [z] are treated by adding either an apostrophe, with pronunciation irrespective of spelling, or less commonly -'s, e.g.

*Dickens'* [ˈdikinziz] *or* [ˈdikinz]/*Dickens's* [ˈdikinziz]

*Johns'* [ˈdʒɔnziz] *or* [dʒɔnz] /*Johns'* [ˈdʒɔnziz]

② Compound Genitive Nouns, Nominal Genitive Phrases

For a compound noun add -'s to the last element, e.g.

*his mother-in-law's interference, the consul general's wife*

This also applies to a noun phrase taken as a whole, as opposed to the headword it modifies, e.g.

*an hour and a half's talk, somebody else's opinion, the University of Minnesota's president*

However, in the case of a coordinate construction, there will be a difference of treatment. If the nouns in such a construction are related to the headword separately, add -'s to each; or, if they are related jointly, add -'s to the last. Contrast:

*Mary's and Bob's books*

*Mary and Bob's books*

The first form means that Mary and Bob own the books separately: Mary owns some, and Bob the others. The second form means that two of them own the books jointly, or share them.

## 2) Genitive Meanings

Alternatively called the possessive case, the genitive indeed expresses the possessive meaning, thus the phrase *Tom's house*, for example, refers to the house that Tom owns or possesses. Possession, however, is not the only meaning that the genitive can express; there are various other meanings. The following is a table of them, with sentential or phrasal analogues illustrating their differences.

| Types of Genitives | Examples | Analogues |
|---|---|---|
| Subjective Genitive | the lady's application | the lady applied |
| Objective Genitive | the boy's release | ... released the boy |
| Genitive of Origin | the manager's letter | the manager wrote a letter |
| Descriptive Genitive | a summer's day | a day in the summer |
| Genitive of Measure | ten days' absence | the absence lasted ten days |

Notes: Subjective genitive indicates that the genitive noun is logically or in meaning the subject or performer of the action indicated by the headword, objective genitive the object or receiver of the action, genitive of the origin or source of the being or living being referred to by the headword, descriptive genitive the attribute or character of it, and genitive of measure the size of it.

### 3) Syntactic Functions of Genitive Nouns

Genitive nouns serve either of the two functions: the **determiner** and the **pre-modifier**. Contrast:

① *the boy's book*   ② *children's book*

The genitive noun in ① serves as determiner, which designates who the book belongs to, or who possesses the book, and the one in ② as pre-modifier, which describes the category or the property of the book, indicating the readership for whom the book is intended.

determiner
限定词
pre-modifier
前置修饰语

### 4) Two Genitives

The genitive discussed above can be referred to as the s-genitive, because that is a form realized by adding an -s to the end of the noun, apart from the possible insertion of an apostrophe before the suffix. But the same noun can also come after a preposition to form an of-phrase, which performs a similar function and expresses a similar meaning. This latter form can be referred to as the of-genitive.

① Comparing the s- Genitive and the of-Genitive

The two genitives overlap in the expression of a few types of meaning or relation. Both can express,

* the possessive relation: *The trunk of an en elephant = an elephant's trunk*

* the subject-verb relation: *The arrival of the prime minister = the prime minister's arrival*

* the verb-object relation:     *the release of these children* = *these children's release*
* the meaning of origin:     *The works of Shakespeare* = *Shakespeare's works*
* the meaning of measure:     *An absence of ten days* = *ten days' absence*

But they are not interchangeable in all cases. In general, s-genitives have a wider usage, applicable to either animate or inanimate nouns, though preferably animate; of-genitives, in contrast, more often applied to inanimate nouns. Contrast:

*the youngest children's toys*     *or*: *the toys of the youngest children*
*John's hat*     *but not*: *\*the hat of John*
*the bottom of the sea*     *but not*: *\*the sea's bottom*

Where the category or the property of something is concerned, only s-genitives are permitted. Contrast:

*children's pictorial*     *but not* *\*pictorial of children*
*men's clothing*     *but not* *\*clothing of men*
*a doctor's degree*     *but not* *\*a degree of doctor*

In idioms containing an s-genitive, no variation is permitted:

*at one's wits end*     *but not* *\*at the wits of one*
*in one's mind's eye*     *but not* *\*in the eye of one's mind*
*to one's heart's content*     *but not* *\*to the content of one's heart*

Cases where only of-phrases are permitted or preferable include **appositive constructions**:

*a map of China*     *but not* *\*China's map*

Notice the difference between these pairs:

  a. *a photo of Tom; Tom's photo*

    *a photo of Tom* = *a photo showing Tom's image*

    *Tom's photo* = *a photo owned by Tom*, necessarily showing his own image

  b. *the story of the old man, the old man's story*

    *the story of the old man* = *the story about the old man himself*

    *the old man's story* = *the story told by the old*, not necessarily about himself

There is also difference in information focus: while *her mother's good figure* is an expression with focus on her mother's figure, *the good figure of her mother* on her mother.

② Independent and Double Genitive

• Independent Genitive

This genitive is one with the noun it modifies omitted, e.g.

*the grocer's = the grocer's shop*

*the Johnsons' = the Johnsons' home*

The use of this genitive occurs if the context makes the identity of the person or thing being talked about clear, e. g.

*My car is faster than John's ( i. e. than John's car).*

*John's is a nice car, too.*

*His memory is like an elephant's.*

This genitive plays a syntactic role similar to a possessive pronoun, so it can be replaced by the latter if the identity of the noun is clear, e. g.

***John's** is a nice car, too.* → ***His** is a nice car, too.*

This genitive is commonly used to indicate one's home or residence, e. g.

*I am going to dine at the **Johnsons**'.*

*The **doctor's** is on the other side of the street.*

Or a public place such as a church, a school or a shop, e. g.

*Joe lives near **St. Paul's**.*

*He was educated at **Merchant Taylor's**.*

*I had my hair cut at the **barber's**.*

*The toys are sold both at **Smith's** and at **Brown's**.*

- Double Genitive

This is an expression combining the two types of genitives, the independent genitive and the of-genitive, the former acting as prepositional object or complement, e. g.

*a friend of my father's*

*a painting of my colleague's*

*a novel of Dickens'*

These examples show that **the independent genitive** in this construction must both be **definite** and **personal**. Thus:

| | |
|---|---|
| *a novel of Dickens'* | but not *\* a novel of a writer's* |
| *a friend of my father's* | but not *\* a funnel of the ship's* |

They also show that the head word before the of-genitive must be preceded by an indefinite determiner, e. g.

| | |
|---|---|
| ***any/some** daughters of Mrs. Green's* | but not *\* **the** daughters of Mrs. Green's* |

Except the cases where the head word is preceded by *this* or *that* to express a strong emotion, e. g.

the independent genitive in this construction must both be definite and personal
在双重属格结构中，独立属格必须是确定特指而且一般指人

>*this* notorious scheme of your colleague's
>
>*that* clever remark of your sister's

or where it is preceded by a wh-word or a numeral, e.g.

>*which/two* novels of Dickens'

In contrast with of-genitive, the double genitive mainly expresses the possessive relation, e.g.

>a car of Berry's     but not *a car of Berry

Notice the difference of implication between

>He is *a friend of my father's.*
>
>He is *a friend of my father.*

The first sentence has an implication that the father does not have only one friend, but a few, and he is one of them. The second does not have such an implication.

**Task 5**  Fill in the blanks with words you choose from the ones supplied in the box before the passage.

| case form | relation | animate | precede | s-genitive | realization |
| independent genitive | two | function | referent | follow | forms |

The genitive is the __(1)__ of a noun indicating its relation with another noun that it modifies, typically a possessive __(2)__. It is realized in __(3)__ processes, i.e. by adding -'s to the end of the noun treated, the realization called __(4)__, or by preceding the noun with *of*, the __(5)__ called of-genitive. The former process is mostly applied to nouns with an __(6)__ referent, and latter an inanimate. The s-genitive may stand alone, called __(7)__, with the noun it modifies omitted, if its __(8)__ is known. An independent genitive may __(9)__ an of-genitive to form a double genitive, which may express a slight different meaning from other __(10)__ of genitive.

# EXERCISES

I. Group these words in the box in terms of morphology, notion and grammatical feature respectively, and then complete the table below the words with your groupings, making sure that each word fills the proper space in the table.

| airmail | anticipation | armchair | audience | beauty |
| dog | equipment | gold | pig-iron | politician |

| M + G<br>N | Simple Words | | Derivatives | | Compounds | |
| --- | --- | --- | --- | --- | --- | --- |
| | Count | Non-count | Count | Non-count | Count | Non-count |
| Individual | | | | | | |
| Collective | | | | | | |
| Material | | | | | | |
| Abstract | | | | | | |

II. Name the grammatical functions of the underlined nouns in the following sentences.

1. Hurry up, <u>Catherine</u>.
2. My <u>family</u> is now in the country.
3. The luggage weighs 20 <u>kilograms</u>.
4. The janitor opens the <u>door</u> every morning.
5. Influenza, a common <u>disease</u>, has no cure.
6. The doctor is a <u>specialist</u> in the diseases of the heart.
7. They called him a <u>coward</u>.
8. She tried to better herself by going to <u>night</u> school.
9. After that, Morris visited Catherin every <u>day</u>.
10. Well, Your <u>Honor</u>, I picked out a dress for my wife

III. Write out the plural forms of the words in the box below. Notice that some of them have two plural forms.

| guy, party, echo, piano, studio, cuckoo, volcano, penny, x, B, 50, BA, veto, photo, mosquito, radio, kangaroo, Euro, loaf, cliff, chief, roof, kerchief, scarf, mouse, goose, ox, hypothesis, phenomenon, medium, index, terminus, nucleus, aircraft, Mary, Germany, lay-by, runner-up |

IV. Correct the errors in the following sentences.

1. I'd found pence and nickels before, but never a dollar!
2. Today this curricula is taught in more than one thousand primary schools in fifty-eight coutries, including the United States.

3. The Mexican explained that his small catch was sufficient to meet his needs and those of his families.

4. Finland and Denmark are culturally very similar countries, but one clear difference between them lies in the size and origin of their immigrant population.

5. Luggages are not allowed to be left there.

6. Some people think that machine is a threat to their jobs.

7. I went to the doctor for an advice about my health.

8. In the garden she took a lot of photography.

9. Ireland has rich experiences and advanced technologies in environmental protection.

10. As the saying goes, looker-ons see more than players. Being a looker-on, I have more right to offer my opinion.

**V. Insert an appropriate unit noun for each of the following words. The unit nouns are given in the box before the words for your choice.**

| an article of | a bench of | an ear of | a fit of |
| a flash of | a flight of | a flock of | a gang of |
| a grain of | a herd of | an item of | a litter of |
| a pack of | a peal of | a shoal of | a spiral of |
| a spoonful of | a swarm of | a troupe of | a truckload of |

1. _____ corn     2. _____ stairs
3. _____ sand     4. _____ incense
5. _____ clothing 6. _____ soup
7. _____ steel    8. _____ goods
9. _____ anger    10. _____ light
11. _____ birds   12. _____ thunder
13. _____ cattle  14. _____ kittens
15. _____ bees    16. _____ fish
17. _____ criminals 18. _____ wolves
19. _____ judges  20. _____ actors

**VI. Rewrite the following sentences, using any of the genitive nouns that is the most appropriate to express the same idea in each.**

1. She was thankful because her little girl recovered quickly.

2. He did that because he loved his wife.

3. He was happy because his wife loves him.

4. The enemy was defeated and it brought the war to the end.

5. Many people criticized Dick when he decided to emigrate to Australia.

6. Last night I read a novel written by Jane Austen.
7. That long report that Mr. Allen wrote has been accepted for publication.
8. The book was bought at the bookshop run by John Wiley.
9. What will this policy the government is following lead to?
10. That dog—Frank's dog—has torn my trousers.

**VII. Multiple choices.**

1. The _____ is broken.

    A. table's leg　　　　　B. table leg　　　　　C. leg of the table

2. _____ house is on the corner.

    A. Mary's and John's　　B. Mary and John's　　D. Mary's and John

3. The meeting will be held at _____.

    A. the Joneses'　　　　B. the Joneses' house　　C. Joneses' house

4. He was not driving Charle's car but _____.

    A. someone else　　　　B. someone else's　　　C. someone elses'

5. A town goes through many crises in _____ time.

    A. ten years time　　　B. ten years'　　　　　C. ten years's

6. The _____ effectiveness will be proved by their performance.

    A. product's　　　　　B. products'　　　　　C. products

7. A sensitive person is aware of _____ wrories.

    A. others'　　　　　　B. others's　　　　　　C. other's

8. _____ was damaged in the fire.

    A. The house of my brother and sister-in-law

    B. The house of my brother and sister-in-law's

    C. My brother and sister-in-law's house

9. _____ called this morning.

    A. The friend of my father's

    B. A friend of my father's

    C. A friend of my father

10. This shop sells _____ only.

    A. woman clothing　　　B. women clothing　　　C. women's clothing

# 10. Determiners

## Aims of the Unit

> In this unit we will discuss some general matters about determiners. We are going to discuss four questions in particular:
> - What are determiners?
> - What are the differences between determiners and modifiers?
> - How can we classify determiners?
> - If there is more than one determiner, what order should they follow?

Words that precede any premodifying adjectives in a noun phrase and which denote such referential meanings as specific reference, generic reference, definite quantity or indefinite quantity are referred to as determiners. While determiners and modifiers (usually adjectives) can both be used to specify the reference of the head noun, premodifiers must appear after determiners.

**Task 1**

Thousands of foreign visitors came to this museum every year.
This company decides to pay the female workers by the hour.
In the underlined part of the above sentences, which words are determiners and which words are modifiers?

## ◆ 10.1 Types of Determiners

Determiners can be grouped into six different subcategories with regard to the varied roles they play in specifying the reference of nouns concerned.

## 10. Determiners

### 1) Articles

There are three types of articles in English, namely, the **definite article** (*the*), the **indefinite article** (*a, an*), and the **zero article.**

### 2) Possessive Determiners

**Possessive determiners** function to specify nouns by relating them to the speaker/writer (*my, our*), the addressee (*your*) or other entities mentioned in a given context (*his, her, its, their*). In function, they are the same as noun genitives like *Mary's*.

### 3) Demonstrative Determiners

**Demonstratives determiners**, namely, *this/these/that/those/such*, function to specify the number of the referent and whether the referent is near or distant in relation to the speaker.

### 4) Indefinite Determiners

There are five different types, namely, **universal determiners** like *all, both, each, every*, **assertive determiners** like *some, certain*, **non-assertive determiners** like *any, either*, **negative determiners** like *no, neither, nor*, **quantifiers** like *enough, (a) few (of), (a) little (of), many (of), much (of), more, most (of), half, several, a bit of, a good deal of, a great amount of, a small number of, a good many of, a lot of, plenty of, a quantity of*, etc.

### 5) Numerals

Numeral determiners include both **cardinal numerals** (*one, two, three*, etc.); **ordinal numerals** (*first, second, third*, etc.); **general ordinals** (*last, next, additional, another, other, further, past*, etc.); **multipliers** (*double, twice, treble, three times*) and **fractions** (one-third, three-fourths)

### 6) Others

Other types of determiners include **genitive noun** (*Jone's, my friend's*), **interrogative determiners** like *what(ever), which(ever), whose, whosever*, **conjunctive determiners** like *what(ever), which(ever), whose, whosever* and **relative determiners** like *which(ever), whose, whosever*.

---

articles (definite article, indefinite article, zero article)
冠词(定冠词、不定冠词、零冠词)
possessive determiners
物主限定词
demonstrative determiners
指示限定词
indefinite determiners
不定指限定词
universal determiners
通用限定词
assertive determiners
肯定限定词
non-assertive determiners
非肯定限定词
negative determiners
否定限定词
quantifiers 量词

numerals
数词
cardinal numerals
基数词
ordinal numerals
序数词
general ordinals
一般序数词
multipliers
倍数词
genitive noun
属格名词
fractions
分数词
interrogative determiners
疑问限定词
conjunctive determiners
连接限定词
relative determiners
关系限定词

**Task 2**  Discuss with your partner why the following central nouns in each sentence can collocate with the underlined determiners respectively.

(1) Why is there <u>less</u> traffic on the street in February than in May?
(2) On account of the typhoon <u>neither</u> shipment will arrive this week.
(3) We had only <u>several</u> rainfalls last summer.

## 10.2  Collocations between Determiners and Nouns

According to the collocations between determiners and three classes of nouns, namely, singular count nouns, plural count nouns and noncount nouns, determiners can be divided into seven types.

### 1) Determiners with All the Three Classes of Nouns

Determiners such as possessive determiners, genitive nouns and the definite article as well as *some*, *any*, *no*, *the other* and *whose* can go with all the three classes of nouns.

| Singular Count Nouns | Plural Count Nouns | Non-count Nouns |
| --- | --- | --- |
| *his* car | *his* cars | *his* money |
| *John's* book | *John's* books | *John's* work |
| *the* car | *the* cars | *the* advice |
| *some* book | *some* books | *some* bread |
| *any* ticket | *any* tickets | *any* news |
| *no* apple | *no* apples | *no* food |
| *the other* girl | *the other* girls | *the other* equipment |
| *whose* bag | *whose* bags | *whose* advice |

### 2) Determiners with Singular Count Nouns Only

Determiners such as *a(n)*, *one*, *another*, *each*, *every*, *either*, *neither*, *many a*, *such a* can collocate with singular count nouns.

  *a* dog    *an* elephant    *one* student    *another* boy    *each* person
  *every* man    *either* player    *neither* child    *many a* gift    *such a* university

## 10. Determiners

### 3) Determiners with Plural Count Nouns Only

Determiners such as *both*, *two*, *three*, *another two/three*, *many*, *(a) few*, *several*, *these*, *those*, *a (great) number of* can only collocate with plural count nouns.

**both** workers  **two** chopsticks  **three** monks  **another two/three** films

**many** children  **(a) few** mistakes  **several** prizes  **these** animals  **those** flowers

**a (great) number of** graduates

### 4) Determiners with Non-count Nouns Only

Determiners such as *a (little) bit of*, *a great amount of*, *a great deal of*, *(a) little*, *much*, *less*, *least* can only collocate with non-count nouns.

**a (little) bit of** water  **a great amount of** rain  **a great deal of** knowledge

**(a) little** milk  **less** courage  **least** punishment

### 5) Determiners with Singular and Plural Count Nouns Only

Determiners such as *the first*, *the second*, *the last*, *the next* can go with either singular or plural count nouns.

| Singular Count Nouns | Plural Count Nouns |
| --- | --- |
| the first rose | the first roses |
| the second visitor | the second visitors |
| the last man | the last men |
| the next meeting | the next meetings |

### 6) Determiners with Singular and Non-count Nouns Only

Determiners such as *this*, *that* can collocate with either singular or plural count nouns.

| Singular Count Nouns | Plural Count Nouns |
| --- | --- |
| this job | this work |
| that job | that work |

### 7) Determiners with Plural and Non-count Nouns Only

Determiners such as *a lot of*, *lots of*, *plenty of*, *enough*, *most*, *such*, *other* can go with plural and non-count nouns, but not with singular nouns.

| Plural Nouns | Non-count Nouns |
| --- | --- |
| *a lot of* people | *a lot of* chocolate |
| *lots of* books | *lots of* food |
| *plenty of* cars | *plenty of* coal |
| *enough* copies | *enough* water |
| *most* essays | *most* work |
| *such* men | *such* bread |
| *other* cards | *other* information |

**Task 3** Discuss with your partner why the underlined determiners in the following sentences appear in such order in each sentence.

(1) The students spent <u>half their</u> time working in the fields.

(2) I bought <u>all the five</u> books on that subject.

(3) Write your answer on <u>every other</u> line.

(4) <u>The first ten</u> bales have arrived; the rest are yet to be shipped.

## ◆ 10.3　Collocations between Determiners

In terms of the positions where they frequently occur in noun phrases, determiners fall into three subclasses: **predeterminers**, **central determiners** and **postdeterminers**.

### 1) Predeterminers, Central Determiners and Postdeterminers

① Predeterminers

**Predeterminers** include: (a) Indefinite Determiners: *all*, *both*; (b) Multipliers & Fraction: *double*, *twice*, *three times*, *one-third*, *two-thirds*, *half*; (c) Demonstrative Determiner: *such (a/an)*; (d) Conjunctive Determiner: *what (a/an)*. Predeterminers are those that precede central determiners.

② Central Determiners

**Central Determiners** include: (a) Articles: *a/an/the*; (b) Possessives: *my*, *your*, *his*, *her*, *its*, *our*, *your*, *their*, *Mary's*; (c) Demonstratives: *this*, *that*, *these*, *those*; (d) Indefinite Determiners: *each*, *every*, *some*, *any*, *either*, *no*, *neither*, *enough*; (e) Genitive Nouns/Interrogative Determiners/

> 在名词中心词之前如果有两个以上限定词出现时,就会产生限定词的先后顺序问题。按其不同的搭配位置,限定词分为:
> predeterminers 前位限定词
> central determiners 中位限定词
> postdeterminers 后位限定词

Conjunctive Determiners/Relative Determiners: Mary's, *what(ever)*, *which(ever)*, *whose*, *whoseover*.

③ Postdeterminers

**Postdeterminers** refer to those that follow central determiners or predeterminers. Postdeterminers can be divided into two subgroups. One group includes: (a) Ordinal Numerals: *first*, *second*, *third*, etc. (b) General Ordinals: *last*, *next*, *additional*, *further*, *past*, etc. The other group includes: (a) Cardinal Numerals: *one*, *two*, *three*, etc. (b) Indefinite Determiners (Quantifiers) to modify plural count/noncount nouns: *enough*, *(a) few*, *(a) little*, *many*, *much*, *more*, *most*, *half*, *several*; *a bit of*, *a good deal of*, *a great amount of*, *a small number of*, *a good many of*, *a lot of*, *plenty of*, *a quantity of*, etc. (c) Demonstrative Determiners: *such*.

## 2) Co-occurrence of Determiners

Predeterminers, central determiners and postdeterminers can modify the central noun separately or together. When more than one determiner co-occurs before a central noun, it can be the following occasions:

① Predeterminer + Central Determiner + Postdeterminer

*all the four* students

*both his two* sisters

② Predeterminer + Central Determiner + Postdeterminer + Postdeterminer

*all these last few* days

③ Predeterminer + Central Determiner

*both his* children

*such a* misfortune

*all this* experience

④ Predeterminer + Postdeterminer

*all other* students

*all three* books

*half such* people

⑤ Central Determiner + Postdeterminer

*some such* alloy

*the author's last* books

*his last few* words

⑥ Central Determiner + Postdeterminer + Postdeterminer

*those last few* months

*the next few* weeks

⑦ Postdeterminer + Postdeterminer

*one such* dictionary

*few such* cases

*many more* copies

There are a few points:

Predeterminers are exclusive with each other, i. e. there can be only one pre-determiner before the head noun in a noun phrase, e. g. *half of all the money John has*, but not *half all the money John has*.

Predeterminers are usually used with central determiners, but sometimes can also be used with postdeterminers, e. g. *both his brothers*, *all four applicants*, *all these last few days*.

Central determiners are also exclusive with each other. That is, there can only be one central determiner before the head noun in a noun phrase, e. g. *the/this/that/these/my/Jack's/the author's* books, but not *the Jack's* brother.

A postdeterminer can co-occur with another postdeterminer, as in *two more tickets*, *the last few* days.

For the postdeterminers, the first sub-group comes before the second sub-group, as in *last three* days.

## EXERCISES

**I. Choose an appropriate determiner to fill in each of the blanks.**

1. Why is there _____ traffic on the streets in February than in May?
   A. less            B. fewer           C. few             D. little

2. On account of the typhoon _____ shipment will arrive this week.
   A. neither         B. all             C. both            D. these

3. There are trees on _____ side of the street.
   A. such a          B. both            C. some            D. each

4. I'd like _____ paper.
   A. a few           B. several         C. a bit of        D. these

5. There must be _____ empty talk but more hard work.
   A. fewer           B. no              C. the least       D. less

6. We had _____ rainfalls last summer.
   A. too much                           B. little
   C. a little                           D. only several

## 10. Determiners

7. The students spent _____ their time working in the fields.
   A. both	B. most	C. more	D. half

8. The additional work will take _____ weeks.
   A. the other	B. another five
   C. other five	D. the more

9. He was on leave _____ days.
   A. the few last	B. few another
   C. few other	D. the last few

10. _____ alloy may be used to replace copper.
    A. Such a	B. Some such
    C. Such some	D. Several such

11. _____ dictionary is enough for me.
    A. Such one	B. One such
    C. Such a one	D. One such a

12. _____ factors should be considered.
    A. These all	B. Such all
    C. All such	D. Some these

13. _____ evenings he did enjoy himself immensely.
    A. The first few	B. The few first
    C. The first some	D. Some the first

14. _____ cases have been reported.
    A. Such few	B. Such some
    C. Few such	D. Some these

15. He has been staying at home _____ days.
    A. these all last few	B. these last few all
    C. all these last few	D. these last all few

16. Set aside a period of the day as "off-limits" during _____ time you will not be interrupted.
    A. what	B. which	C. that	D. whatever

17. Sometimes earthquakes cause tidal waves and, as _____, these can be deadly.
    A. in a case of Japan	B. in the case of Japan
    C. the case of Japan	D. a case of Japan

18. I know now, of course, there is _____ as a free lunch.
    A. no such a thing	B. not such thing
    C. not a thing	D. no such thing

19. The writer wrote a number of books, but _____ books were not very popular.
    A. last two his          B. his last two
    C. two his last          D. last two of his

20. It was more expensive than _____ we were normally able to afford.
    A. the any other magazines      B. the other any magazines
    C. any the other magazines      D. any of the other magazines

Ⅱ. Correct the errors in the following sentences.

1. The police fired into air to clear the demonstrators from the street.
2. He was a man of a few words, but when he spoke it was worth listening to.
3. By the way of an introduction to the subject, let me give you a brief history.
4. You can never use my car, and at any time should you put your hands on it.
5. I haven't read Cymbeline, but I have read all other Shakespeare's plays.
6. I don't' like this kind of apples.
7. The farmers are hoping that there will be a great many rainfall this year than there was last year.
8. The third sister of his is such a spitfire.
9. He came to see me once three nonths.
10. Would you like any more soup?

Ⅲ. Put the following Chinese sentences into English.

1. 水管工是安装和修理水管的人。
2. 一定还有别的办法做这件事。
3. 小明完全有机会获得成功。
4. 为了完成任务我们夜以继日地工作。
5. 我作文快写完了，只要再有5分钟就行。
6. 少说空话多干实事。
7. 百万富翁有许多钱财，也有许多烦恼。
8. 每隔几分钟电话铃就响一次。
9. 他新编的两本英语语言学著作都将在2011年年底出版。
10. 我兄弟花了一千美元买了一辆旧汽车，但我买到同样货色却几乎花了两倍价钱。

# 11. Verbs

## Aims of the Unit

> In this unit we will discuss some general matters about verbs. We are going to discuss five questions in particular:
> - How are verbs classified according to their different roles in the formation of verb phrases?
> - How are verbs classified according to word formation and grammatical forms?
> - What are the collocations of infinitive?
> - How are -ing participles and -ed participles used in sentences?
> - How can we make a choice between the infinitive and -ing participle according to the preceding verbs?

**Task 1**  Identify the underlined verbs in the following sentences as ① transitive verb, ② intransitive verb, ③ linking verb, ④ primary auxiliary verb, ⑤ modal verb or, ⑥ semi-auxiliary verb.

(1) You <u>can</u> <u>trust</u> me. Nobody <u>will</u> <u>know</u> that you <u>are</u> here.//
(2) Tim <u>works</u> very hard. He <u>is bound</u> to <u>succeed</u>.
(3) Dennis <u>likes</u> music, so <u>does</u> his wife.
(4) The drunk driver <u>had</u> <u>run</u> away when the police <u>came</u>.

## ◈ 11.1  Classification of Verbs (Ⅰ)

### 1) Main Verbs and Auxiliaries

According to the different roles played in the formation of verb phrases, verbs fall into two major classes: **main verbs** and **auxiliaries**. Main verbs function as the head and convey the basic meaning of a verb phrase. A verb phrase may consist of a main verb only; this is called "a simple verb phrase". A verb phrase may also take the form of a main verb preceded by one or more auxiliaries; this is called "a complex verb phrase".

<small>main verbs 主动词  
simple verb phrase 简单动词词组  
complex verb phrase 复杂动词词组  
primary auxiliaries 基本助动词  
modal auxiliaries 情态助动词  
semi-auxiliaries 半助动词</small>

We *study* English.

You *should have read* the book.

Auxiliaries help main verbs to express various grammatical and modal meanings. Auxiliaries can be classified into three categories: **primary auxiliaries**, **modal auxiliaries** and **semi-auxiliaries**.

① Primary Auxiliaries

There are three primary auxiliaries: *be*, *do*, *have*, which have only grammatical functions.

Auxiliary *be* helps the main verb to form the progressive aspect or the passive voice. Auxiliary *do* is usually used to help the main verb to form negation and questions, or to express the emphatic affirmative. Auxiliary *have* helps the main verb to form the perfective and the perfective progress aspect, e. g.

I *am listening* to a Beethoven symphony.

The milkman *didn't* come yesterday.

He *did* annoy everyone that evening.

*Do* come and join us.

Joan *has seen* that movie.

I *have been working* here for 20 years.

② Modal Auxiliaries

There are fourteen modal auxiliaries including some past tense forms: *can/could*, *may/might*, *will/would*, *shall/should*, *must*, *ought to*, *dare*, *need*, *used to* and *had better*. Modal auxiliaries express modal meanings; their past tense forms do not necessarily express past time. In a finite verb phrase, only one modal auxiliary can be used, followed by the bare infinitive or the base form of the main verb.

It *may* show before nightfall.

*Would* you let me use your pen a minute?

Paul *might have been* injured.

③ Semi-auxiliaries

Semi-auxiliaries are between main verbs and auxiliaries. They have certain notional meanings like main verbs on the one hand; on the other, they can precede the main verbs to form complex verb phrases. All semi-auxiliaries are followed by infinitives. Semi-auxiliaries are: *be able to, be about to, be apt to, be bound to, be certain to, be destined to, be doomed to, be due to, be going to, be liable to, be likely to, be obliged to, be supposed to, be sure to,* had better, have (got) to, appear to, chance to, come to, fail to, get to, happen to, seem to, tend to, turn out to, be to, be willing to, etc.

*She **is likely to** pass the exam if she works hard enough.*

*He **tends to** get up late on Sunday morning.*

## 2) Transitive Verbs, Intransitive Verbs and Linking Verbs

According to whether or not the main verbs must be followed by complementation and the kinds of elements that form the complementation, main verbs can be divided into **transitive verbs**, **intransitive verbs** and **linking verbs.**

① Transitive Verbs

Transitive verbs must be followed by an object or two objects, namely indirect object and direct object.

*She is **playing table tennis**.*

*The owner **gave me a discount**.*

Some transitive verbs can be followed by an object and an object complement.

*The lawyer **found her guilty**.*

② Intransitive Verbs

Intransitive verbs are not followed by an object.

*All of us know he often **lies**.*

Some intransitive verbs are followed by an adverbial so that the meaning of the sentence can be complete.

*He is at a meeting and can't **get away**.*

③ Linking Verbs

Linking verbs can be followed by a subject complement.

*She tends to **become hysterical**.*

Many main verbs can belong to more than one of the three verb classes mentioned above. For instance, the verb *smell* belongs to all the three verb classes mentioned above.

*You can **smell** the fragrance of grass.*

*The fish is not fresh. It **smells**.*

*This soup **smells** good.*

### 3) Dynamic Verbs and Stative Verbs

Main verbs can be divided into **dynamic verbs** and **stative verbs** according to their lexical meanings. Dynamic verbs refer to actions while stative verbs refer to relatively stable states of affairs.

① Dynamic Verbs

Durative verbs refer to actions that last for a period of time. They normally can be used in both the progressive aspect and the non-progressive aspect. Dynamic verbs are subcategorized into **durative verbs**, **transitional verbs** and **momentary verbs**. The first subclass refers to durative verbs, such as *drink*, *eat*, *fly*, *play*, *rain*, *run*, *sit*, *stand*, *sleep*, *talk*, *watch*, *write*, *work*, etc.

> She **works** at a chemical factory.
> She **has been working** there for a long time.
> They **talked** and **talked** until midnight.
> They **were talking** about the house.

The second subclass refers fo transitional verbs, such as *arrive*, *become*, *chamge*, *come*, *get*, *go*, *grow*, *leave*, *reach*, *turn*, etc.

> Winter is here. The leaves of the trees **are turning** yellow.
> I **turned** my head and sow the profile of a man.
> The weather **is changing** for the betler.
> Shanghai **has changed** a lot in the past 10 years.

The third subclass refers to momentary verbs, such as *hit*, *jump*, *kick*, *knock*, *open/close* (a door), *put* (something on the table), *shut*, *take out*, etc. With momentary verbs, the non-progressive form inclicates a single movement and the progressive form a repeated movement.

> The child **jumped** for joy.
> The child **was jumping** for joy.
> He **opened** the door and ran out of the house.
> He was **opening and closing** the door to make sure that it worked properly.

② Stative Verbs

Stative verbs refer to present or past states. Stative verbs are normally not used in the progressive form except for certain cases in which there is a change of meaning. Stative verbs can be divided into four categories.

The first category includes two basic stative verbs *be* and *have*.

> **I'm** now a college teacher and was once a tour guide.
> The hare **has** a short tail.

---

durative verbs
持续动作的动词
transitional verbs
改变或移动的动词
momentary verbs
短暂动作的动词

The second subclass of stative verbs are the verbs that indicate the notion of being and having, such as *apply to*, *belong to*, *lack*, *resemble*, *fit*, *weigh*, etc.

This principle doesn't **apply to** every situation.

Suzhou accent slightly **differs from** Shanghai accent.

This dress **fits** her well.

The third subclass of stative verbs refers to a **sense perception**, such as *hear*, *feel*, *see*, *taste*, *smell*, etc.

I can't **hear** him clearly.

The beef steak **tastes** delicious.

The fourth subclass includes verbs that refer to feelings, a state of mind or an opinion, such as *assume*, *believe*, *consider*, *detest*, *fear*, *hate*, *hope*, *imagine*, *know*, *like*, *love*, *mean*, *mind*, *notice*, *prefer*, *regret*, *remember*, *suppose*, *think*, *understand*, *want*, *wish*, etc.

I **assume** she will get a promotion.

I **love** watching plays.

Sometimes stative verbs can become dynamic verbs and may be used in the progressive form when there is a transfer of meaning.

The little boy is **being** naughty (is acting in a naughty way).

We're **having** a wonderful time (are enjoying ourselves).

sense perception
感觉

**Task 2**

Discuss with your partner about the following questions.
(1) What are the two finite forms of main verbs?
(2) What are the three non-finite forms of main verbs?
(3) Do modal auxiliaries have the non-finite forms?
(4) Which of the following verbs are regular verbs and which are irregular verbs?

① let ② reduce ③ come ④ stop ⑤ bring ⑥ go ⑦ clean ⑧ work

## ◆ 11.2　Classification of Verbs（Ⅱ）

According to word formation and grammatical forms, English verbs can be divided into **single-word verbs** and **phrasal verbs**, **finite verbs** and **non-finite verbs**, **regular verbs** and **irregular verbs**.

single-word verbs
单词动词
phrasal verbs
词组动词
finite verbs
限定动词
non-finite verbs
非限定动词
regular verbs
规则动词
irregular verbs
不规则动词

## 1) Single-word Verbs and Phrasal Verbs

A single-word verb consists of only one word. Most verbs are singe-word verbs. A phrasal verb is composed of two or more words. Phrasal verbs are subclassified into three categories:

① Verb + Preposition

Many graduates *apply for* the same position.

The police are *probing into* this case.

② Verb + Adverb Particle

Her car *broke down* on the way to work.

Please *turn* the light *off*!

③ Verb + Adverb Particle + Preposition

You shouldn't *give in to* him if you are right.

He decides to *cut down on* smoking.

Phrasal verbs like single-word verbs can be transitive or intransitive. There are some constructions also grouped under the category of phrasal verbs, such as "**verb + noun + preposition**" and "**verb + noun**".

If you wish to *make a fool of* yourself, that is your affair.

Time would be needed for democracy to *take root*.

The car has *changed hands* twice.

## 2) Finite Verbs and Non-finite Verbs

According to the forms that verbs take in sentences, they can be divided into finite and non-finite verbs.

① Finite Verbs

Finite verbs function as the predicate or the first part of the predicate of sentences. They have different finite forms in accordance with tense and subject-verb concord principle. English main verbs have two finite forms. The two finite forms are the present tense and the past tense.

He *is/was* a super star.

I *studied* English before/*studies* English every day.

② Non-finite Verbs

Finite verbs are marked for tense, while non-finite verbs have no tense distinction. Non-finite verbs can't be used as the first part of the predicate nor can they denote tense. There are three non-finite forms: the infinitive, the -ing participle and the -ed participle.

Tom asked her to **marry** him.

Doctor Neil stood there **gazing at** the patient.

**United**, we stand; **divided**, we fall.

Most auxiliaries have the present and past tense forms but no non-finite forms except for *be*. The modal auxiliaries do not have the non-finite forms or the base forms.

I **could** read story books when I was four.

I **did** love him at that time.

### 3) Regular Verbs and Irregular Verbs

A majority of verbs are regular verbs that derive their past tense and -ed participle forms by adding -ed to the base form, while the past tense and -ed forms of irregular verbs are unpredictable.

① Regular Verbs

Regular verbs derive their past tense and -ed participle forms by adding -ed to the base form.

help→ helped→ helped        work→ worked→ worked

clean→ cleaned→ cleaned    stay→ stayed→ stayed

② Irregular Verbs

There are just a limited number of irregular verbs that can be divided into four groups: the first group of irregular verbs has only one and the same form for the base, past tense and -ed participle; the second group has one base form and another form for the past tense and -ed participle; the third group has three different forms for the base, past tense and -ed participle; in the fourth group the -ed participle shares the same form with the base while the past tense has another form.

let→ let→ let                        cut→ cut→ cut

hang→ hung→ hung            smell→ smelt→ smelt

go→ went→ gone                see→ saw→ seen

become→ became→ become    run→ ran→ run

**Task 3**   Correct the mistakes in the following sentences.

(1) Echo bought a book to be read on the journey.

(2) I don't think much of him, be honest with you.

(3) This book seems to be translated into English.

(4) It is impossible him to find such a nice place to livein.

## 11.3 Infinitive

The infinitive form is one of the three non-finite forms of English verbs. There are two kinds of infinitive: **to-infinitive** and **bare infinitive**. The bare infinitive is the infinitive without *to* and takes the same form with the base form of the verb. Infinitives can be combined with adjectives, nouns and verbs.

### 1) Adjective + Infinitive

"Adjective + infinitive" combinations act as complements in SVC patterns. With different kinds of adjectives, the combinations can vary in meaning. Semantically, these combinations fall into three groups.

① In this group the subject of the main clause is also the **logical subject** of the infinitive. The adjectives appearing in this pattern are all dynamic adjectives that show emotional feelings, good or bad luck, mental state and **character or behavior traits**.

I'm **sorry to interrupt** you.

He was **lucky to be admitted** by this famous university.

He's **determined to further** his study abroad.

He was **foolish to make** the same mistake.

You are **nice to help** a stranger.

If the subject of the main clause is not the logical subject of the infinitive, *for* is used to introduce the logical subject.

I'm **afraid for my daughter to go** to school by herself.

The child is quite **willing for his mother to go** with him.

The sentences with adjectives showing character or behavior trait can be transformed into a corresponding it-pattern.

It was **foolish of him to make** the same mistake.

It is **nice of him to help** a stranger.

② In this group the subject of the main clause is the logical object of the infinitive. The adjectives appearing in this pattern are generally stative adjectives that denote durable states rather than temporary dynamic qualities.

This problem is **difficult to solve**.

He is **impossible to please**.

*This car is **expensive to repair**.*

These sentences can be transformed into an anticipatory it-construction.

*It is **difficult to solve** this problem.*

*It is **impossible to please** him.*

*It is **expensive to repair** this car.*

③ In this group the subject of the main clause may be the logical subject or logical object of the infinitive. In most cases, the adjective can be turned into a corresponding adverb in deep structure.

*She is **quick to respond** to my question. = She responds to my question quickly.*

*My mother was **hesitant to make** a decision. = My mother made a decision hesitantly.*

### 2) Noun (Phrase) + Infinitive

In the "noun (phrase) + infinitive" combinations the infinitive is the **postmodification** in noun phrases.

> postmodification
> 后置修饰语

① Semantic Relations

Semantically the noun (phrase) and the infinitive may form different relations. Sometimes, the noun (phrase) is the logical subject of the infinitive.

*She is always the **first student to arrive** at school.*

*The **key to unlock** the door can't be found anywhere.*

Sometimes the noun (phrase) is the logical object of the infinitive. Therefore, a verb-object relation exists between the infinitive and the noun (phrase).

*This is **the most important thing to do**.*

*He has **a large family to support**.*

> 有时候不定式结构与它所修饰的名词是一种同位关系

Sometimes the noun (phrase) is in apposition to the infinitive.

*I had an **impulse to tell** her the truth.*

*She has no **intention to marry** him.*

② Active or Passive

As postmodification, the infinitive may appear in active or passive voice. In some cases, both active and passive forms are possible.

*Give me **a list of guests to invite/to be invited**.*

*The **man to consult/to be consulted** is Mr. Johnson.*

But in other cases, an active form seems more natural than the passive.

*I have got **a lot of letters to write**.*

*There is **a lot of work to do**.*

In still other cases, a passive form sounds more appropriate.

The **cases to be investigated** must not be made public in press.

The **question to be discussed** at the meeting is crucial to the whole company.

③ "Noun + Infinitive" and "Noun + Preposition + -ing"

Some nouns can be followed by both an infinitive or a "preposition + -ing" as postmodifier with no difference in meaning. These nouns are: *attempt, chance, effort, freedom, intention, necessity, opportunity, reason, time, way,* etc.

There is no **necessity to buy/of buying** a new car.

The doctor made a bold **attempt to save/of saving** the patient.

With some other nouns, an infinitive rather than a "preposition + -ing" is used as postmodifier. These nouns include: *ability, agreement, ambition, anxiety, curiosity, disposition, mind, obligation, permission, refusal, reluctance, temptation, tendency, wish,* etc.

disposition 性情
reluctance 勉强
temptation 诱惑
tendency 趋势
aptitude 习性
delay 耽搁
genius 天才
motive 动机
objection 异议

We should develop students' **ability to handle** practical problems.

She is under no **obligation to help** you.

There are still other nouns which should be followed by a "preposition + -ing" as postmodifier. These nouns are: *aptitude, delay, difficulty, excuse, experience, interest, genius, habit, idea, motive, objection, passion, plan, possibility, skill, success,* etc.

There is no **hope of passing** the exam.

You can obtain the **experience of teaching** by tutoring.

### 3) Verb + Infinitive

Some verbs can be followed by an infinitive to form a verb-object relation. These collocations fall into three types: **verb + infinitive**, **verb + object + infinitive** and **verb + (object) + infinitive**.

pledge 誓言
profess 自称
swear 发誓
threaten 威胁
undertake 从事
venture 冒险
volunteer 自愿
vow 立誓

① There are verbs that can be directly followed by an infinitive as object. These verbs include: *agree, aim, apply, arrange, choose, claim, decide, demand, desire, determine, endeavor, expect, hope, learn, manage, offer, pledge, prepare, pretend, profess, promise, refuse, resolve, seek, swear, threaten, undertake, venture, volunteer, vow,* etc.

We must **agree to differ**.

He **claimed to marry** this ordinary-looking girl.

The boss **demanded to fire** him.

② Some verbs can not be directly followed by an infinitive unless a noun or pronoun comes between the verb and the infinitive. These verbs can be subcategorized into five types.

- **Verbs of perception** such as *see*, *hear*, *watch*, *feel*, etc.

*I watch him enter the gate of the hospital.*

- Causative verbs such as *have*, *let*, *make*, etc.

Be sure to **have your daughter come** with you.

- Some phrasal verbs such as *arrange for*, *ask for*, *rely on*, etc.

*I arrange for them to meet in the coffee bar.*

- Verbs showing mental state such as *consider*, *declare*, *find*, *consider*, *prove*, *think*, *believe*, *discover*, *feel*, *imagine*, *judge*, *suppose*, *understand*, etc. The infinitive after these verbs is invariably *to be*. After such verbs as *consider*, *declare*, *find*, *prove*, *think*, the infinitive *to be* can be omitted.

*He declared himself to be innocent.*

*I know her to be a nice person.*

*He proved himself (to be) innocent.*

- Verbs having the force of "advice", "permission" and "forbiddance", such as *advise*, *allow*, *forbid*, *permit*, *recommend*, *require*, *urge*, etc.

*I advise him to start exercise as soon as possible.*

③ With some verbs such as *ask*, *can't bear*, *hate*, *intend*, *like*, *prefer*, *want*, etc. the object can occur in the "verb + infinitive" construction or in the "verb + object + infinitive" pattern.

*Do you intend to marry him?*

*I didn't intend you to marry him.*

*I like to have a cup of coffee.*

*I don't like people to make fun of me.*

> verbs of perception
> 感知动词
> causative verbs
> 使役动词

**Task 4**  Put the verbs in brackets into the -ing participle or the -ed participle.

(1) I saw him _____ (go) to the dining-room.

(2) Just get job _____ (finish up) as soon as possible.

(3) A tiger can be trained if _____ (catch) young.

(4) The joke set the whole company _____ (laugh).

## 11.4　Participles

In this part we will discuss the other two non-finite forms of verbs the **-ing participle** and the **-ed participle**.

### 1) Collocation of -ing Participle with Verbs

① Verb + -ing Form

An -ing participle can be used after verbs as object. These verbs include: *admit, acknowledge, anticipate, advocate, appreciate, avoid, can't help, can't resist, can't stand, consider, contemplate, defer, delay, deny, detest, dislike, don't mind, ensure, enjoy, escape, excuse, evade, facilitate, fancy, favor, finish, give up, imagine, include, keep (on), mind, miss, pardon, postpone, practice, put off, resent, report, risk, stop, suggest*, etc. If the logical subject of the -ing participle is also the subject of the main clause, it needn't be expressed. If the -ing form has a logical form of its own, it must be expressed.

I **detested watching** scenes of violence.

She **denied lying** to the teacher.

Please **pardon my disturbing** you.

I don't **mind him moving** to another house.

② Verb + Object + Preposition + -ing Form

Some of the verbs listed above can also take a corresponding that-clause as object. They are: *acknowledge, admit, advocate, anticipate, appreciate, deny, fancy, imagine, suggest, mean, mention, propose, recall, recollect, understand*, etc.

He **acknowledged having cheated** in the final exam.

He **acknowledged that** he had cheated in the final exam.

Some verbs can't be directly followed by an -ing form unless there is an object and a preposition between the verb and the -ing form. These verbs include: *trick, mislead, shame, surprise, trap, stop, prevent, restrain, hinder, save*, etc. The prepositions commonly used in this collocation are *into* and *from*.

He **tricked her into marrying** him.

Her sudden question **surprised him into betraying** himself.

---

anticipate 预期
advocate 提倡
contemplate 沉思
defer 推迟
detest 憎恶
evade 逃避
facilitate 使便利
fancy 想象
resent 怨恨
restrain 抑制
hinder 阻碍
trap 诱捕

*A sailor **saved him from drowning***.

In some of these collocations such as "prevent/stop somebody from doing something" the preposition *from* can be omitted. But it cannot be left out if the preceding verb occurs in the passive voice.

*The father **prevents the young man** (**from**) **seeing** his daughter again.*

*I can't be **stopped from chasing** my dream.*

### 2) -ed Participle as Premodifier

In a noun phrase -ed participles can be used as premodifier. Most of these -ed participles used as premodifier are derived from transitive verbs while a few of them come from intransitive verbs.

① -ed Participles Derived from Transitive Verbs

As premodifier, transitive -ed participles usually denote a passive meaning or a sense of completion. -ing participles derived from transitive or intransitive verbs, however, express an active meaning or a sense of incompletion. Compare:

| | |
|---|---|
| ***frozen** meat* | *a **freezing** winter morning* |
| *a **finished** article* | *the last **finishing** touch* |
| *a **conquered** army* | *a **conquering** army* |
| ***written** language* | ***writing** paper* |

As premodifier, some -ed participles cannot be used alone unless they are combined with a negative prefix "un-" or when they are combined with an adverb to form a compound.

| | |
|---|---|
| ***uninvited** guests* | *a **badly-built** house* |
| ***untold** sufferings* | *a **newly-born** baby* |
| *an **unedited** story* | ***half-baked** ideas* |
| *an **unexpected** happening* | ***far-fetched** reasons* |

② -ed Participles Derived from Intransitive Verbs

The use of intransitive -ed participles as premodifier is limited to only a few verbs: *retired, escaped, faded, withered, fallen, expired, risen, returned, vanished, grown*. These -ed participles imply a sense of completion instead of passive meaning.

| | |
|---|---|
| *a **retired** teacher* | *an **expired** lease* |
| *an **escaped** prisoner* | *the **risen** sun* |
| ***faded** color* | *a **returned** student* |

*a **withered** flower*  *the **vanished** treasure*
***fallen** leaves*  *a **grown** man*

A few -ed participles cannot be used as premodifiers unless they are combined with an adverb to form a compound. For example, you can say *a well-behaved boy* or *a widely-travelled businessman* but *behaved* and *travelled* can't be used as premodifiers.

### 3) -ed Participle as Complement

Verbs that can be followed by an -ed participle as object complement fall into three groups.

① The first group comprises verbs of conception and verbs denoting mental state such as *see, hear, feel, find, think*, etc.

*I found the bird **stolen**.*
*He saw the students **assembled** in the hall.*

② The second group consists of causative verbs such as *make, get, have, keep*, etc.

*He got his car **repaired** at last.*
*She keeps herself **informed** of the latest development in computer industry.*

③ The third group includes verbs denoting hope, expectation, order, such as *like, want, wish, order*, etc.

*I don't like the dish **cooked** this way.*
*I wished the task **finished** as soon as possible.*

---

**Task 5**  Put the verbs in brackets into the infinitive or the -ing participle.

(1) Have you heard of Smith the carpenter _____ (hurt)?

(2) His ambition, _____ (win) the men's singles in the 2008 Olympic Games, was understandable.

(3) Once _____ (leave) the premises, you have to buy another ticket to reenter.

(4) You ought to know better than _____ (believe) all the gossip you hear.

## 11.5 Notes about Infinitive and -ing Participle

There are verbs that can be followed either by an -ing form or by an infinitive. With some of these verbs, no semantic difference will be produced by choosing either of these two patterns, while with others, different choices result in different interpretations.

### 1) Either Infinitive or -ing Participle without Change of Meaning

Verbs that can be followed by an infinitive or an -ing form as object are: *attempt, begin, can't bear, continue, deserve, dread, hate, intend, like, loathe, love, need, neglect, omit, plan, prefer, require, start*, etc. No great change will take place when either of these two forms is used, but in some cases alternation can produce slightly different meanings.

dread 惧怕
loathe 厌恶
neglect 忽视

① After process verbs such as *begin, cease, continue, start* and emotive verbs such as *can't bear, deserve, dread, hate, intend, like, loathe, love, need, neglect, omit, plan, prefer, require*, the infinitive is commonly used to refer to a specific act while the -ing participle is used to refer to a general act.

I can't **bear getting up** early in the morning.

I can't **bear to** see him again.

I **prefer going** to bed early in the evening.

I **prefer to buy** the red coat.

② After *need, want, require* and *deserve*, an active -ing form can be used to denote a passive meaning which can also be expressed by a passive infinitive.

This book **deserves reading** again and again.

This book **deserves to be read** again and again.

This car **needs repairing**.

This car **needs to be repaired**.

③ After *begin* and *start*, both infinitive and -ing form can be used, but normally *begin* is used when the infinitive is a stative verb.

She **began to** see what he meant.

We **began to believe** what he said.

④ After *attempt, intend* and *plan*, the infinitive is more commonly used, but when they are in the progressive form, only the infinitive can be used.

I intended **to visit/visiting** Thailand this year.

I'm intending **to visit** France this winter.

### 2) Either Infinitive or -ing Form with Different Meanings

With some verbs, an infinitive can produce a rather different meaning from an -ing form. These verbs can be divided into four subclasses.

① After *remember*, *forget* and *regret*, the infinitive refers to a second act that follows the first, while the -ing form to a previous event.

I **remember giving** the book back. It is not with me.

Please **remember to give** the book back or you'll have to pay overdue fine.

I **regret to tell** you that I failed the exam.

I **regret failing** the exam.

② After *stop*, *leave off*, *go on*, the -ing participle functions as object, while the infinitive as adverbial of purpose.

They **stopped watching** TV at 9:30.

They were tired of hard work all day so they **stopped to watch** TV at 9:30.

③ After *try*, *mean*, *can't help* the choice between an infinitive and an -ing form is determined by the meaning of these verbs.

His silence **means refusing** your advice.

He didn't **mean to accept** your help.

**Trying doing** it once again and you can succeed.

He **tries to finish** the experiment by doing it once again.

④ After *encourage*, *permit*, *allow*, *recommend*, *advise*, *authorize*, either the -ing participle or the infinitive with a logical subject can be used.

This company doesn't **allow leaving** early.

This company doesn't **allow the employees to leave** early.

## EXERCISES

Ⅰ. **Identify the underlined verbs in the following sentences as (1) transitive verb, (2) intransitive verb, (3) link verb, (4) primary auxiliary verb, (5) modal verb or (6) semi-auxiliary verb.**

1. What he said still hold.
2. I have to save some money to buy a car.
3. Pam held my hand, not knowing what to do.
4. It just happened that a policeman was nearby.

5. When we mentioned this, she went red.
6. I know he has been injured before.
7. I happened to know the place he lived.
8. We should go out while the weather is fine.
9. Be patient. Dad is sure to be back soon.
10. Shall I help you, or do you want to do it yourself?

II. Mark the underlined finite verbs with F and the nonfinite verbs with N in the following sentences.

1. I have been here before.
2. You may go if you like.
3. Is this the book recommended by the teacher?
4. Scot went to the hospital to see his friend.
5. How much did it cost to send the telegram?
6. No one could tell me where to get the book.
7. Clem insisted on doing it in his own way.
8. We watched the children playing in the garden.
9. Peter says he will come as soon as he has a chance.
10. Confined to bed, she needed to be waited on in everything.

III. Fill in the blanks with the proper infinitive forms of the given verbs.

1. The question _____ (discuss) is very important.
2. He doesn't like the news _____ (spread).
3. I don't want you _____ (involve) in the case.
4. Jessica was nowhere _____ (find).
5. Nobody likes _____ (laugh at).
6. I should _____ (tell) him, but I forgot.
7. We planned _____ (go) to Shanghai, but we didn't.
8. Ben was _____ (set out) at six, but was late.
9. We hope _____ (finish) the work by Friday.
10. I had meant _____ (visit) him yesterday, but I was ill.
11. You are lucky _____ (receive) a good education.
12. My sister would like _____ (emigrate), but her husband disagreed.
13. My aunt wished _____ (travel) around the country with his friends.
14. Andy seems _____ (sit) there all day.

15. It's a great pleasure _____ (work) with you all the time.

16. The chairman was reported _____ (visit) in Europe.

17. Her great claim to fame is _____ (choose) for the last Olympic squad.

18. This scientist, _____ (see) daily in the British Museum, has devoted his life to the history of science.

19. He happened, at the moment, _____ (stand) near a small conservatory at the end of the garden.

20. Her hands and feet were firmly holding onto the ladder, but his body remained _____ (hang) in the air.

Ⅳ. Rewrite the following sentences, using infinitive phrases.

1. Paul was sent to hospital in order that he could get better treatment.
2. Tom is looking for a house in which he can live.
3. The youngest person that entered the program was only fourteen.
4. We are happy that we have found such a nice place to live in.
5. The case which will be investigated is not to be made public.
6. Tom studies hard in order that he can pass the examination.
7. Joey jumped for joy when he saw his old friend again.
8. Mike opened his mouth as if he was going to speak.
9. Many of us considered that the speaker had overstated his case.
10. I would have given up my life if I could have saved her.

Ⅴ. Complete the sentences by using the -ing participle or the -ed participle form of the verb in brackets.

1. Mrs. Allison will charm everyone at the party. She is a _____ (charm) woman.
2. Has something troubled you? Did you receive some _____ (trouble) news?
3. Will your _____ (increase) salary enable you to buy a new car?
4. The committee didn't approve the _____ (suggest) changes.
5. Did you try to encourage your son? Did you give him any _____ (encourage) advice?
6. Was the _____ (attempt) experiment a success?
7. The _____ (fall) snow was frozen hard.
8. More traffic will be able to pass on the _____ (widen) road.
9. I can't bear the smell of _____ (burn) toast.

## 11. Verbs

10. One should always be careful with _____ (load) guns.
11. The _____ (rage) wind destroyed a great deal of property.
12. Dick jumped out of the way of the _____ (approach) train.
13. We need another copy of the _____ (sign) contract.
14. The _____ (return) package has no stamps on it.
15. There is a _____ (refresh) breeze on the porch.

**VI. Rewrite the following sentences, using an -ing form or -ed form as a premodifier in the noun phrases.**

1. This report encourages us very much.
2. This is an agreement that will last long.
3. We have a supply of fuel, but it is limited.
4. Those seats are reserved.
5. This lawyer has a number of clients who are very satisfied.
6. People didn't at all expect that kind of result.
7. These circumstances really worry us very much.
8. The writer made his point with an emphasis that terrified us.
9. A writer people know well has adopted Sheila as his daughter.
10. He gave a lecture that bored all of us.

**VII. Put the verbs in brackets into the correct forms, choosing between the -ing participle and the infinitive.**

1. We'd better hurry up; I hate _____ (arrive) late.
2. Don't hesitate _____ (call) if you have any problem.
3. I don't want you _____ (become) too confident.
4. I stopped _____ (eat) sugar years ago.
5. A phone call sent him _____ (hurry) to London.
6. Any appeal _____ (leave) is against the regulation.
7. The rooms need _____ (clean) before we move in.
8. Don't omit _____ (lock) the door.
9. I didn't remember _____ (phone) them last night.
10. Why should we risk _____ (break) the law?
11. _____ (make) a long story short, I quite agree with you.
12. People _____ (live) closest to the river bank were the worst affected.
13. I can't bear _____ (see) the children treated rudely.
14. Shanghai has too many people _____ (chase) too few jobs.
15. Polly began _____ (understand) what he meant.

# 12. Adjectives and Adverbs

## Aims of the Unit

> In this unit we will discuss some general matters about grammar. We are going to discuss six questions in particular:
> - What is the classification of adjectives?
> - What are the chief uses of adjectives and adjective phrases?
> - What is the classification of adverbs?
> - What are the chief uses of adverbs and adverb phrases?
> - Do the adverbs with two forms (with -ly and without -ly) have identical meaning?
> - What are the comparison and comparative constructions of adjectives and adverbs?

Adjectives and adverbs are chiefly used as modifying elements in a sentence. In this unit, we shall talk about classification and chief uses of adjectives and adjective phrases, adverbs and adverbs phrases as well as comparison and comparative constructions.

### ◆ 12.1 Classification of Adjectives

Adjectives may be divided into **one-word** and **compound adjectives**, **central** and **peripheral adjectives**, **dynamic** and **stative adjectives**, **gradable** and **non-gradable adjectives**.

#### 1) One-word and Compound Adjectives

In terms of word formation, adjectives may be classified into one-word adjectives and compound adjectives. A one-word adjective may consist of only

---

one-word and compound adjectives
单词形容词和复合形容词
central and peripheral adjectives
中心形容词和外围形容词
dynamic and stative adjectives
动态形容词和静态形容词
gradable and non-gradable adjectives
等级形容词和非等级形容词

one free morpheme, such as *big*, *small*, *bad*, *good*, *hot*, *cold*; it may also consist of a free root plus a prefix or a suffix or both, such as *unkind*, *impossible*, *lovely*, *voiceless*, *monolingual*, *unthinkable*, etc.

Compound adjectives are formed in different ways: "adjective + adjective", such as *bitter-sweet*, *light-blue*; "adjective/adverb + v-ing participle", such as *good-looking*, *hard-working*; "adjective/adverb + v-ed participle", such as *newfangled*, *well-meant*; "noun + adjective", such as *grass-green*, *duty-free*; "noun + v-ing participle", such as *ocean-going*, *law-abiding*; "noun + v-ed participle", such as *hand-made*, *suntanned*; "adjective + noun + v-ed participle", such as *kind-hearted*, *absent-minded*, etc.

## 2) Central and Peripheral Adjectives

In terms of syntactic function, adjectives can be divided into two groups: **central adjectives** and **peripheral adjectives**. Most adjectives can be used both as modifier in a noun phrase and as subject/object complement. These adjectives are labeled "central". Take the adjective *green* as an example:

***Green** apples are sour.* (modifier in a noun phrase)

*Those apples are **green**.* (subject complement)

*They have painted the door **green**.* (object complement)

Peripheral adjectives refer to the few which cannot meet both these requirements. Some peripheral adjectives can only act as premodifiers, e. g. *chief*, *main*, *principal*, *utter*, *sheer*, etc. Other peripheral adjectives can only be used as complement, e. g. *asleep*, *afraid*, *alike*, etc.

*This is **utter** nonsense.* → *\* The nonsense is **utter**.*

*This child is **asleep**.* → *\* This is an **asleep** child.*

## 3) Dynamic and Stative Adjectives

Semantically, adjectives can be **dynamic** or **stative**. Such adjectives as *tall*, *short*, *big*, *small* describe static characteristics of animate or inanimate objects, and most adjectives are stative adjectives. Dynamic adjectives, such as *ambitious*, *careful*, *generous*, *fill*, *patient*, *witty*, describe the dynamic properties of people or things, and they are different in use from stative adjectives. For instance, dynamic adjectives can go with the progressive aspect of the verb *be*, while stative adjectives cannot. Dynamic adjectives can appear in imperative sentences with *be* as the start, while stative adjectives cannot.

Lastly, dynamic adjectives can occur in causative constructions in which it is impossible to use stative adjectives.

> She is being **witty**. → *She is being **tall**.
> Be **patient/careful**! → *Be **pretty**.
> I persuaded her to be **generous**. → *I persuaded her to be **pretty**.

### 4) Gradable and Non-gradable Adjectives

Morphologically, adjectives can be **gradable** and **non-gradable**. Most adjectives are gradable adjectives, whose gradability is manifested in the forms of their comparative degree and superlative degree and in ability to accept modification by intensifiers. All dynamic and most stative adjectives are gradable adjectives: *careful, witty, patient, big, small, pretty, ugly*, etc.

> *big, bigger, biggest*
> *good, better, best*
> *difficult, more difficult, most difficult*

The few non-gradable ones include some denominal adjectives that denote classification or provenance: *atomic* scientist, *Chinese* carpet. Some other adjectives, such as *perfect, excellent, extreme*, are also non-gradable because their lexical meanings have already denoted a high or extreme degree.

**Task 1** Give an example for each type of adjective and illustrate the roles or role of each adjective played in each sentence.

## 12.2 Chief Uses of Adjectives and Adjective Phrases

### 1) Adjective (Phrase) as Modifier in Noun Phrases

Most adjectives can function both as modifier and as complement. In many cases, these two functions are interchangeable. For example, *The boy is intelligent* can be transformed into *He is an intelligent boy*; likewise, *The boy is so intelligent* can be turned into *He is so intelligent a boy*.

As modifiers in the noun phrase, adjectives usually appear after the determiner and before the headword, but sometimes they may also take a post-head position. When two or more pre-modifying adjectives co-occur on the same level, they are usually coordinated in the normal order of shorter members preceding the longer, e.g.

*It was a **rainy**, **windy**, **freezing** day.*

When two or more pre-modifying adjectives appear on different levels, their normal order is like this: (determiner)—adjective denoting the speaker's evaluation—(adjective denoting) size, shape, age—adjective denoting color—adjective denoting nationality, origin, material—adjective denoting use or purpose (i.e. classifier)—headword, e.g.

*a **well-known German medical** school*

*an **interesting little red French oil** painting*

Adjectives can also be used as post-modifiers. This normally occurs when the headword is a some-/any-/no- compound, e.g.

*I'd like something **cheaper**.*

Adjectives with a prepositional phrase or an infinitive as complementation also occur after the headword they modify, e.g.

*It was a conference **fruitful of results**.*

*Students **brave enough to take this course** deserve to succeed.*

It is not uncommon, however, that an adjective is separated from its complementation by the noun it modifies, that is, the adjective precedes the headword, while the complementation follows it, e.g.

*It is a **different** book **from that one**.*

*That is a **difficult** problem **to solve**.*

For some adjectives, a pre-head or post-head position does not make any difference in meaning. For example, *It is the only possible solution* is semantically equivalent to *It is the only solution possible*. But for some other adjectives, different positions give different meanings, e.g.

*the members **present*** (being in the place)

*the **present** members* (at the present time)

*the person **responsible*** (obliged to take care)

*the **responsible** person* (being relied on)

### 2) Adjective Phrases as Complement

Predicative adjectives are used in predicative structure and function as subject as well as object complements. In this section we are going to talk about four kinds of **adjective complementation**.

> predicative adjectives
> 补语形容词
> adjective complementation
> 形容词补足语成分

① Predicative Adjectives

There are two groups of **predicative adjectives**: one group of adjectives denoting health conditions, such as *well*, *ill*.

He's very **well**.

You look **ill**.

The other are adjectives with a- as prefix, such as *alike*, *alone*, *alive*.

The two brothers are very much **alike**.

I was **alone** in the house.

He was **asleep**.

Predicative adjectives cannot be placed before a noun as pre-modifier, but sometimes they can be used before a noun when they are themselves modified by an adverb. For example, instead of "*an asleep child", we can say "a fast asleep child". But sometimes the synonyms of these predicative adjectives can be used as pre-modifiers. For example, *alike—similar*, *live—living*, *alone—lonely/solitary*, etc.

The animals are **alive**. → They are **live/living** animals.

The children were **asleep**. → I saw the **sleeping** children.

The woman was **afraid**. → I saw the **frightened** woman.

② Adjective + Prepositional Phrase

Prepositional phrases are most commonly used as adjective complementation, and adjective phrases composed of "adjective + prepositional phrase" are most frequently found in the position of subject complement. Different adjectives usually go with specific prepositions to express different meanings (see Section 13.3).

He was **absent from** the meeting.

I feel **ashamed of** playing so badly.

You should not be **blind to** the beauties of nature.

He felt **confident of** victory.

He is **content with** what he has.

The adjectives in the sentences cited above can also be used alone as subject complement, but there are a few adjectives that cannot be so used unless they are followed by a prepositional phrase.

I'm very **fond of** Edgar's music.

He is **intent on** his studies.

③ Adjective + to-infinitive

There are different SVC patterns in which the complement is realized by "adjective + to-infinitive". These patterns vary in meaning with the different adjectives, and each pattern represents a different group of adjectives (see Section 11.3)

>He is **impossible to teach**.
>She is **stupid not to follow** your advice.
>The government should be **quick to react**.

④ Adjective + that-clause

The adjectives that can take a that-clause as complementation include *sure, glad, amazed, surprised, confident, certain, proud, sad, alarmed, annoyed, astonished, disappointed, pleased, shocked*, etc. In spoken language, the conjunction that is usually omitted.

>I'm **sure (that) you'll succeed**.
>I'm **glad (that) you like it**.
>She was **amazed (that) he should arrive so soon**.

This kind of that-clause can sometimes be replaced by a corresponding prepositional phrase or a to-infinitive.

>I'm **sure that you will get success**.
>= You are **sure of success**.
>= You are **sure to get success**.
>I'm **certain that he will come**.
>= He is **certain to come**.

## 3) Nominal Adjectives as Subject/Object

>**The Chinese** are very industrious.
>**The young in spirit** enjoy life.
>**The beautiful** is not always the same as **the good**.
>We will nurse **your sick**, clothe **your naked** and feef **your hungry**.
>Helen was singing her **sweetest** (song).

In some idiomatic expressions, an adjective is used as a noun and served as a prepositional object.

| | |
|---|---|
| above (the) **normal** | at **large** |
| for **short** | from **bad** to **worse** |
| in **brief/short** | in **general/particular** |

### 4) Adjective Phrases as Adverbial

① As Modifier of Adjectives

Tina has **fiery** red hair.

Cathy is wearing a **dark** blue dress.

Mrs Brown has reached a **good** (= very) old age.

In informal speech, adjectivves such as *awful*, *deilish*, *dreadful*, *full*, *jolly*, *mightyt*, *plain*, *real*, *terrible*, etc. are ususally used as adverbs as modifier of adjectives denoting degree.

Pam was **awful** surprised.

It's **mighty** helpful.

This is a **real** nice house.

② As Modifier of Verbs Denoting the State of Subject/Object when Action Is Happening

Drink it **hot** (= when it is hot).

Mr Brown sells them **new** (= when they are new).

Most of fruit and vegetables are eaten **raw** (= when they are raw).

③ As Modifier of the Whole Sentence Denoting Time, Cause, Result, Concession, Accompanying Situation

**Ripe**, these apples are sweet.

**Glad to accept**, the boy nodded his agreement.

He dropped on the rock, **dead**.

They came back, **happy and gay**.

All magnets behave the same, **large or small**.

④ As Modifier of Verbs Denoting Manner in Informal Speech

The car is running **good** now.

You should learn to speak **plain**.

Grace pays her rent **regular**.

⑤ Adjective Phrases as Parenthesis

**True**, it is no easy job to learn English well.

**More remarkable still**, he is in charge of the project.

Jim fell quite 20 feet, but, **strange to say**, he was not hurt.

**Task 2**  Complete the following sentences by arranging the words in parentheses in the correct order and inserting them in the blanks.

(1) Mrs. Brown has _____ children. (three, very intelligent, healthy)

(2) _____ carvings were donated to the museum. (original, twenty, wood, African)

(3) My concert was a _____ success. (long, brother's, first, public)

(4) _____ sunset filled the sky. (beautiful, pink, pale, really)

(5) There are _____ chairs in the living room. (dark, three, very, comfortable, blue)

## 12.3   Classification of Adverbs

Like adjectives, adverbs are a class of words that chiefly function as modifying elements, but what is modified by an adverb is normally a verb, an adjective, a preposition, a conjunction or another adverb. As a clause element, adverb phrases may be used as adverbials of time, place, manner, etc.; they may also be used as disjuncts, expressing the speaker's attitude or assessment on an accompanying clause, or as conjuncts, playing the role of connectives.

**1) In Terms of Word Formation, Adverbs Fall into Two Groups: Simple Adverbs and Derivative Adverbs.**

① Simple adverbs are those that consist of only one free morpheme, such as *hard*, *free*, *high*, *late*, etc.; they are mostly identical in form with corresponding adjectives.

② Derivative adverbs are those that are derived from adjectives by adding a suffix -ly, such as *constantly*, *gradually*, *internally*, etc. and most adverbs are derivatives.

**2) Semantically, Adverbs Can Be Subdivided into:**

① Adverbs of Manner (*bravely*, *quickly*, *slowly*, etc.)
② Adverbs of Degree (*very*, *badly*, *greatly*, etc.)
③ Adverbs of Time (*now*, *late*, *early*, *then*, etc.)
④ Adverbs of Frequency (*always*, *often*, *seldom*, etc.)

⑤ Adverbs of Place (*above*, *here*, *there*, *home*, etc.) as well as Conjunctive and Explanatory Adverbs (*therefore*, *moreover*, *however*, etc.)

A conjunctive adverb is an adverb that connects two independent clauses. Conjunctive adverbs show cause and effect, sequence, contrast, comparison, or other relationships, such as *therefore*, *moreover*, *however*. Explanatory adverbs are used for explanation like *namely*, *as*, etc.

## 12.4　Chief Uses of Adverbs and Adverb Phrases

Adverbs and adverb phrases are chiefly used as modifiers in phrases and as adverbials in clauses or sentences.

### 1) Adverbs as Modifier in Phrases

As a phrase element, adverbs are chiefly used:

① As Modifier of Verbs

They **completely** ignored my views.
I **entirely** agree with her.

② As Modifier of Adjectives

He had an **unusually** deep voice.
I'm feeling **kind of** tired.

③ As Modifier of Adverbs

He drives **extremely** carelessly.
Do it **right** now.

④ As Modifier of Prepositions or Conjunctions

There's the house **right** in front of you.
His parents are **dead** against the trip.

⑤ As Modifier of Determiners

**Virtually** all the students took part in the discussion.
They recovered **roughly** half their equipment.

⑥ As Modifier of Nouns or Whole Noun Phrases

It takes **quite** some time.
She's **rather** a fool.

As modifier of whole noun phrases, only these few adverbs, *quite*, *rather* are possible to be used as modifier of whole noun phrases. There are a number of adverbs, most of adverbs of time and place, can be used as post-modifiers of nouns.

| | |
|---|---|
| the way **ahead** | your friend **here** |
| the direction **back** | that man **there** |
| the hall **downstairs** | a step **forward** |
| the noise **backstage** | the neighbors **upstairs** |
| his trip **abroad** | the meeting **yesterday** |
| his journey **home** | the meal **afterwards** |
| the sentence **below** | the day **before** |
| the photo **above** | their stay **overnight** |

Some of the adverbs cited above can also be used as pre-modifiers, and, therefore, maybe viewed as adjectives.

| | |
|---|---|
| the **downstairs** part of the house | a house with three **upstairs** rooms |
| the **backstage** noise | his **home** journey |
| an **away** match | the **then** capital of the country |
| in **after** years | the **above** sentence |

These uses of adverbs are mostly found in informal style.

### 2) Adverb Phrases as Adverbial in Clauses or Sentences

As a clause element, adverb phrases are chiefly used as **adjuncts**, **disjuncts**, and **conjuncts**.

① When used as an adjunct, the adverb phrase describes the time, place or manner concerned with the action, process or state denoted by the verb. In this use, the adverb phrase is relatively mobile, being able to take the initial, medial or end position.

*Recently*, they had an accident.

They *recently* had an accident.

They had an accident *recently*.

By contrast, manner adjuncts appear more often at the end position.

They live *frugally*.

He always drives *carefully*.

Sometimes for rhetorical reasons, a manner adjunct may occur at the head of the sentence.

*Quietly* she walked on and on.

*Noiselessly*, the girl crept across the floor and stole out of the house.

Place adjunct normally appear at the end of the sentence.

*The porter will take your luggage **upstairs**.*

*I couldn't find it though I had looked **everywhere**.*

② Disjuncts serve the function of modifying the whole, denoting the speakers' attitude.

***Frankly**, I can do nothing about it.*

***Briefly**, she didn't want speak to him.*

***Officially**, he's on holiday; **actually**, he is in hospital.*

***Luckily**, she was in when I called.*

***Honestly**, I think you are mistaken.*

***Theoretically**, this is a arvellous piece of scientific writing.*

Sometimes a disjunt appears at the end of the sentence separated by a comma.

*The expedition was a success, **scientifically**.*

(= *from a scientific point of view, disjunct*)

*The expedition was a success **scientifically**.*

(= *in a scientific manner, adverbial of manner*)

③ Conjuncts differ from adjuncts and disjuncts in that they do not modify anything nor comment on the accompanying clause, but function as a transitional means from one sentence to another sentence and are often placed at the beginning of a sentence.

*They have their umbrellas up; **therefore**, it must be raining.*

*Do it now. **Otherwise** it will be too late.*

*Tom hasn't arrived yet. He may, **however**, come later.*

They can also be realized by certain noun phrases.

*The expression is ungrammatical; **all the time** it is part of the common tongue.*

Conjuncts are different from coordinators or subordinators. A conjunct differs from a coordinator in that it can sometimes be preceded by a coordinator.

*This car is smaller **and therefore** cheaper.*

It also differs from a subordinator because what is introduced by a conjunct is not a subordinate clause. Compare:

***Though** they knew the war was lost, they continued fighting.*

*They knew the war was lost. They continued fighting, **though**.*

**Task 3**  Put the adverbs in brackets in their appropriate positions. In many cases, more than one position is possible.

(1) You have studied this chapter (thoroughly).
(2) I appreciate it (very much).
(3) Such enormous distances are impossible to imagine (practically).
(4) Will you come this way (kindly)?
(5) The house needs repainting (badly).

## 12.5 Two Forms of Adverbs

There are adverbs that have two forms: one is identical with a corresponding adjective, the other is with -ly. With some of these adverbs, the two forms carry the same meaning; with some others, the meanings of the two forms are slightly different; with still other adverbs, the meanings conveyed by the two forms are entirely different. This section will deal with the meanings of some such adverbs.

**Task 4**  Choose the correct word to fill in the blank in each sentence.

(1) Come _____! I want to tell you something. (close, closely)
(2) She's _____ related to the Duke of Halifax. (close, closely)
(3) Let's meet _____ after lunch; then I'll take you _____ to your room. (direct, directly)
(4) This is a sentence _____ quoted from Latin. (direct, directly)
(5) You can eat _____ in my restaurant whenever you like. (free, freely)
(6) You can speak _____ in front of George—he knows everything. (free, freely)

### 1) Two Forms with No Difference in Basic Meaning

There are adverbs with two forms which are identical in meaning but are used in different contexts.

Drive **slowly** onto the ferry.

The workers decided to go **slow**.

It goes as **quickly** as lightning.

You must think **quick** with the mind and act **quick** with the body.

He **rightly** guessed what had brought her there.

He guessed **right**.

It serves you **right**.

She complained **loudly** of having been kept waiting.

Don't talk so **loud/loudly**.

Speak **louder**, I can't hear you.

Who laughed **loudest**?

We must aim **high**.

They searched **high** and low but didn't find anything.

He was **highly** praised.

He told the facts **fairly**.

You must play **fair**.

I can **easily** finish it today.

**Easy** come, **easy** go.

Can you see **clearly** from here?

You can see **clear** to the mountains today.

Fix the post **firmly** in the ground.

Always hold **firm** to your beliefs.

He answered me very **directly** and **openly**.

He came **direct** to London.

This achievement is **surely** unprecedented.

It's **sure** hot in this room.

## 2) Two Forms Different or Slightly Different in Meaning

These adverbs also include some of the items cited in the preceding section.

He stopped **dead**. (completely)

He was **dead** tired. (extremely, very)

He looks **deadly** pale. (deathly)

He lives **close** to the school. (near, not far away)

Watch **closely** what I do. (carefully and thoroughly)

The bullet went **clean** through his chest. (used to emphasize that an action takes place completely)

*This knife cuts **cleanly**.* (easily and smoothly in one movement)
*At the crossroads we turned **sharp** to the left.* (turning suddenly to the left or right)
*The road turns **sharply**.* (suddenly)
*He arrived at ten **sharp**.* (exactly)

### 3) Two Forms Entirely Different in Meaning

The following pairs are entirely different in meaning.

*He is working **hard**.* (with great effort)
*He could **hardly** see anything.* (almost not)
*He was **justly** punished.* (fairly)
*I wonder **just** how good he is at spoken English.* (only)
*He arrived too **late** for the train.* (after the expected time)
*His studies haven't been improving **lately**.* (recently)
*That is the thing which worries me **most**.* (very much)
*The guests at the party were **mostly** young men.* (mainly)
*She is **pretty** good at mathematics.* (very)
*She dances **prettily**.* (elegantly, gracefully)

## ◈ 12.6  Comparison and Comparative Constructions

As has been shown, most adjectives and adverbs are gradable and can be used in comparative clauses. When appearing in comparative constructions, adjectives and adverbs take special grammatical forms which are called "forms of comparison".

### 1) Comparison of Adjectives and Adverbs

With gradable adjectives and adverbs, there are three degrees of comparison: **positive/absolute degree**, **comparative degree** and **superlative degree**. The positive/absolute degree is just the base form of an adjective or adverb. The comparative and superlative degrees may be regular or irregular. Most adjectives and adverbs have regular comparison; only a few of them are irregular.

① Regular Comparison of Adjectives and Adverbs
Comparison in relation to a higher or the highest degree is expressed by the

> positive/
> absolute degree
> 原级
> comparative
> degree
> 比较级
> superlative
> degree
> 最高级
> synthetic form
> 综合形式
> analytic form
> 分析形式

inflected forms in -er or -est, or by their equivalents with *more* or *most*; the former is known as the **synthetic form** and the latter the **analytic form**. Comparison of adverbs is similar to that of adjectives. Adverbs of one syllable form their comparative degree -er and their superlative in -est. Adverbs of more than one syllable usually take *more* and *most* forms.

| | | |
|---|---|---|
| *low* | *lower* | *lowest* |
| *soon* | *sooner* | *soonest* |

But *just*, *real*, *right*, *wrong*, etc. can only take the analytic form. In fact, except *big*, *black*, *clean*, *fair*, *fast*, *great*, *hard*, *high*, *low*, *old*, *quick*, *small*, *thick*, *thin*, *wide*, *young*, etc. which adopt the synthetic form, the rest **monosyllabic words** also can take the analytic form, e.g.

She is **more mad** than Bob is.
They have been **most kind** to me.
Jill is **less tall** than Jack (is).

Many **disyllabic words** can either take the synthetic form or the analytic form, e.g.

| | | |
|---|---|---|
| *polite* | *politer/more polite* | *politest/most polite* |
| *often* | *oftener/more often* | *oftenest/most often* |

Words ending in -y, -er, -le, -ow, -ure often take the inflected forms, e.g.

| | | |
|---|---|---|
| *early* | *earlier* | *earliest* |
| *clever* | *cleverer* | *cleverest* |
| *simple* | *simpler* | *simplest* |
| *narrow* | *narrower* | *narrowest* |
| *obscure* | *obscurer* | *obscurest* |

But *eager* and *proper* can only take the analytic form, e.g.

| | | |
|---|---|---|
| *eager* | *more eager* | *most eager* |
| *proper* | *more proper* | *most proper* |

Words ending in -ful and -ish can only take the analytic form, e.g.

| | | |
|---|---|---|
| *doubtful* | *more doubtful* | *most doubtful* |
| *foolish* | *more foolish* | *most foolish* |

Adverbs formed by "adjective + -ly" can only take the analytic form, e.g.

| | | |
|---|---|---|
| *quickly* | *more quickly* | *most quickly* |

② Irregular Comparison of Adjectives and Adverbs

There are only a small number of adjectives and adverbs whose comparative and superlative degrees take irregular forms. These adjectives and adverbs are

## 12. Adjectives and Adverbs

called irregular adjectives/adverbs. For example:

| | | |
|---|---|---|
| good/well | better | best |
| ill/bad/badly | worse | worst |
| many/much | more | most |
| few | fewer/less | fewest/least |
| little | less/lesser | least/least |
| far | father/further | fathest/furthest |
| old | older/elder | oldest/eldest |
| late | later/latter | latest/last |
| in | inner | in(ner)most |
| out | outer | out(er)most |
| up | upper | up(per)most |
| fore | former | foremost |
| down | — | downmost |
| top | — | topmost |
| mid | — | midmost |
| under | — | undermost |
| hind | — | hindmost |
| eastern | — | easternmost |
| western | — | westernmost |
| northern | — | northernmost |
| southern | — | southernmost |

**Task 5**  Reword the following sentences in the two ways suggested below:

The example *He is less stupid than I thought he was* is better expressed by either *He is not so stupid as I thought he was.* or *He is cleverer than I thought he was.*

(1) Your house is less near than I thought.
(2) A donkey is less beautiful than a horse.
(3) She is less ugly than you said she was.
(4) I am less light than you.
(5) A cigarette is less strong than a cigar.

## 2) Comparative Constructions

There are three types of comparative construction:

① "as ... as" Construction

The basic pattern of "as ... as" construction is "as + adjective/adverb + as", e. g.

John is **as bright as** Bob.

The negation form of the pattern is either *John is **not as bright as** Bob* or *John is **not so bright as** Bob*.

There are cases in which the subjects of the comparative and the main clause are identical but the comparative elements are different, e. g.

*The girl was **as bright as she was beautiful**.*

*The swimming pool isn't **as wide as it is long**.*

*He is **not so wise as he is witty**.*

*She is **not so witty as she is pretty**.*

There are also cases where both the subjects and the comparative elements are different, e. g.

*The swimming pool isn't twice **as wide as that one is long**.*

Another pattern of "as ... as" construction is "as much/many + noun + as-clause", in which *much* and *many* are determiners. The negative form of this pattern is "not as/so much/many + noun + as-clause", e. g.

*You can take **as much butter as you need**.*

*She wrote **as many essays as her brother** (**did**).*

*He didn't drink **as/so much wine as his roommate**.*

There is, in addition, a variant form of "as ... as" construction, "as + adjective + noun phrase + as-clause", e. g.

*George is **as efficient a worker as Jack**.*

It should also be noticed that this variant form is sometimes interchangeable with the pattern "noun phrase + as ... as construction" with little or no difference in meaning. The only difference lies in the fact that in the variant pattern nucleus falls on the noun, while in the latter pattern nucleus falls on the adjective, e. g.

*George is **as efficient a worker as Jack**.*

*George is **a worker as efficient as Jack**.*

② "more ... than" Construction

The basic pattern of "more ... than" "construction is comparative degree + than-clause", e. g.

*This parcel is **heavier than that one**.*

*This parcel is **less heavy than that one**.*

*This parcel is **not so/as heavy as that one***.

Another pattern of "more ... than" construction is "more adjective/less/fewer + noun + than-clause". As in the case of "as ... as" construction, the noun is always embedded in the comparative structure, e. g.

*I have done **more work than he***.

*You have made **fewer mistakes than I have***.

A variant form of "more than" construction is "a/an + comparative adjective + noun + than-clause", e. g.

*John is **a more efficient worker than Jack***.

= *John is **a worker more efficient than Jack***.

*John is **more efficient a worker than Jack***. (less frequently)

Another variant form of "more than" construction is "the + comparative adjective/adverb + of-phrase". In this pattern, the definite article is obligatory with comparative adjectives, but optional with comparative adverbs, e. g.

*John is **the brighter of the two boys***.

*Of the two boys John behaves (**the**) **more politely***.

A third variant form of "more than" construction is "more/less of a + noun + than clause". Here *more* and *less* are used as indefinite pronouns, and the noun that follows is usually a singular gradable noun, e. g.

*He is **more/less of a sportsman than his brother***.

= *He is **more/less sportsmanlike than his brother***.

③ (The) + Superlative Adjective/Adverb + Scope of Comparison

The superlative construction is used when three or more than three people or things are compared. In this construction there is usually a scope of comparison which may be expressed by a prepositional phrase, a relative clause, or a non-finite clause. Sometimes the scope of comparison is understood in the context and need not be expressed, e. g.

*The Sahara is **the largest desert in the world***.

*This is **the most interesting book I have ever read***.

*Shakespeare was **the greatest dramatist ever known***.

*I will do it with **the greatest pleasure***.

The negative form of the superlative construction is "the least ... " which, in practical usage, is usually replaced by the superlative degree of antonymous adjectives or adverbs, e. g.

*This is **the least difficult book I have ever read***.

= This is **the easiest book I have ever read**.

The idea of highest degree can also be expressed by other constructions. In some contexts, the positive or comparative degree expresses the same meaning as is usually conveyed by the superlative, e.g.

George did **more work** this morning **than anyone else**.

= George did the most work.

**Nothing** in my life shook me **so deeply as** my first visit to China.

= My first visit to China moved me the deepest.

④ "the more ... the more" vs "more and more"

"the more ... the more" is commonly used to denote two parallel processes on a proportional increase. In this construction, the first part constitutes a subordinate clause, while the second the main clause, e.g.

**The older** I get, **the happier** I am.

= When I get older, I become happier.

"more and more" is a coordinate adverb phrase commonly used as pre-modifier in adjective/adverb phrases. In contrast with "the more ... the more", "more and more" is usually used to denote one process that is on a continual increase, e.g.

The car was running **faster and faster**.

His health is getting **better and better**.

## EXERCISES

I. Choose the correct words in the brackets to complete the sentences.

1. Uncle spoke (low, lowly) but (clear, clearly).
2. The baby was (sound, soundly) asleep.
3. Tell me (straight, straightly) what you think.
4. They danced (deep, deeply) into the night.
5. Sam always holds (firm, firmly) to his beliefs.
6. The word was (wrong, wrongly) spelt.
7. Vivien returned (short, shortly) after sunset.
8. The car stopped (short, shortly) in front of me.
9. We love our motherland (dear, dearly).
10. They are (wide, widely) different in opinions.

## 12. Adjectives and Adverbs

**II. Fill in each of the blanks with a proper adjective or adverb in its correct form, using "the" before it where necessary.**

1. Shakespeare is _____ -known than Marlowe.
2. Robert listened carefully but he didn't speak _____.
3. There are ten rather deep lakes near here; Green Lake is _____.
4. Cynthia is the _____ -working woman that I know.
5. Of all animals the cheetah runs _____.
6. Henry is an efficient worker, and his brother is still _____ than him.
7. The _____ I see of her, the _____ I like her.
8. A: Do they drink _____ beer?
   B: Yes, _____ than we do.
9. A girl as _____ as a mouse cannot climb that high.
10. They say she is _____ woman alive.

**III. Correct the mistakes in the following sentences.**

1. They don't drive rather fast.
2. You did fairly well, but he did fairly badly.
3. The tour bus is very full.
4. I found the film absolutely moving.
5. I bought the book because it was very recommended.
6. I'm afraid there's nothing to eat; the fridge is very empty.
7. I guess he is lazier than sick.
8. Tess is the happiest when left alone.
9. Of all the books, which one do you like better?
10. His illness has taken a turn for the good.

**IV. Translate the following sentences into Chinese.**

1. He is no more a writer than a painter.
2. I have written no less than five papers this semester.
3. Tom is no wiser than Bob.
4. I regard him less as my teacher than as my friend.
5. It is more than probable that he will fail.

# 13. Prepositions

## Aims of the Unit

In this unit we will discuss the functions and use of prepositions and prepositional phrases. We are going to discuss the following questions in particular:
- What is a preposition?
- What are simple prepositions? What are complex prepositions?
- How do prepositions collocate with adjectives, verbs and nouns?
- What are the transformational relations like between prepositional phrases and subordinate clauses?

**Task 1**

Are all the italicized words in the following sentences propositions?
(1) They talked *over* the problem to see if they could solve it.
(2) They talked *over* the counter when William visited Peter's shop.
(3) They called *up* all young men.
(4) She called *on* her friends.
(5) He kept *on* his overcoat because it was so cold.
(6) He kept *on* the pavement because of the heavy traffic.
(7) Keep *off* the grass.
(8) Draw the curtain to keep *off* the sun.

## ◈ 13.1 Types of Prepositions

### 1) Simple Prepositions

In English grammar, a preposition is a word (one of the parts of speech and a member of a closed word class) that shows the relationship between other words and phrases in a sentence (See the table of simple prepositions below).

Prepositions commonly convey the following relationships: agency (*by*), comparison (*like, as ... as*), direction (*to, toward, through*), place (*at, by, on*), possession (*of*), purpose (*for*), source (*from, out of*), and time (*at, before, on*).

**A Table of Simple Prepositions**

| aboard  | about   | above   | across  | after      |
|---------|---------|---------|---------|------------|
| against | along   | amid    | among   | around     |
| atop    | before  | behind  | below   | beneath    |
| beside  | between | beyond  | by      | despite    |
| as      | at      | down    | during  | for        |
| from    | in      | inside  | into    | like       |
| off     | on      | onto    | out     | outside    |
| near    | of      | over    | past    | regarding  |
| round   | since   | than    | through | throughout |
| to      | toward  | under   | unlike  | until      |
| till    | up      | upon    | with    | within     |

**Task 2**  Fill in the blanks in the following sentences with appropriate prepositions and state the relationship they convey.

(1) I'm going to visit my aunt this weekend, and my brother is coming _____ well.

(2) The Chinese tradition of the New Year is different _____ the American one.

(3) The boys stood anxiously _____ line to buy the tickets for the football game.

(4) Classes are over at last How _____ going for a picnic tomorrow?

(5) Many cultures believe that anything _____ the shape of a ring is good luck.

(6) He gave great importance _____ what his father said.

(7) People use more than words when they communicate _____ each other.

(8) The secret of happiness is to fill one's life _____ activity.

(9) The teacher told his students to make of the opportunities _____ hand.

(10) You are asking _____ trouble if you let your child play with fire.

## 2) Complex Prepositions

A complex preposition is a word group (such as *along with* or *on account of*) that functions like an ordinary one-word preposition.

**Task 3**  Spot the complex prepositions in the following sentences:

(1) Thanks to the Interstate Highway System, it is now possible to travel from coast to coast without seeing anything.

(2) But our deeds are like children that are born to us; they live and act apart from our own will. Nay, children may be strangled, but deeds never: they have an indestructible life both in and out of our consciousness.

(3) To ensure that it was not for lack of appetite that the spider had rejected the moth, I offered the spider an edible scarab beetle, which it promptly took.

(4) In addition to my other numerous acquaintances, I have one more intimate confidant. My depression is the most faithful mistress I have known. No wonder, then, that I return the love.

(5) The shipwrecked sailors were at the mercy of the wind and waves.

(6) He is working hard now with an eye to the future.

From the above task, it can be found that complex prepositions can be divided into three groups:

∗ two-word prepositions (a word + a simple preposition), also known as compound prepositions, such as *apart from*

∗ three-word prepositions (a simple preposition$_1$ + a noun + a simple preposition$_2$), also known as phrasal prepositions, such as *by means of*

∗ four-word prepositions (a simple preposition$_1$ + a determiner + a noun + a simple preposition$_2$), such as *on the eve of*

① Two-word Prepositions

**A Table of Two-word Prepositions**

| according to | ahead of | along with | apart from | as for |
|---|---|---|---|---|
| as to | because of | but for | due to | irrespective of |
| next to | out of | owing to | previous to | prior to |
| regardless of | instead of | thanks to | together with | up to |

The big auditorium was oddly silent **except for** a few scattered giggles.

Why don't you stay at home and watch TV **instead of** going to the cinema?

She bought whatever caught her eye **regardless of** the price.

He sent her some books, **together with** a dictionary.

It is a good book **save for** the last chapter.

She was cheated **out of** $1,000 by the young man.

She never would have been able to make a success of the dining-room **but for** the kindness and assistance of the men.

② Three-word Prepositions

**A Table of Three-word Prepositions**

| by force of | by means of | by reason of | by way of | for fear of |
|---|---|---|---|---|
| for lack of | in addition to | on behalf of | in case of | in comparison with |
| in connection with | in contrast to/with | in consequence of | in danger of | in defiance of |
| in excess of | in line with | in place of | in point of | in return for |
| in search of | in spite of | in terms of | in view of | on account of |
| on top of | with/without regard to | with respect to | without prejudice to | with/without reference to |

Harry achieved his aim **by force of** sheer determination.

**In consequence of** the shipwreck many families were in mourning.

**In point of** composition, her letter does not seem defective.

**In defiance of** the order to finish the work, Joe went away leaving half of it undone.

**In terms of** sentence structure, legal sentences are, almost without exception, complex.

It must be understood that this concession is made **without prejudice to** any future decisions of the committee.

If he thought a thing was right, he should do it **without regard to** consequence.

③ Four-word Prepositions

**A Table of Four-word Prepositions**

| at the expense of | at the mercy of | at the rate of | for the benefit of | for the purpose of |
|---|---|---|---|---|
| for the sake of | in the care of | in the event of | in the interest(s) of | in the pay of |
| in the teeth of | in the wake of | in the way of | in the process of | on/at the brink of |
| on the eve of | on the ground(s) of | on the part of | on the point of | on the strength of |
| on the watch for | on the part of | on the point of | on the strength of | on the watch for |
| on the verge of | to the exclusion of | under the guise of | with an eye to | with the exception of |

The boy was left **in the care of** his uncle.

**In the event of** an accident, the police must be called at once.

The ship could scarcely hold her course **in the teeth of** the wind.

He declined the invitation **on the ground(s) of** a previous engagement.

Incompetence **on the part of** a judge cannot but lead to miscarriage of justice.

In the hall he found Roberts **on the point of** departure.

Such irresponsible conduct can only work **to the prejudice of** our cause.

**With the exception of** David Coleman all in the room were smoking.

## 13.2 Collocation of Prepositions

### 1) Prepositions after Adjectives

Adjectives can collocate with prepositions to form adjective phrases.

① Some adjectives can only be followed by specific prepositions.

**Task 4**

Fill in the following blanks with proper prepositions.

(1) Don't be afraid _____ difficulties.

(2) He was absent _____ the meeting.

(3) I am not accustomed _____ the cold.

(4) Jack was blind _____ his own fault.

(5) He is intent _____ winning.

(6) Joe was very disappointed _____ not finding her at home.

**A Table of Adjectives Followed by Specific Prepositions**

| be anxious about | be ashamed of | be aware of |
| be busy with | be capable of | be characteristic of |
| be conscious of | be content with | be crazy about |
| be famous for | be dependent on | be fatal to |
| be fit for | be fond of | be equal to |
| be full of | be keen on | be loyal to |
| be nervous about | be ready for | be short of |
| be rich in | be worthy of | be popular with |
| be subject to | be suitable for | be valid for |
| be wary of | be obedient to | be peculiar to |

## 13. Prepositions

② There are adjectives that can be followed by different prepositions without change in meaning.

Amenda was **angry with** John.

Amenda was **angry at** John's remark.

You're **safe from** danger now.

You're **safe in** accepting the offer.

He is always considerate **of/to/towards/about** others.

③ Some adjectives can collocate with different prepositions to express different meanings.

He is **good at** computer games.

That medicine is **good for** headache.

He is **guilty of** murder.

I felt **guilty about** leaving without saying goodbye.

Rose is **alive to** the feeling of shame.

The cat is **alive with** lice.

### 2) Prepositions after Verbs

① Some verbs can only be followed by specific prepositions to form verbal phrases (verb + preposition).

**Task 5**

Fill in the following blanks with proper prepositions.

(1) I shall prevail _____ him to make the attempt.

(2) You can appeal _____ a higher court and apply for a fresh trial.

(3) We concentrated _____ doing one job at a time.

(4) He fell _____ the habit of not attending to other people's advice.

### A Table of Verbs Followed by Specific Prepositions

| abide by | accord with | adhere to |
| --- | --- | --- |
| answer for | benefit from | bet on |
| brag of | browse through | cater for |
| cling to | chase after | coincide with |
| comment on | comply with | confess to |
| contribute to | conform to | cope with |
| crave for | dispose of | gossip about |

| elaborate on | flirt with | grab at |
|---|---|---|
| intervene in | indulge in | lag behind |
| lament for | dwell on | meditate on |
| mingle with | originate from | plunge into |
| prey on | ponder over | preside over |
| probe into | resort to | emigrate to |
| lust for | recoil from | restrain from |
| consent to | deviate from | |

② Some verbs can be followed by objects and specific prepositions (verb + object + preposition).

**Task 6**  Fill in the following blanks with proper prepositions.
(1) They excluded him _____ the club.
(2) They took me _____ their confidence.
(3) Bad weather robs a holiday _____ half its pleasure.
(4) He released her _____ her promise.

**A Table of Verbs Followed by Objects and Specific Prepositions**

| accuse ... of | banish ... from | blame ... for |
|---|---|---|
| charge ... with | coax ... into | compare ... with |
| convict ... of | cure ... of | confer ... on |
| deprive ... of | devote ... of | eliminate ... from |
| entitle ... to | excuse ... for | exempt ... from |
| impose ... on | inform ... of | insert ... into |
| mistake ... for | multiply ... by | name ... after |
| prevent ... from | regard ... as | relieve ... of |
| rob ... of | warn ... of | substitute ... for |

③ Some verbs can be followed by adverbial particles and specific prepositions (verb + adverb particle + preposition).

**Task 7**

Fill in the following blanks with proper prepositions.

(1) Mr. Smith is looked up _____ by all his students.

(2) The family came up _____ fresh problems.

(3) She got off _____ him soon after she began to work at the institution.

(4) We shouldn't put the shortage down _____ bad planning.

**A Table of Verbs Followed by Adverb Particles and Specific Prepositions**

| break away from | catch up with | come up to |
| --- | --- | --- |
| do away with | face up to | get down to |
| get on with | keep away from | look back upon |
| look forward to | make up for | |

④ Some verbs can be followed by objects, adverbial particles and specific prepositions (verb + object + adverb particle + preposition).

**Task 8**

Fill in the following blanks with proper prepositions.

(1) You shouldn't take your resentment out _____ me.

(2) Flowers can bring a dull room back _____ life.

**4) Collocations of Verbs with Nouns**

① Prepositions after Nouns

There are nouns that are usually followed by certain prepositions.

**Task 9**

Fill in the following blanks with proper prepositions.

(1) His application _____ the post is being carefully considered.

(2) Have you any faith _____ herb medicine?

(3) There seems to be a solution _____ this problem.

(4) Is there any need _____ all this hurry.

### A Table of Nouns Followed by Certain Prepositions

| absence form | agreement with | attitude towards |
|---|---|---|
| bearing on | belief in | candidate for |
| comment on | credit to | competition with |
| concern about | conformity to | heir to |
| demand for | delight in | devotion to |
| outlook on | disgrace to | exception to |
| equivalent of | indifference to | guess at |
| incentive to | insight into | key to |
| liking for | objection to | prejudice against |
| qualification for | operation on | prelude to |
| protest against | prospect of | remedy for |
| symptom of | triumph over | relief from |
| passion for | reference to | regret for |

② Prepositions Preceding Nouns

There are also nouns that are usually preceded by certain prepositions.

**Task 10** Fill in the following blanks with proper prepositions.

(1) A young man should be _____ his guard against bad company.

(2) We did it _____ your request.

(3) _____ all probability, the mail will arrive tomorrow.

(4) _____ my surprise, he passed the entrance of our institute.

### A Table of Preposition Preceding Nouns

| at hand | at intervals | at length |
|---|---|---|
| at liberty at present | beyond recognition | in progress |
| in return | in season | in haste |
| in person | for sale | as a rule |
| as a result | at all costs | at any rate |
| on the spot | from the beginning | in the end |
| on the contrary | on the whole | to some extent |
| in a word | under the weather | |

## 13.3 Roles of Prepositional Phrases in Sentences

A prepositional phrase can perform the following syntactic functions: adverbials, attributes, subject/object complements. Sometimes they can be used as subjects/objects.

### 1) Prepositional Phrases as Adverbials

He left *on a cold winter morning*.
I arrived at the concert hall *in good time*.
He has been here *since Monday*.
We have friends *all over the world*.

### 2) Prepositional Phrases as Attributes

The boy *at the back of the classroom* is Peter's younger brother.
She seems to know the solution *to the problem*.
Here is a cheque *for $30*.
They lived in a flat *above the shop*.

### 3) Prepositional Phrases as Subject/Object Complements

The museum is just *across the street*.
It is not *within my power*.
He found everything *in good order*.
A cold kept him *in bed* for three days.

### 4) Prepositional Phrases as Subjects/Objects

*Between 11 and midnight* suits me.
*After Saturday* would be a good time to go away for a few days.
He came out *from behind the door*.
*Over the fence* is out.
They were mostly elected *from among the workers*.

### 5) Prepositional Phrases as Parenthesis

*In my opinion*, you'd better go with us.
*Of course* I will help you.

**Task 11**  Identify the syntactic functions the prepositional phrases perform in the following sentences.

(1) Bake it for two hours.
(2) At first he opposed the marriage, but in the end he gave his concert.
(3) They flew from Paris to Rome.
(4) The house opposite ours was burnt down last week.
(5) The man next to Bill was talking to him.
(6) Good advice is beyond price.
(7) He was always on the move.
(8) The fort was under attack.
(9) He was called as David.
(10) We found her in better spirits that evening.
(11) He thought it beneath him to do such a thing.
(12) From London to New York is a long distance.
(13) From freezing to boiling is 180 degrees on the fahrenheit scale.
(14) He walked out from among the crowd.

## 13.4　Transformation between Prepositional Phrases and Subordinate Clauses

Prepositional phrases, which are chiefly used as adverbials in clauses and as modifiers in noun phrases, have transformational relations with some subordinate clauses and perform the same syntactic functions.

### 1) Prepositional Phrase vs That-Clause

In some contexts, a prepositional phrase can be transformed into a corresponding that-clause.

I'm sure *of his honesty*.
= I'm sure *that he is honest*.
She lamented *for the lost opportunity*.
= She lamented *that she had lost the opportunity*.

## 2) Prepositional Phrase vs Adverbial Clause

Sometimes, a prepositional phrase is interchangeable with an adverbial clause.

We come back **because of the rain**.
= We came back **because it rained**.
**But for** music, life would be dull.
= **Were it not for music**, life would be dull.

## 3) When a Prepositional Phrase Is Used as Post-modifier in a Noun Phrase, It Can Sometimes Be Turned into a Relative Clause

Most of the products **on display** are new ones.
= Most of the products **which are displayed** are new ones.
The person **in charge** should bear greater responsibility.
= The person **who was in charge** should bear greater responsibility.

# EXERCISES

### I. Fill in each blank with a proper preposition.

1. The Chinese tradition of the new year is different _____ the American one.
2. Many cultures believe that anything _____ the shape of a ring is good luck.
3. His latest two novels have many things _____ common.
4. He gave great importance _____ what his father said.
5. To show their support _____ the player they love, the fans are all dressed in the same sport clothes with the number "7" on them.
6. He is quick _____ seizing the rebound, but his shooting is poor.
7. People use more than words when they communicate _____ each other.
8. It was so black you could not see a hand _____ front of your face.
9. Coaches like those players who have a very positive attitude _____ the sport they are in.
10. For over a century every small boy dreamed _____ becoming a pilot.

### II. Multiple choice.

1. His ill-health may well be _____ malnutrition.
   A. due to        B. next to        C. thanks to        D. up
2. _____ the many delays, we shall get to our destination in time.
   A. In the way of              B. In case of
   C. In spite of                D. In the event of

3. I wish I could do something _____ the kindness I have received from you.

   A. in terms of  B. in return for

   C. in the way of  D. in search of

4. Expenditure is twenty pounds _____ income.

   A. in point of  B. in the pay of

   C. in the wake of  D. in excess of

5. _____ rigorous training, the football team has secured promotion.

   A. But for  B. As for  C. Thanks to  D. Save for

6. The ship was sunk by a collision; but _____ diving apparatus the cargo was retrieved.

   A. for the sake of  B. by way of

   C. by reason of  D. by means of

7. I consulted the lawyer _____ my claim.

   A. in view of  B. with reference to

   C. with a view to  D. with an eye to

8. Yesterday John went to see a house _____ buying it.

   A. with a view to  B. with respect to

   C. with regard to  D. in process of

9. The work is not very profitable _____ cash, but he is getting valuable experience from it.

   A. in view of  B. in terms of

   C. with a view to  D. for the sake of

10. The children were left _____ an aunt.

    A. in the event of  B. in the pay of

    C. in the wake of  D. in the care of

III. Decide which one of the four choices given is most suitable to complete the sentence.

1. Is the city noted _____ (in, about, on, for) its champagne?
2. Jock was completely devoid _____ (of, at, in, to) humour.
3. His attitude was destructive _____ (in, towards, about, to) achievement.
4. The bed was alive _____ (in, with, at, on) bugs.
5. Mary is still inseparable _____ (to, with, about, from) her mother.
6. The tides vary _____ (at, on, with, to) the moon.
7. She admitted him _____ (into, to, in, at) her plans.
8. The word derives _____ (at, in, from, on) Latin.

9. Harry swore _____ (at, in, by, on) the Bible he was telling the truth.

10. Everyone blames you _____ (on, for, in, against) a certain mistake.

**IV. Fill in each blank with a proper preposition.**

1. I'll find some one to fill in _____ you.

2. Not many criminals get away _____ their crimes.

3. Robert worked hard so that he could get ahead _____ the others.

4. The great leaders of the world have always stood up _____ their principles.

5. If you want to be trusted, you should never go back _____ your word.

6. There is some confusion _____ whether the word can be left out.

7. By midnight the effect _____ the drops will have worn out.

8. A key _____ the back door is always kept on a high ledge above the door.

9. There's a limit _____ every man's patience.

10. The Hawkinses bought a horse _____ $15.000.

**V. Fill in each blank with a proper preposition.**

Rewrite each of the following sentences using a prepositional phrase introduced by the word(s) given.

1. Many of the war prisoners died on the march either because they were starving or because they had been severely wounded. (from)

2. I assure you that I am willing to stand down. (of)

3. I think the chief let us go simply because he sympathized with us in our plight. (out of)

4. There are criminals who will commit murder only because they want money. (for)

5. She was obliged to wear thick, high boots, as she was afraid of poisonous snakes. (for fear of)

6. If it had not been for Wallis, we would have lost the match. (but for)

7. The proposal that we should take better care of child health was rejected. (concerning)

8. Since this news was received, everybody has been happy. (since)

9. He worked so well that he astonished every one of us. (to)

10. Every precaution was taken that the plan might not fail. (against)

# Part Four

## Grammar and Text

# 14. Inversion

## Aims of the Unit

> In this unit we will discuss some general matters about inversion. We are going to discuss seven questions in particular:
> - What is inversion?
> - Which parts of the sentence can be inverted?
> - What is the main function of inversion?
> - What are the two types of inversion?
> - What do questions and inversion have in common?
> - When do we use inversion in a sentence with negative adverbials?
> - When do we use inversion in conditionals?

In the English language, there are inversions that are part of its grammar structure and are quite common in their use. For instance, inversion always occurs in interrogative statements where verbs or auxiliaries are placed before their subjects. Similarly, inversion happens in typical exclamatory sentences where verbs and subjects are inverted, such as the following examples:

*Where in the world **were you**!*

*Boy, **is syntax** easy!*

**Task 1**

Discuss: What do these sentences have in common?
(1) Not only is he difficult to understand, but he is also funny.
(2) Never have I understood less about women.
(3) Scarcely have they been on time.

## 14.1 Definition of Inversion

By inversion, we mean the reversal or rearrangement of the normal order of words and phrases in a sentence by placing a prepositional phrase or other expressions at the beginning of the sentence followed by an inverted word order.

There are two types of inversion. One is subject-verb inversion, where the subject and the main verb switch positions and the word order becomes "verb + subject".

*On the top of the hill* ***stood an old oak tree***.
*Across the table* ***sat a group of three noisy boys***.
*Here* ***lies the greatest pleasure of greenhouse gardening***.

From the above examples, we can see that subject-verb inversion normally occurs after (mainly place) adverbial in initial position. The subject must be realized as a noun phrase, and should generally be longer than the verb. It is sometimes possible to insert existential *there*. For example,

*In a hole in the ground* ***there lived a rabbit***.

The other is subject-auxiliary inversion, where the subject occurs in postponed position while some other **dependent of the verb** is preposed. A considerable range of elements may invert with the subject in this way. In the great majority of cases the **preposed element** is usually a complement of the verb "be". When the subject and the auxiliary switch positions and the word order becomes "auxiliary + subject (+ verb)". Look at the following examples:

*Hardly* ***had I*** *arrived home when my phone rang.*
*When* ***does the bus*** *leave?*
*You're hungry,* ***aren't you****?*

> **Task 2**
>
> Discuss: Do you think that differences in word order mean differences in meaning? Please paraphrase the following sentences.
> (1) Once he did not offer to help.
> (2) Not once did he offer to help.
> (3) Very rarely is an effort made to develop character in depth.
> (4) Very rarely an effort is made to develop character in depth.

*dependent of the verb*
动词从属成分
*preposed element*
前置成分

## 14.2 Grammatical Inversion

Based on the motivation of inversion, a distinction can be made between **grammatical inversion** and **rhetorical inversion**. Grammatical inversion refers to a change of word order which is usually not optional but required by certain grammatical rules. In other words, grammatical inversion occurs for the sake of grammaticality of the sentence.

Grammatical inversion is mostly used in questions, and questions in English are usually characterized by inversion of the subject and the first verb in the verb phrase. Specifically, the verb "be", or an auxiliary verb, or a modal verb, should be placed in front of the subject. We can move an auxiliary verb or linking verb to the front of the clause, e.g.

>  **Is everybody** *watching*?
>  **Is English** *spoken all over the world*?
>  **Have the windows** *been cleaned*?
>  **Is this** *the last example*?
>  **Are we** *finished yet*?

Grammatical inversion can also be realized by moving a modal verb to the front of the clause, for instance:

>  **Would she** *have been listening*?
>  **Will the work** *be finished soon*?
>  **Might they** *have been invited to the party*?

The present simple and the past simple have no auxiliary verb. We make questions by adding the auxiliary *do/does* for the present simple or *did* for the past simple, e.g.

>  **Does he** *live here*?
>  **Did everybody** *laugh*?
>  **Do you** *enjoy reading these lists*?

In **reporting clauses** after a direct speech, grammatical inversion can be used and it is optional, e.g.

>  "*You'll never even get near Greece in this,*" **said Mary**.
>  "*I think it's time to go,*" **said Susan**.

---

grammatical inversion
语法倒装
rhetorical inversion
修辞倒装
reporting clauses
引出直接引语或间接引语的分句;转述分句

"*It's time for you, but not for me,*" **replied Gary**.

"*Maybe we should collect our thoughts for a moment,*" **commented Lany**.

When the subject in the reporting clause is a common noun, either grammatical inversion or a normal order can be used. But if the subject in the reporting clause is a pronoun, the normal order is maintained, e. g.

"*And what about all the rubbish, then?*" **asked the woman**.

"*And what about all the rubbish, then?*" **the woman asked**.

"*Will she be back?*" **I asked**.

Grammatical inversion can be used after *so*, *neither*, *nor*, etc. when the clauses introduced by them indicate agreement or disagreement, e. g.

*He's a real perfectionist which can be a pain for some people. But I happen to like that. And* **so do millions of fans and critics around the world**.

*But I don't have any use for it in my daily life, and* **neither do most of the people I know**.

*(The gate makes a lot of noise when we open it.)* **So does the back door**, *where we all go in and out*.

## ◆ 14.3   Rhetorical Inversion

Rhetorical inversion, or stylistic inversion, a rhetorically motivated change of word order, is aimed for the discourse to achieve some certain rhetorical effects. Rhetorical inversion is very rarely used in speech, but it is relatively commonly used in formal writing. While the normal word order is also grammatically correct, rhetorical inversion is also widely used, especially in literary works.

Generally, rhetorical inversion begins with a negative and is mostly used to stress the uniqueness of an event or to achieve emphasis, cohesion, or a better balance of a sentence. Rhetorical inversion generally begins with a negative word or phrase, or a negative sentence opener. If a negative adverb or adverbial expression is put at the beginning of a clause for emphasis, an inversion is obligatory and usually "an auxiliary verb + subject" follows, e. g.

***Never have I** seen such a mess*!

***Not only do I** enjoy classical music, but I also have regular music lessons*.

## 14. Inversion

*Not only does God* sow the seed of His word, but He continues to cultivate it.

Note that when there is no purpose for emphasis, if *not only* is followed by *but also* or simply *but*, we need make sure the parts that follow each set of words are formatted the same way, e. g.

*Not only* the mother *but also* the children are sick.

He *not only* swims with ease, *but also* plays amazing music.

Note that the inversion does not always occur right after the negative form, but sometimes takes place in the clause followed by the clause with negative form, e. g.

*Not until* men first charted the stars thousands of years ago, and linked their fates with events in the sky, **did personal birthdays** become important.

= Birthdays did not become important until men first charted the stars thousands of years ago, and linked their fates with events in the sky.

*At no point* in the progression **can we** insert a cut-off and say: this step is too abrupt.

= We cannot insert a cut-off at any point in the progression and say: this step is too abrupt.

Yet **nowhere has there** been a guide to their identification.

Time expressions such as *never, rarely, seldom*, etc. are usually followed by "auxiliary verbs *have, has* or *had* + subject + past participle" and often include comparatives, e. g.

*Seldom have I* seen anything more remarkable.

*Never have I* seen such a vast crowd.

*Seldom has he* seen anything stranger.

*Never have I* been more insulted!

Time expressions such as *hardly, barely, no sooner, scarcely*, etc. are used to talk about a succession of events in the past that happen one after another.

*Hardly had she* arrived when problems started.

*Scarcely had I* sat down when the doorbell rang.

*No sooner had he* finished dinner than he started feeling ill.

Rhetorical inversion can occur after an adverbial particle in initial position to create a vivid image of an action or a scenario, e. g.

*The door opened, and **in marched the minister** himself.*

Sometimes, inversion occurs with be-verbs, linking verbs and verbs that show direction or movement, like *come, go, run*, etc. This type of inversion is optional. Note that sometimes we have an adverb, like *first* and *down*, and sometimes we have an adverb phrase, like *into the room*. These adverbs and adverb phrases usually show location or direction, e. g.

*Into the room ran the lady*.

*First comes love, then comes marriage*.

*Down came the rain* and *washed the spider out*.

Sentences beginning with *only* or *little* as a **restrictive sentence opener** also follow an inverted word order. In this case, the use of rhetorical inversion is obligatory. For instance, e. g.

> restrictive sentence opener
> 限制性句首词

*Only rarely were women* doing similar work to men.

*Only then did I* understand what I had done.

*Only after her death was I* able to love her.

*Little did she* understand what she was doing.

*Little did I* realize the danger I faced.

*Little did I* dream that I would be awarded this generous scholarship.

We can see that rhetorical inversion should be used when *only* is used with a time expression, such as *only after*, *only when*, *only then*, etc.

Note that no inversion occurs after "negative" sentence openers which do not affect the verb, e. g.

*Little wonder* he looked so nervous.

*Not long after that*, I knew I must go to China.

*No doubt* the man on the stairs is her husband.

*No matter* when and how the invaders come, they would be wiped out clean.

*No other city* has this particular smell.

In conditional clauses, an auxiliary verb can be put before the subject instead of using *if*. In this case, the conditional *if* is dropped and the inverted form takes the place of the if-clause. In other words, *if* is omitted: even though the word *if* does not appear in the clause, we still have the meaning of an if-clause. The conditional forms are inverted as a means of sounding more formal. For instance, e. g.

*Were I you*, I wouldn't do it.

= If I were you, I wouldn't do it.

*Had I* understood the problem, I wouldn't have made those mistakes.

= If I had understood the problem, I wouldn't have made those mistakes.

*Had he* understood the problem, he wouldn't have committed those mistakes.

*Should he* decide to come, please telephone.

## 14. Inversion

Rhetorical inversion also occurs after the fronted -ing or -ed clause which denotes existence or appearance. Note that the -ing phrase or -ed phrase is the complement of the verb *be*, e.g.

*Standing looking out at the daylight* **is the dean**.

*Not helping the situation* **was little Susie**, *who was throwing newspaper on the spreading fire*.

*Attached to the back of the house* **was an enclosed courtyard**.

*Found in San Francisco* **is Lombard Street**, *the so-called crookedest street in the world*.

*Lost among the old tables and chairs* **was the priceless Victorian desk**.

In **subject-dependent inversion** the subject occurs in postponed position while some other dependent of the verb is preposed. A considerable range of elements may invert with the subject in this way. In the great majority of cases the preposed element is a complement, usually of the verb *be*. For example:

*Slightly harder* than describing what they do is **explaining why they do it**.

In the structure "so + adjective ... that" combining with the verb *be*, rhetorical inversion can be found, e.g.

*So strange* **was the situation** *that I couldn't sleep*.

*So difficult* **is the test** *that students need three months to prepare*.

> subject-dependent inversion
> 主语-动词从属成分倒装

**Task 3**

Discuss: How do you rephrase the following sentences by means of stylistic inversion? They have to be as similar in meaning to the sentences written before as possible. Discuss and decide on the starter of each sentence before rewriting it. For example,

I don't think the children have the faintest idea what we have planned for them.

Starter: Little

→Little do the children know what we have planned for them.

(1) It wasn't until we got home that we found out why the car was making such a strange noise.

(2) In order to get to the solution, we had to start again from the beginning.

(3) Whatever you do, don't try to open up the back of the television.

(4) Such appalling incompetence is virtually unheard of in this company.

(5) This is the first time that so many people have died as a result of a signal failure.

(6) It was the biggest family gathering since Alison's wedding.

(7) The guard dogs refused to leave the kennel before they had been fed.

(8) The day was unbearably hot until the sun went down.

(9) The plane had only just taken off when the engine trouble started.

## EXERCISES

Ⅰ. **Choose the most appropriate answer with inverted word order if necessary.**

1. There _____ that he will agree to your plan.
   A. hope is little   B. is hope little   C. is little hope   D. little hope is

2. The view of the canyon was breathtaking. Never before _____ such beauty.
   A. had seen we   B. had we seen   C. we had seen   D. we hadn't seen

3. _____. See you tomorrow!
   A. Comes here my bus          B. Here comes my bus
   C. Here my bus comes          D. My bus comes here

4. —We will probably go shopping in the afternoon.
   —_____. Why don't we go shopping together?
   A. I will so   B. So I will   C. So will I   D. Will so I

5. _____ the truth, he wouldn't have invited them.
   A. Had known he   B. Had he known   C. He had known   D. Known he had

6. —She should have helped them. She wasn't busy at that time.
   —_____. Why didn't you help them?
   A. Neither were you          B. Neither you were
   C. Were you neither          D. You were neither

7. No sooner _____ the receiver than the telephone began to ring again.
   A. down had I put   B. down had put I   C. had I put down   D. I had put down

8. —Can you give me a pen, please? —Sure. _____.
   A. Here is it   B. Here it is   C. Is it here   D. It is here

9. _____ so busy, we would go there with you.
   A. Were we not   B. Weren't we   C. We were not   D. We weren't

10. Not only _____ my car poorly, but they also overcharged me.
    A. did they repair           B. repair they did
    C. they did repair           D. they didn't repair

## 14. Inversion

**II. Change the sentences so that they use inversion. For example.**

We had hardly arrived when Julie burst into the house.

→ Hardly had we arrived when Julie burst into the house.

1. John had never been to such a fantastic restaurant.

2. I in no way want to be associated with this project.

3. They had no sooner eaten dinner than the ceiling crashed onto the dining table.

4. I had scarcely finished writing my essay when the examiner announced the end of the exam.

5. I seldom leave my house so early.

6. People rarely appreciate this musician's talent.

7. We would understand what had happened that night only later.

8. They had met such rude people nowhere before.

9. He understood little about the situation.

10. The children should on no account go on their own.

11. My happiness was such that I arranged a big party.

12. I waited for you to come back many a time.

13. We little realised the dangers that were awaiting us.

14. If you should need a good make-up remover, please let me know.

15. The beautiful scenery I had been told about lay below me.

16. My brother went off without saying a word.
    _____

17. You will never again have such an opportunity.
    _____

18. Immediately he learnt about his mother's incurable disease, he cried his eyes out.
    _____

19. My humiliation was such that I did not know what to do.
    _____

20. I well remember when I saw her for the first time.
    _____

**III. Apart from common inversions, some unusual inversions are employed in literature by writers in order to achieve some special artistic effects. Read carefully the following excerpts and think about why the authors wanted to use inversion and what the main function of inversion in prose or poetry is.**

1. Shelly describes his favorite literary and political personality Milton in the following lines:

   "Blind, old, and lonely, when his country's pride,
   The priest, the slave, and the liberticide,
   Trampled and mocked with many a loathed rite … "

2. Similarly in the poem "Love in Jeopardy" by Humbert Wolfe, there is an inversion of an unusual kind. He wrote:

   "Here by the rose-tree
   they planted once
   of Love in Jeopardy
   an Italian bronze."

# 15. Ellipsis and Substitution

## Aims of the Unit

> In this unit we will discuss some general matters about ellipsis and substitution. We are going to discuss seven questions in particular:
> - What is ellipsis?
> - What is substitution?
> - What is the relationship between ellipsis and substitution?
> - What are the three levels on which grammatical ellipsis occurs?
> - How many types can ellipsis be divided into according to how we can recover the full structure? What are they?
> - What functions can rhetorical ellipsis usually perform?
> - What are the three levels on which substitution occurs?

Sometimes when people fail to understand something they read or hear not because they don't understand the words being used, but because of the words that aren't being used.

When speaking or writing, it is common to avoid repeating things and to ensure the flow of the text. There are two methods to do that: **Ellipsis** and **Substitution**, which are economical ways of language use, enabling us to avoid the unnecessary repetition of words. For instance,

(1) I was to take the east path and Jack was to take the west path.

(2) I was to take the east path and Jack, the west.

In both speaking and writing, this tendency either to leave out words that we think are unnecessary or to use another single word or a short phrase in place of a longer phrase, however, can cause considerable confusion for learners, especially when listening, as there is no chance to go back and try to work out the meaning.

ellipsis 省略
substitution 替代

> **Task 1**  Discuss: In the following dialogue, B1 and B2 are two possible answers to A's questions. What do these answers have in common? How are they different from each other?
>
> A: —Is anyone here an Economics major?
> B1: —I am.
> B2: —I am one.

## 15.1  Definition of Ellipsis and Substitution

In grammar, **ellipsis** refers to the linguistically appropriate omission of parts of a sentence, i.e. a word or series of words, which are mutually understood in the context and thus unnecessary, and the omitted word or words can usually be presumed from what has already taken place in the text. Ellipsis is usually used where the words omitted would be redundant. For example,

*I went to the mall on Monday, and she on Sunday.*

*I went to the mall on Monday, and she went to the mall on Sunday.*

In the first example, the words *to the mall* are omitted because they are understood from the context what the speaker is referring to. The second example is a contextually identical sentence.

The omission of an element of language occurs for reasons associated with grammar and rhetoric. Based on the motivation of ellipsis, a distinction can be made between **grammatical ellipsis** and **rhetorical ellipsis**.

**Substitution** means the replacement of a part of a sentence with a substitute word or phrase in the same grammatical position. So a speaker or writer can choose to replace one item with another or entirely omit that item if he wishes to avoid repeating a word, phrase or clause. In elliptical sentences, an item is replaced by nothing.

> grammatical ellipsis
> 语法省略
> rhetorical ellipsis
> 修辞省略

## 15.2  Grammatical Ellipsis

Ellipses are common to both formal and informal English, but there is an important difference. From the above two examples, we can see that in formal

## 15. Ellipsis and Substitution

English, the omitted words in the elliptical sentence must be ones that would appear twice in the full sentence. In formal English, therefore, we are allowed to omit only what would otherwise be duplicated. There is no such requirement with informal English, however. For example,

A. *Seems like a good idea.*

B. *It seems like a good idea to me.*

Sentence A is an elliptical sentence where the word *it* is simply left out. Sentence B is a full sentence with no duplication of the omitted word.

Elliptical phenomena seem to be able to shed light on basic questions of form-meaning correspondence: in particular, the usual mechanisms of grasping a meaning from a form seem to be bypassed in the interpretation of elliptical structures, ones in which there is meaning without form. In **generative linguistics**, the term "ellipsis" has been applied to a range of phenomena in which a perceived interpretation is fuller than that which would be expected based solely on the presence of linguistic forms.

Ellipsis is a common syntactic device in everyday language. It depends on the words that precede it, e.g.

*Take another piece if you want to (**take another piece**).*

Here, the elliptical sentence is normal and functions as well as the full structure but sounds more economical of words and concise. The omitted element can usually be recovered by considering the context of what has been said or written. In speech and writing, sounds and letters are often left out of words, e.g.

*She said **he'd** come.*

Such contractions as *he'd* are informal and usually arise from speed of delivery, economy of effort, and the rhythm of the language. After *and*, *but*, and *or* we often leave out a repeated subject or a repeated subject and auxiliary verb, especially when the clauses are not long, e.g.

*He got up and (**he**) had breakfast.*

*She was late for the class but (**she**) didn't give an explanation.*

*We should call her or (**we should**) send her an email.*

The subject pronoun cannot be left out after *after*, *before*, *because*, *when*, and *while*. For example,

*We'll watch the video **after we** finish lunch.*

*They turned off the lights **before they** left.*

---

generative linguistics
生成语言学,也称转换生成语法,20 世纪 50 年代兴起的一种语言学说。创建人是 N. 乔姆斯基。1957 年他的第一部专著《句结构》出版,标志着这种学说的诞生。目前该学派有东北语言学会与欧亚语言学会两个国际性组织,出版《语言学探索》等国际性学术刊物。

He is under great stress **because he** has too much work.

She was horrified **when she** saw the whole mess they had left.

Note that elliptical speech or writing is so concise that sometimes listeners and readers must supply missing elements through guesswork or special knowledge, and if they cannot, they fail to understand. In the above example, *he'd* is elliptical for either *he had* or *he would*. Information can be left out or hinted at for reasons of style or discretion. In such areas as politics, diplomacy, negotiation, remarks are often elliptical in nature and intent.

**1) Grammatical Ellipsis: the Nominal Group, the Verbal Group, and the Clause**

① Nominal Ellipsis

In **nominal ellipsis**, a noun or noun phrase can be omitted when it is repeated mechanically otherwise.

I'll ask my mom about the pencils and whether she has any (**pencils**).

Note that in similar situations, **substitution** words such as *one* or *ones* can be used. For example,

—Who has a pencil?

—I have **one**.

② Verbal Ellipsis

Of the various ellipsis mechanisms, **verbal ellipsis**, a particularly frequent form of ellipsis, has probably been studied the most and it is therefore relatively well understood. In verbal ellipsis, a verb or verb phrase can be omitted when it is repeated mechanically otherwise. The ellipsis must be introduced by an auxiliary verb or by the particle *to*. For example,

—Have you read much?

—I am trying to (**read much**).

He will help, and she will (**help**), too.

Steve has never been to Mexico, but his brother has (**been to Mexico**).

They said I would love the movie, but I don't think I would (**love the movie**).

Note that we can use a different auxiliary or modal verb from that used in the first part of the sentence, e.g.

I know you have never learned to drive, but I really think you **should have**.

I thought I would be able to come tomorrow, but in fact I **can't**.

Verbal ellipsis can occur both forwards and backwards. That is, the ellipsis can both precede and follow its antecedent, e.g.

---

nominal ellipsis
名词性省略
verbal ellipsis
动词性省略
clausal ellipsis
分句性省略

*The man who wanted to order the salmon **did**.*

*The man who wanted to **did** order the salmon.*

If the verb is in its simple tense, we use a proper form of the **substitution** verb *do*, e. g.

—*Who ran to school?*

—*I **did**. ( did = ran to school )*

③ Clausal Ellipsis

In **clausal ellipsis**, the entire clause or a large part of it can be omitted when it is repeated mechanically otherwise. Clausal ellipsis is typically done with *yes/no* responses (as well as *if so* and *if not*) or wh-question words, e. g.

—*Are you all right?*

—*Yes (, **I am all right**).*

—*I need them.*

—*What ( is it that **you need** ) ?*

In speech or writing, words may be omitted because they relate to what someone has just said or what has just been written.

—*When can I see you?*

—*( **You can see me** ) Tomorrow.*

Reduced relative clauses and reduced adverbial clauses are also often considered to be examples of ellipsis. With these, the missing words haven't necessarily been mentioned, but they are clearly recoverable, e. g.

*The dark-haired girl ( **who is** ) standing over there just smiled at you.*

*When ( **you are** ) teaching grammar, you need to find good examples.*

One trait that many types and instances of ellipsis have in common is that the appearance of ellipsis is optional. Whether or not ellipsis is used is up to the speaker and to the communicative aspects of the situational context in which the sentence is uttered. This optionality is a clear indication of ellipsis.

## 2) Textual Ellipsis, Situational Ellipsis, Structural Ellipsis and Telegraphic Ellipsis

According to how we can recover the full structure, ellipsis can be divided into four types.

① Textual Ellipsis

Textual ellipsis could be defined as when we omit something that has already been mentioned (so doesn't need to be repeated), or when what is

textual ellipsis
语篇省略
situational ellipsis
情景省略
structural ellipsis
结构省略
telegraphic ellipsis
电信省略

missing is clearly recoverable from the text. It is a type where the recoverability of the full structure depends on what occurs before or after. Textual ellipsis has more grammatical rules, and can be found in both speech and writing, e. g.

*Those who can (**pay**) should pay.*

Here, the elliptical *Those who can* depends on what follows for the interpretation of *Those who can pay*. Textual ellipsis is probably most commonly found in the second clause after the coordinating conjunctions *and*, *or* or *but*. For instance,

*I went to the bakers to get some wholemeal rolls and (**I went**) to the butchers for lamb chops.*

② Situational Ellipsis

In contrast with textual ellipsis in situational ellipsis, recoverability depends on knowledge of the situational context. Situational ellipsis is, unsurprisingly, where the situation or context makes the missing element clear. It's informal and mostly used in conversation, e. g.

(**Have you/they**) *Got any money?*

(**Would you like a cup of**) *Tea?*

③ Structural Ellipsis

In structural ellipsis recoverability depends on syntax. For example,

*Poll shows (**that the**) Labour (**Party is**) 10 points ahead.*

The above example is a headline of a news report, whose full structure can be recovered with the help of our knowledge of syntax.

④ Telegraphic Ellipsis

Telegraphic ellipsis is often used in making notes or writing a diary. For example:

*Went out. Had a meal. Came home and watched TV. Then bed.*

Grammatical ellipsis is a device for achieving economy by avoiding repetition. It contributes to clarity and emphasis, enabling attention to be focused on important information. It shares these characteristics with pronouns and other forms of substitution such as the auxiliary verb *do* in the following example:

*Mary liked the musical as much as I **did**.*

**Task 2**

Discuss and decide whether the following sentences have ellipsis. If yes, please tell whether the ellipsis is nominal, verbal or clausal.

(1) Fred can play the guitar; Mary can play the guitar, too.

(2) Lucy did three tasks while Susan had done two.

(3) He has done it before, which means he will again.

(4) Gorge has attempted Problem 1 twice, and Problem 2 also.

(5) They have been eating the pears more than they have the apples.

## ❖ 15.3 Rhetorical Ellipsis

Elliptical sentences are actually incomplete in structure but complete in meaning. Ellipsis can be an artful and arresting means of securing economy of expression. When well used, ellipsis can create a bond of sorts between the writer and the reader. The writer is saying, in effect, that he needn't spell everything out for the reader; he knows the reader will understand. Rhetorically, omitting a word or phrase that is easily inferred from the context can perform several functions.

### 1) Helping to Achieve Brevity and Conciseness

By omitting the unnecessary elements of a sentence or of those that have already occurred in the context, the speaker/writer can effectively avoid **redundancy, give prominence to** the more important information, and shorten the intervals of communication. Ellipsis is highly effective in saving space as in public signs, labels, instructions, newspaper headlines and so on, and takes less time for readers to finish reading, e.g.

*No smoking!*
*Stop!*
*Road closed.*
*Handle with care.*
*Man in Belgium charged for Paris attacks.*

### 2) Building Up Tension and Expressing Quick Thoughts

It seems as though a character or the narrator is leaving something

---
redundancy
冗长
give prominence
突出

unfinished, unsaid, or un-started. The following example is an excerpt from *To the Lighthouse* by Virginia Woolf:

"*The vast flapping sheet flattened itself out, and each shove of the brush revealed fresh legs, hoops, horses, glistening reds and blues, beautifully smooth, until half the wall was covered with the advertisement of a circus; a hundred horsemen, twenty performing seals, lions, tigers ... Craning forwards, for she was short-sighted, she read it out ... 'will visit this town,' she read.*"

In this instance, the characters Mrs. Ramsay and Charles Tansley walk through town and notice details about what they see all around them. Ramsay has seen a poster for a traveling circus, and Charles Tansley feels slighted that she is more interested in this than in him. Woolf's novel uses much stream-of-consciousness, and the ellipses indicate jumps in their consciousness. For example, there is a whole list of animals coming through with the circus, but the ellipsis cuts off the list, indicating that there are more animals but their brains have moved on. The second ellipsis indicates an omission of the first half of Mrs. Ramsay's sentence.

**3) Emphatic and Vivid**

In advertising, for example, a group of sentence fragments may gain special advertising effectiveness. Let us compare the following two advertisements.

A. *Baked. Drenched. Tested to the extreme. A Motorola cellular phone.*

B. *The Motorola cellular phones are baked, drenched, and tested to the extreme.*

Obviously, through use of an elliptical structure, Sentence A is far more brief, eye-catching and forceful than Sentence B. What's more, it conveys attitudes that Sentence B lacks. Sentence A implies a kind of appreciation for the phone, by splitting the sentence into several fragments and rearranging its word order. Therefore skillful arrangement of elliptical sentences may add to certain special effects by giving prominence to the most important information.

## ◈ 15.4  Substitution

Like ellipsis, substitution is another grammatical process to achieve the economy of expression. The easiest way to understand substitution is to consider it as a form of ellipsis. Something is missing, but instead of just leaving it out, we substitute it with another word, usually *so*, *one(s)*, *do(es)*, *did*. Substitution usually works on three levels: the nominal group, the verbal group, and the clause.

### 1) Nominal Substitution

In nominal substitution, *one(s)* and *the same* are taken as the most common substitute items. The meaning or function of *one(s)* is that it carries over the *head*, which is a count noun of a preceding nominal group, and brings with it its own modifying or redefining elements. The following are some examples to illustrate the points made above.

*If you want to buy an electric fan, you may be interested in this* **one** *in the window.* ( *one = electric fan* )

—*I've lost my bike and I can't have an easy trip to work, you know?*

—*Get a new* **one**! ( *one = bike* )

*I've heard many strange stories, but this* **one** *is perhaps the strangest one of all.* ( *one = story* )

The other substitute for nominal groups is *same*. When *same* occurs as a substitute, it presupposes the whole of the preceding nominal group, and is typically accompanied by the definite article. *Same* can be a substitute for a noun phrase, an adjective phrase or a prepositional phrase acting as complement, or a nominal clause, e.g.

*Winter is always damp in Hainan.* **The same** *is often true of Summer.* ( *the same = damp* )

*Yesterday I felt under the weather, and today I feel* **the same**. ( *the same = under the weather* )

*His speech didn't say anything new.* **The same** *applies to most political speeches.* ( *the same = the fact that his speech didn't say anything new* )

### 2) Verbal Substitution

The verbal group, like the nominal group, also consists of head expressing typically all action, event or relation and modifier. With the verbal substitution, the head is *do* ( *does, did, doing, done* ), sometimes *do so*, e.g.

*I speak English much more fluently than I* **did** *five years ago.* ( *did = spoke English* )

*You mustn't put the fruit on the chair. You can* **do** *on the table.* ( *do = put the fruit* )

Note that the substitute *do* can not occur in the sentence with verbs like *seem*, *look*, *appear*, for all these kinds of verbs have the attribute of state but not action.

### 3) Clausal Substitution

In clausal substitution, the substituting part is an entire clause rather than an element within the clause. The substitute items used in these types of substitution are *so* (for positive substitution) and *not* (for negative substitution). In substituting for that-clauses, *so* and *not* substitute for reported speech and reported beliefs or assumption, but the substituted clauses are always declarative ones.

We often use *so* instead of repeating a whole positive clause after such verbs of thinking as *assume*, *believe*, *expect*, *guess*, *hope*, *imagine*, *presume*, *reckon*, *suppose*, *think*, etc., e. g.

—*Will you be working on Saturday?*
—*I suppose **so**, unless we get everything done today.*
*I will have finished the project by the weekend, or at least I hope **so**.*

We also use *so* to substitute a whole positive clause after *be afraid*, *appear*, *seem*, *say*, etc. While with *appear* and *seem* frequently occurring with an initial anticipatory *it*, e. g.

*It appears **so/not**.*

With negative clauses we use positive verb plus *not* with *assume*, *be afraid*, *guess*, *hope*, *presume*, *suspect*, etc. For example,

—*He is not very likely to pass, is he?*
—*No, I am afraid **not**.*
—*Do you think it will rain tomorrow?*
—*I hope **not**.*

Note that we usually use *so* after verbs such as *think* and *say* in the negative clauses. For example,

*I know she liked the book, even though she didn't say **so**.*
*The children may be back in time, but I don't think **so**.*

## 15. Ellipsis and Substitution

**Task 3**

Discuss: What are some important principles of using *one(s)* as a substitute? Can you tell whether the *one* in each of the following sentences is the numeral *one*, the pronoun *one* or the substitute *one*?

(1) Hi, Tonny, do you still have some apples? I only want *one*.

(2) *One* never knows what might happen in future.

(3) Mummy, will you buy me a bike? I want that red *one* in the window.

(4) Ten set out, but only *one* came back.

(5) I'd like a cup of coffee so I pour myself *one*.

## EXERCISES

**I. In the following sentences, underline the words which are usually omitted.**

1. If you need any money, I've got some money.
2. I could have gone to her party, but I didn't want to go to her party.
3. Would you like a candy? I've got a lot of candies.
4. They will come soon but I don't know exactly when they will come.
5. John bought a coat and Lynn bought a hat and gloves.
6. I don't know if Mike has gone, but I think he has gone.
7. He was the greatest footballer ever, and remains the greatest footballer ever.
8. I believe that this party can win the next election and will win the next election.
9. Some of the water which falls as rain flows on the surface as streams. Another part of the water is evaporated. The remainder of the water sinks into the ground and is known as ground water.
10. —How many players were there?
    —There were five players.
11. —What time are you coming?
    —I am coming about nine.
12. He is poor but he is honest.
13. You can have tea or you can have coffee.
14. —Do you want large eggs?
    —No, I will have small eggs.
15. I thought that she would be interested, but she wasn't interested.
16. —I haven't got the letter.
    —I haven't got the letter either.

17. —Are you and David getting married?

 —We hope to get married.

18. Prosperity is a great teacher; adversity is a greater teacher.

19. Some people go to priests; others go to poetry; I go to my friends.

20. Wise men talk because they have something to say; fools talk because they have to say something.

**II. Read the following paragraph and translate it into Chinese. Pay special attention to ellipsis if any.**

I learned this, at least, by my experiment; that if one advances confidently in the direction of his dreams, and endeavors to live the life which he has imagined, he will meet with a success unexpected in common hours. He will put some things behind, will pass an invisible boundary; new, universal, and more liberal laws will begin to establish themselves around and within him; or the old laws be expanded, and interpreted in his favor in a more liberal sense, and he will live with the license of a higher order of beings. In proportion as he simplifies his life, the laws of the universe will appear less complex, and solitude will not be solitude, nor poverty poverty, nor weakness weakness. If you have built castles in the air, your work need not be lost; that is where they should be. Now put the foundations under them.

**III. Rewrite the following sentences, providing whatever is omitted without change of meaning.**

1. My mistake.
2. Anything I can do for you?
3. An hour in the morning is worth two in the evening.
4. He was always the first to come and the last to leave.
5. To some life is pleasure, and to others suffering.
6. He can be happy in hard times as in good tines.
7. If I could see her again!
8. When pure, water is a colourless liquid.
9. Henry looked about as if in search of something.
10. She studies very hard though still rather weak.
11. This conclusion proved correct.
12. When necessary you can help us to do something.
13. Answer these questions, if possible without referring to the book.
14. Errors, if any, should be corrected.
15. She stayed in her aunt's during the winter vacation.

# 16. Cohesion in English Text

## Aims of the Unit

> In this unit we will discuss the functions and uses of cohesion in English text. We are going to discuss the following questions in particular:
> - What's the meaning of cohesion?
> - What's a cohesive text?
> - What devices can be employed to keep a text cohesive?
> - How can language users choose some devices to keep a text cohesive?

**Task 1** Compare the following two texts, and find out the differences between them.

(1) In the last twenty years or so, some undeveloped countries have increased their food production. Their populations have at the same time grown faster. The standard of living hasn't improved. The increase in food production has been achieved at the expense of using up marginal land. There has been no gain in the productivity of land labor.

(2) In the last twenty years or so, some undeveloped countries have increased their food production. Their populations, however, have at the same time grown faster, and so their standard of living hasn't improved. What's more, their increase in food production has been achieved at the expense of using up marginal land. As a result, there has been no gain in the productivity of land labor.

## ◈ 16.1  Definition of Cohesion

**Cohesion** is the grammatical and lexical linking within a text and the linking holds a text together and gives it meaning. The grammatical or lexical linking between elements of a text shows the relationship between different sentences or between different parts of a sentence. It is related to the broader concept of **coherence**, e.g.

A: *Is Jenny coming to the party?*
B: *Yes, she is.*

In the example, there is a link between *Jenny* and *she* and also between *is ... coming* and *is*, where *she* refers to *Jenny*, and *coming* is omitted after *is*.

*If you are going to* **London***, I can give you the address of a good hotel* **there***.*

The link is between *London* and *there*, where *there* is substituted for *London*. The above examples are cohesive utterances. Sometimes there is no grammatical or lexical link in a text, but it can be coherent if it is constructed with a series of sentences that develop a main idea, e.g.

A: *Could you give me a lift home?*
B: *Sorry, I'm visiting my sister.*

In the above sentences, no grammatical or lexical link can be found between A's question and B's reply, but it is coherent because A and B share the knowledge: B's sister lives in the opposite direction to A's home. It's the meaning in the text that keeps the text cohesive.

## 16.2 Types of Cohesive Devices

reference
照应,所指
logical cohesion
逻辑衔接
grammatical cohesion
语法衔接
lexical cohesion
词汇衔接

A cohesive text can be created in many different ways. In *Cohesion in English*, M.A.K. Halliday and Ruqaiya Hasan identify five general categories of cohesive devices that create coherence in texts: **reference**, **ellipsis**, **substitution**, **lexical cohesion** and **conjunction**. Here three types of cohesion are introduced: **logical cohesion**, **grammatical cohesion** and **lexical cohesion**. Logical cohesion is based upon the transitional words or phrases which show temporal orders, spatial orders, and causes and effects, etc.; grammatical cohesion upon structural content; and lexical cohesion upon lexical content and background knowledge.

### 1) Logical Cohesion

In the logical cohesion, some transitional words or phrases to show time, space, listing, concession, causes and effects, etc. are employed to show the link between sentences in the text. The transitional words or phrases are usually conjunctions or conjunctive adverbs. They are *afterwards*, *later*, *then*, *nearby*, *next to, firstly, finally, next, last,* and *besides, besides, furthermore, moreover, likewise, otherwise, similarly, but, however, nevertheless though, because, for, therefore, hence, accordingly, consequently, thus,* etc. Some prepositions or prepositional phrases, infinitives or non-infinitives or verbless causes can also keep the text cohesive. They are, for example, *since then, on the right/left, to the east/west/north/south, for example/instance, in the other words, on the other hand, on the contrary, for all that, for that reason, in addition, in the same way, in that case, in brief, in short, in conclusion, as a result, if so, if not, to sum up, what's more,* etc.

**Task 2**  Read the text, and find out the logical cohesion.

> Flu season occurs annually in countries that have cold weather in the winter. Although the influenza virus is alive throughout the world in all four seasons, it seems to have its greatest impact on humans during the winter. Scientists are not sure why. They think it's because in the winter people are indoors and close together for longer periods of time. Also, the virus might be able to live longer and be stronger in colder weather. Finally, indoor air can dry up the mucous that helps protect people from the virus.

### 2) Grammatical Cohesion

In linguistics, grammar refers to the logical and structural rules that govern the composition of clauses, phrases, and words in any given natural language. Grammar helps language users organize utterances to form cohesive text. The grammatical cohesive devices generally concern the use of tense/aspect, reference, substitution, and ellipse.

① Tense-aspect Cohesion

The tense/aspect of verbs is a very important grammatical concept in English because it can show the time of occurrence of events. The chronological order can keep the text cohesive. In a narration, the past perfect form, past future form or past tense should be used in agreement with the time when an event happens if the background information is presented with the past tense. This so-called tense-aspect-agreement can make the narrative text cohesive, e.g.

He was watching TV. It was about 10:45 pm. All of a sudden, he felt something in his chest. It was a fullness that he had never felt before. The feeling was dull and painless. But it quickly became a very strong "chest ache". His chest felt full, sort of like his belly did after Thanksgiving dinners. He could feel a little bit of sharpness in the area of his heart. Then he felt a tiny electric current go down his left arm and into his left hand. His hand felt numb. He thought he would be in hospital the following days.

In the above paragraph, the past continuous is used in the beginning sentence, and the past tense is used in the following sentences except ... *he had never felt before* and ... *he would be in hospital the following days* in which the past perfect and the past future are used accordingly to show the events in the past and in the future. The agreement of uses of tense-aspect keeps the narration cohesive.

② Reference-based Cohesion

In a broad sense, there are two referential devices that can create cohesion: **anaphoric reference** and **cataphoric reference**.

> anaphoric reference 后照应
> cataphoric reference 前照应

Anaphoric reference occurs when the writer refers back to someone or something that has been previously identified to avoid repetition, e.g.

Lyn lived with her husband in **a house** that they had bought for a song in near by Seyer Street. **The house** was cheat partly because it was falling down.

He ordered **a book** sometime ago. **It** has now arrived.

Cataphoric reference is the opposite of anaphora: a reference forward as opposed to backward in the discourse. Something is introduced in the text before it is identified, e.g.

Please tell us **the story of Franklin**.

Is this **the train for Shanghai**?

Here is **the student I told you about**?

③ Ellipse-based Cohesion

Ellipsis is another cohesive device. It happens when, after a more specific mention, words are omitted when the phrase needs to be repeated. A simple conversational example:

A: *Where are you going?*

B: *To dance.*

The full form of B's reply would be: "I am going to dance."

A simple written example:

*The younger child was very outgoing, the older much more reserved.*

The omitted words from the second clause are *child* and *was*.

④ Substitution

A word is not omitted, as in ellipsis, but is substituted for another more general word. For example, —*Which ice-cream would you like?* —*I would like the pink one*, where *one* is used instead of repeating *ice-cream*. This works in a similar way to pronouns, which replace the noun. For example, *ice-cream* is a noun, and its pronoun could be *it*, as in *I dropped the ice-cream because it was dirty*.

**Task 3**  Read the passage in the following box and find out the grammatical links.

> On the moon, there's no air to breathe, no breezes to make the flags planted there by the Apollo missions flutter. However, there is a very, very thin layer of gases on the lunar surface that can almost be called an atmosphere. Technically, it's considered as an exosphere.
>
> In an exosphere, the gases are so spread out that they rarely collide with one another. They are rather like microscopic cannon balls flying unimpeded on curved, ballistic trajectories and bouncing across the lunar surface. In the moon's atmosphere, there are only 100 molecules per cubic centimeter. In comparison, Earth's atmosphere at sea level has about 100 billion molecules per cubic centimeter. The total mass of these gases is about 55,000 pounds (25,000 kilograms), about the same weight as a loaded dump truck.

### 3) Lexical Cohesion

Lexical cohesion refers to the way in which related words are chosen to link elements of a text. Obviously, lexical cohesion cannot be separated from logical cohesion and grammatical cohesion. Here lexical cohesion refers to the repetition of the same key words in a text, the use of **synonyms**, **antonyms** and **hyponymy** words.

synonyms
同义词
antonyms
反义词
hyponymy
下义词
superordinate
上义词

① Repetition of the Same Words

The saying "*one picture is worth 1,000 words*" suggests the importance to a writer of thinking by **examples**. By putting the right **examples** in a paragraph or composition, a writer can tell his or her idea to a reader. But the art of using the right **examples** is not easy to learn. Choosing **examples** calls for imagination. Using **examples** well calls for both reasoning and control. **Examples** must make abstract ideas more concrete. At the same time, **examples** must not lead a reader away from a writer's central purpose. Clear thinking is needed for good writing. Clear thinking alone helps a writer choose **examples** that will explain the idea of an essay. **You must** have a plan instead of a grocery list. **You must** write with your mind as well as your pen because a composition is an act of thought.

In the text above, the word *examples* are repeated eight times and *you must* are repeated twice. They keep the text cohesive and forceful.

② Synonyms or Antonyms

Sometimes the language users don't want to repeat the same words, but they use words with the same meaning or words with opposite meaning to keep texts cohesive. For example,

A: *Which dress are you going to wear?*

B: *I will wear my green frock.*

In the conversation above, Speaker B uses the **synonyms** *dress* and *frock* for lexical cohesion. Sometimes language users also use **antonyms** to keep the utterance cohesive as shown in the following text in which *virtue* and *vice*, *good* and *evil* are antonyms.

Sow virtue and the harvest will be virtue; sow vice and the harvest will be vice. Good companions help you to sow virtue; evil companions help you to sow vice.

③ Hyponyms

Sometimes language users use hyponyms, that is, specific words in meaning (hyponyms) to substitute for the general words in meaning (superordinates) to keep the text cohesive. For example,

Henry's bought himself a new **Jaguar**. He practically lives in the **car**.

You can save money if you rent that house **furniture**. The **air-conditioners** and the **TV set** are quite new.

In the two sentences, they are cohesive because *Jaguar*, *air-conditioners* and *TV set* are all hyponyms of *car* and *furniture* respectively. The speaker and the listener can understand each other.

## ◆ 16.3  Choice of Cohesive Devices

The cohesive devices in texts are discussed in the sections above. It doesn't mean that language users can use the devices at their will. The cohesive devices chosen in texts are determined by the topics, the potential audience and the shared knowledge they have. Take a conversation for example,

A: *That's the telephone*

B: *I'm in the bath.*

A: *Okey.*

In the conversation, A and B talk about different stuff in their utterances, but the conversation is meaningful and cohesive because they share the background knowledge. Speaker B can't answer the phone because he is taking a bath. People usually favor a more economical use of language, so they use no cohesive devices discussed above. On the other hand, a text can't be coherent though some cohesive devices are employed if it has no central idea at all. See the following example,

Sayner, Wisconsin, is the **snowmobile** capital of the word. The buzzing of **snowmobile** engines fills the air, and their tanklike tracks crisscross the **snow**. The **snow** reminds me of Mom's **mashed potatoes**, covered with furrows I would draw with my fork. **Her** mashed **potatoes** usually make me sick, **that**'s why I play with **them**. I like to make a hole in the middle of the **potatoes** and fill **it** with melted butter. **This** behavior **has been** the subject of long chats between me and my analyst.

Although the repetitions of *snowmobile*, *snow* and *potatoes*, pronouns such as *her*, *them*, *it*, *this* and *that*, and present perfect in the last sentence keep the text cohesive, the text is not coherent at all because it lacks unity of a text, that is, it has no central idea. Native language users never write in such way.

**Task 4**    Read the following text, and point out the cohesive devices employed in it.

> The moon is the easiest celestial object to find in the night sky—when it's there. Earth's only natural satellite hovers above us bright and round until it seemingly disappears for a few nights. The rhythm of the moon's phases has guided humanity for millennia-for instance, calendar months are roughly equal to the time it takes to go from one full moon to the next.
>
> Moon phases and the moon's orbit are mysteries to many. For example, the moon always shows us the same face. That happens because it takes 27.3 days both to rotate on its axis and to orbit Earth. We see either the full moon, half moon or no moon (new moon) because the moon reflects sunlight. How much of it we see depends on the moon's position in relation to Earth and the sun.
>
> Though a satellite of Earth, the moon, with a diameter of about 2,159 miles (3,475 kilometers), is bigger than Pluto. (Four other moons in our solar system are even bigger.). The moon is a bit more than one-fourth (27 percent) the size of Earth, a much smaller ratio (1:4) than any other planets and their moons. This means the moon has a great effect on the planet and very possibly is what makes life on Earth possible.

# EXERCISES

**I. Reconstruct the following sentences into a cohesive paragraph.**

### A Busy Morning

a. First, I had to go to the post office.
b. Half of the letters were addressed to American business companies.
c. I got up at 6:30 am.
d. When I left the train station, I took my boss's car to the garage for repairs.
e. When I arrived at the office, my boss had several things for me to do.
f. I left the house at 7:45.
g. The other half were addressed to foreign companies.
h. After typing the letters, I had to run several errands.
i. Yesterday morning was quite hectic for me.
j. Then I had to pick up a train ticket for my boss's wife.
k. He asked me to type twenty letters for him.
l. By 1:00, I was exhausted, so I decided to have a long leisurely lunch.

**II. Read the following short story and fill in the blanks with proper words to keep the text cohesive.**

### The Fire Alarm

Jennifer's ears were "talking" to her. They were making little sounds, like little bubbles bursting. A "bubble" was bursting almost every second. It was not painful, __1__ annoying. She knew the cause.

__2__ she was cleaning the whiteboard __3__ her class ended last night, the fire alarm went off. __4__ leaving the building immediately, she walked around to see what the problem was. The blaring alarm sounded like the busy signal on a phone, __5__ 1,000 times louder. The school seemed to be empty. __6__ she walked by one room, and saw about seven students inside.

Just then the night supervisor came by. She told everyone to leave immediately. The students were packing their hair-care equipment into their bags. The night supervisor waited impatiently. __7__, after almost five minutes, all the students and their teacher left the building. They apologized for being so slow.

The firemen never arrived. __8__, a school police officer showed up. He walked around the area with the supervisor. It was a false alarm. The officer used his key to finally turn off the alarm.

__9__ it was too late for Jennifer. She had listened to the loud alarm for too long.

She should have known better. Even __10__ she drove home, her ears felt strange.

**Ⅲ. Improve the cohesion in the following text.**

The day of the exam approaches. There are several things you can do to make life easier. You should make sure that you get regular exercise, that way you won't feel tired at night and you won't stay awake worrying. You can find someone who is doing the exam and can share the revision with you. You can organize little tests and quizzes for each other. This can make the process much more fun than working on your own. It helps to write short notes of the most important study points on pieces of paper and look at them just before you got to bed. Don't do any studying. Eat a proper breakfast and take some emergency snacks with you, wear comfortable clothes and take your favorite pen and pencil with you. Don't forget your watch.

# Appendix 1: Solutions to Tasks

**Notes:**

1. This appendix does not have solutions to all the tasks in the book.

2. The solutions provided here are the authors' suggestions or materials from other resources. They are better considered as "further comments" than as "answers".

## 1. Introduction: Grammatical Hierarchy

**Task 1**  Here is the dissection of the sentence:

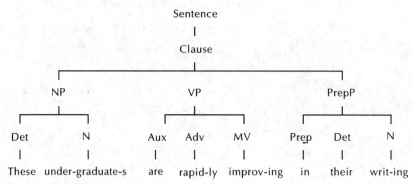

**Task 4**

(1) prepositional phrase

(2) adjective phrase

(3) noun phrase

(4) noun phrase

(5) finite verb phrase

(6) finite verb phrase

(7) non-finite verb phrase

(8) adverb phrase

(9) non-finite verb phrase

(10) adjective phrase

**Task 5**

(1) non-finite clause

(2) independent clause

(3) subordinate clause

(4) independent simple clause/simple sentence

(5) independent complex clause/complex sentence

(6) subordinate clause

(7) non-finite clause/nominative absolute construction

(8) verbless clause

**Task 6**

(1) complete sentence/simple sentence

(2) complete sentence/compound sentence

(3) complete sentence/complex sentence
(4) complete sentence/compound-complex sentence
(5) incomplete sentence/elliptical sentence
(6) incomplete sentence/amorphous sentence
(7) incomplete sentence/amorphous sentence
(8) incomplete sentence/amorphous sentence
(9) incomplete sentence/amorphous sentence
(10) incomplete sentence/amorphous sentence

## 2. Sentence Components

**Activity 1**

| | Agree/Disagree |
|---|---|
| 1. All the sentences must explicitly or implicitly contain the subject and the predicate. | √ |
| 2. The subject complement is another name for the predicative. | × |
| 3. Not all adverbials in a sentence are grammatically obligatory. | √ |
| 4. Components like the object and the adverbial can be arbitrarily moved within the sentence. | × |
| 5. All English sentences begin with the subject. | × |
| 6. Theoretically, the subject of an English sentence can be infinitely complex in form. | √ |
| 7. If the subject of an English sentence is singular, the precidate verb must be singular, too. | √ |
| 8. All English sentences have an object. | × |
| 9. Not all noun phrases following the main verbs are objects. | √ |
| 10. The position of the object is filled by a nominal expression. | √ |

**Task 1**

(1) noun   (2) pronoun   (3) infinitive and gerund   (4) noun clauses
(5) adjective and participle   (6) adverb   (7) prepositional phrases

**Task 2**

(1) East Market   (2) absurd   (3) hot   (4) attractive   (5) interesting   (6) on the top
(7) open   (8) on the table

**Task 3**

(1) pronoun   (2) adjective   (3) interrogative adverb   (4) adverb   (5) predicate
(6) gerund phrase   (7) clause

## 3. Subject-verb Concord

**Task 1**

(1) has  (2) is  (3) costs  (4) comes  (5) are  (6) is

**Task 2**

(1) is  (2) are  (3) is  (4) was  (5) Has  (6) are  (7) is  (8) have

**Task 3**

(1) provide  (2) is  (3) is  (4) are, are

**Task 4**

(1) is  (2) are  (3) means  (4) is  (5) was  (6) is  (7) are

**Task 5**

(1) is  (2) are  (3) are  (4) looks  (5) are  (6) has  (7) are  (8) was

**Task 6**

(1) is  (2) is  (3) remain  (4) were  (5) are  (6) plays  (7) is  (8) am  (9) is

## 4. Sentence Constructions and Analysis

**Task 1**

(1) SVoO and SVOC  (2) SVoO and SVOC  (3) SVC and SVO  (4) SVoO and SVOC (or SVoO)  (5) SVA and SVO  (6) SV and SVO

**Task 2**

Types of verbs:

The main verb in an SVC pattern is a **linking verb.**

The main verb in the SV pattern is an **intransitive verb.**

Some **intransitive verbs** must be followed by an adverbial, like those in SVA.

The main verb in the SVO pattern is a **monotransitive verb.**

Some **transitive verbs** must be followed by an adverbial like those in SVOA.

The main verb in the SVoO pattern is a **ditransitive verb.**

The main verb in SVOC is a **complex transitive verb.**

**Task 3**

I depend on you <u>to do it</u>.

You'd better keep the door <u>open</u>.

His action made him <u>respected</u>.

I found him <u>out</u> just now.

**Task 4**

When you attach a subordinate clause **in front of** a **main clause**, use a **comma**; when you attach a subordinate clause **at the end of** a **main clause**, you will generally use **no punctuation**. Therefore, A and C are right.

**Task 5**

There *is* a train due to arrive.

There *was* a lot of rain last year.

There *will be* an English lecture at three this afternoon.

There *has been* much talk about it.

## 5. Uses of Sentences

**Task 1**

(1) Does grandpa like telling stories?

(2) His stories are always true.

**Task 2**

(1) The balloon is not red.

(2) The baby is not crying.

(3) The man does not have a horse.

(4) The television is not broken.

(5) The children are not happy.

**Task 3**

(1) Is Jack leaving today?

(2) Did Robert eat the last doughnut?

(3) Can you understand why I am unset?

(4) Is there a physician in the house?

(5) Have you received a pay raise this year?

(6) Does Laura know how to serve her customers effectively and efficiently?

(7) Did the doctor tell us to add cereal to the baby's formula?

(8) Did the repairs to the TV set cost more than the TV set was worth?

(9) Do all of your friends try to cheer you up when you are sad?

**Task 4**

(1) What   (2) What   (3) Who   (4) Where   (5) When   (6) Why   (7) When   (8) What

(9) Why   (10) Why

**Task 5**

(1) How   (2) How   (3) What   (4) What   (5) What   (6) What   (7) How   (8) How

## 6. Tense and Aspect Systems

**Task 1**

(1) work; am studying   (2) is raining   (3) always rains   (4) are saying; is talking   (5) drives

**Task 2**

(1) has not been   (2) been   (3) have found   (4) working   (5) getting   (6) been working

**Task 3**

(1) moved   (2) have not bought   (3) has already written   (4) Did they spend   (5) went

(6) have already traveled

**Task 4**

(1) saw   (2) were playing   (3) was falling   (4) went   (5) was reading   (6) did

**Task 5**

(1) had been smoking  (2) had not finished  (3) had not been  (4) had not been completed
(5) had not been expecting  (6) had been

**Task 6**
(1) will win; will win; will win  (2) am going to buy; will try; will go

**Task 7**
(1) will you be wearing  (2) will be snowing  (3) will be relaxing  (4) will be taking

**Task 8**
(1) am going to hill  (2) am going to repaper; will help

## 7. Voice System

**Task 1**
(1) The bird, performer, active
(2) A nest, receiver, passive
(3) Tom, performer, active
(4) The blackboard, receiver, passive
(5) Many people, performer, active
(6) The match, receiver, passive
(7) The shoemaker, performer, active
(8) The ball, receiver, passive

**Task 2**

| She recognized me at once. |
| --- |
| → I She recognized at once. |
| → I She *was recognized* at once. |
| → I She *was recognized by* at once. |
| → I *was recognized by her* at once. |

| I bought him a gift. |
| --- |
| →*He* I bought a gift. |
| →*He* I *was bought* a gift. |
| →*He He was bought* a gift. |

| I bought him a gift. |
| --- |
| →*A gift* I bought him. |
| →*A gift* I *was bought* him. |
| →*A gift was bought for* him. |

| They saw a man standing in front of the house. |
| --- |
| →*A man* They saw standing in front of the house. |
| →*A man* They *was seen* standing in front of the house. |
| →*A man was seen* standing in front of the house. |

| John wanted her to go to the office at once. |
| --- |
| → *She* John wanted to go to the office at once. |
| → *She* John *was wanted* to go to the office at once. |
| → *She* John *was wanted by* to go to the office at once. |
| → *She was wanted by John* to go to the office at once. |

**Task 3**

(1) F  (2) F  (3) F  (4) T

**Task 4**

(1) is visited: simple present

(2) was put off: simple past

(3) will be completed: simple future

(4) were being looked after: past continuous

(5) will have been chosen: future perfect

(6) to have been largely given: perfect, subject complement

(7) being expelled: simple, object

(8) to be drawn: simple, post attribute

**Task 5**

(1) unnecessary  (2) improper  (3) impossible

**Task 6**

(1) active, active  (2) be + v-ed, SVC  (3) active, passive  (4) passive, passive

(5) passive, passive  (6) active, passive  (7) active, passive  (8) active, passive

# 8. Mood System

**Task 1**

(1) Real  (2) Uncertain  (3) Unreal

**Task 2**

(1) indicative mood  (2) imperative mood  (3) subjunctive mood

**Task 3**

(1) base form  (2) notional  (3) uncertain  (4) nominal  (5) adverbial  (6) formulaic

**Task 4**

(1) only  (2) unreal  (3) objective  (4) supposition  (5) concession  (6) manner

**Task 5**

(1) similar  (2) were-subjunctive  (3) main  (4) unreal  (5) future  (6) unwelcome

# 9. Nouns

**Task 1**

One day a <u>man</u> went into a <u>chemist's</u> <u>shop</u> and said, "Have you anything to cure a <u>headache</u>?"

The <u>chemist</u> took a <u>bottle</u> from a <u>shelf</u>, held it under the <u>gentleman's nose</u> and took out the <u>cork</u>. The <u>smell</u> was so strong that <u>tears</u> came into the <u>man's eyes</u> and ran down his <u>cheeks</u>.

"What did you do that for?" he said angrily, as soon as he could get back his <u>breath</u>. "But that <u>medicine</u> has cured your <u>headache</u>, hasn't it?" said the <u>chemist</u>.

"You <u>fool</u>," said the <u>man</u>, "It's my <u>wife</u> that has the <u>headache</u>, not me!"

| Function \ Form | Subject | Object | Attribute | Subject Complement |
|---|---|---|---|---|
| Singular | man, smell, medicine, chemist, man | shop, headache, bottle, shelf, nose cork, breath, headache, headache | | fool, wife |
| Plural | tears | eyes, cheeks | | |
| Genitive | | | chemist's, man's, gentleman's, | |

**Task 2**

| Words \ Criteria for Classification | Morphology | Notion | Grammatical Property |
|---|---|---|---|
| people | simple | collective | countable |
| horse | simple | individual | countable |
| management | derivative | abstract | uncountable |
| man-power | compound | abstract | uncountable |

**Task 3**

(1) Monica: subject    class: attribute    adviser: appositive    library: prepositional object

(2) Tom: subject    machine: object    substitute: object complement    one: prepositional object

**Task 4**

(1) sibilant    (2) consonant    (3) preceded    (4) regular    (5) irregular    (6) unchanged

(7) source    (8) change    (9) uncountable    (10) singular

**Task 5**

(1) case form    (2) relation    (3) two    (4) s-genitive    (5) realization    (6) animate

(7) independent genitive    (8) referent    (9) follow    (10) forms

# 10. Determiners

**Task 1**

(1) determiners: Thousands of   modifier: foreign

(2) determiner: the   modifier: female

**Task 2**

(1) less can collocate with noncount nouns

(2) neither can collocate with singular count nouns

(3) several can collocate with plural count nouns

**Task 3**

(1) half: pre-determiner,   their: central determiner

(2) all: pre-determiner, the: central determiner, five: post-determiner

(3) every: central determiner, other: post-determiner

(4) The: central determiner, first: first sub-group of post-determiner, ten: second sub-group of

Appendix 1: Solutions to Tasks

post-determiner

## 11. Verbs

**Task 1**

(1) ⑤,①,⑤,①,④

(2) ②,⑥,②

(3) ①,④

(4) ④,②,②

**Task 2**

(1) The two finite forms of main verbs are the present tense and the past tense.

(2) The three non-finite forms of main verbs are the infinitive, the -ing participle and the -ed participle.

(3) Modal auxiliaries have no non-finite forms.

(4) Regular verbs are: ② reduce; ④ stop; ⑦ clean; ⑧ work

Irregular verbs are: ① let; ③ come; ⑤ bring; ⑥ go

**Task 3**

(1) Echo bought a book **to read** on the journey.

(2) I don't think much of him, **to be honest** with you.

(3) This book seems to **have been translated** into English.

(4) It is impossible **for him** to find such a nice place to live in.

**Task 4**

(1) going   (2) finished up   (3) caught   (4) laughing

**Task 5**

(1) being hurt   (2) to win   (3) having left   (4) to believe

## 12. Adjectives and Adverbs

**Task 1**

One word adjective: kind, e.g. she is a kind girl. (premodifier)

Compound adjective: well-known, e.g. Madam Curie is a well-known female scientist. (premodifier)

Central adjective: new, e.g. I like my new hairstyle. (premodifier)

This idea isn't new. (subject complement)

Peripheral adjective: digective, e.g. He has some digestive problem. (premodifier)

Alive, e.g. We don't know whether he's alive or dead. (subject complement)

Dynamic adjective: cunning, e.g. He was as cunning as a fox. (subject complement)

Stative adjective: deep, e.g. She fell into the deep hole. (premodifier)

Gradable adjective: beautiful, e.g. She is more beautiful than her elder sister. (subject complement)

Non-gradable adjective: utter, e.g. To my utter amazement, she agreed. (premodifier)

**Task 2**

(1) three very healthy, intelligent children/three healthy, very intelligent children

(2) Twenty original African wood carving

(3) My brother's first long public concert

(4) A nearly beautiful pale pink sunset

(5) Three very comfortable dark blue chairs

**Task 3**

(1) ... have thoroughly studied ... /studied this chapter thoroughly.

(2) ... very much appreciated it/appreciate it very much.

(3) ... are practically impossible ...

(4) Will you kindly come this way?

(5) The house badly needs repainting / ... repainting badly.

**Task 4**

(1) close  (2) closely  (3) directly, direct  (4) directly  (5) free  (6) freely

**Task 5**

(1) not so near as/farther than

(2) not so beautiful as/uglier than

(3) not so ugly as/prettier than

(4) not so light as/heavier than

(5) not so strong as/weaker than

## 13. Prepositions

**Task 1**

(1) adv.  (2) preposition  (3) adv.  (4) preposition  (5) adv.  (6) preposition

(7) adv.  (8) adv.

**Task 2**

(1) as  (2) from  (3) in  (4) about  (5) in  (6) to  (7) with  (8) with  (9) at  (10) for

**Task 3**

(1) Thanks to  (2) apart from  (3) for lack of  (4) In addition to  (5) at the mercy of

(6) with an eye to

**Task 4**

(1) of  (2) from  (3) to  (4) to  (5) on  (6) at

**Task 5**

(1) on  (2) on  (3) on  (4) into

**Task 6**

(1) from  (2) into  (3) of  (4) from

**Task 7**

(1) to  (2) against  (3) with  (4) to

**Task 8**

(1) on  (2) to

**Task 9**

(1) for  (2) in  (3) to  (4) for

# Appendix 1: Solutions to Tasks

**Task 10**

(1) on  (2) at  (3) In  (4) To

**Task 11**

(1) adverbials  (2) adverbials  (3) adverbials  (4) attributes  (5) attributes

(6) subject complement  (7) subject complement  (8) subject complement

(9) subject complement  (10) object complement  (11) object complement

(12) subject  (13) subject  (14) object

## 14. Inversion

**Task 1**

These are all inverted sentences. Inverted sentences are sentences with an irregular verb placement of the verb before the subject.

**Task 2**

(1) On one occasion he did not offer to help.

(2) He did not offer to help on any occasion at all.

(3) An effort to develop character in depth is not made very often.

(4) On a few occasions an effort to develop character in depth is made.

**Task 3**

(1) <u>Only when</u> we got home did we find out why the car was making such a strange noise.

(2) <u>Only by</u> starting again from the beginning were we able to get to the solution.

   or ... from the beginning did we manage to get to the solution.

(3) <u>Under no circumstances</u> should you open up the back of the television.

(4) <u>Seldom</u> do you hear of/about such incompetence in this company.

(5) <u>Never</u> before have so many people died as a result of a signal failure.

(6) <u>Not since</u> Alison's wedding was there such a big family gathering/gathering of family.

(7) <u>Not until</u> the guard dogs had been fed would they leave the kennel.

(8) <u>Only after</u> the sun went down wasn't the day hot.

(9) <u>No sooner</u> had the plane taken off than the engine trouble started.

## 15. Ellipsis and Substitution

**Task 1**

These two sentences are both shortened forms of the answer: *I am an Economics major.*

*I am.* is an answer with Ellipsis where an *Economics major* is omitted.

*I am one.* is an answer with substitution where *one* substitutes for *an Economics major*.

**Task 2**

(1) no ellipsis  (2) nominal ellipsis  (3) verbal ellipsis  (4) clausal ellipsis  (5) verbal ellipsis

**Task 3**

Ⅰ. The principles of using *one/ones* as a substitute:

- *One/ones* can only replace the countable noun(s) as the head word.

- *One/ones* must always take on the element of the determiner to form the substitute element, e.g., *this*

one, that one, another one, the largest ones.
- *One/ones* can not replace the proper noun, for the proper noun has already defined in meaning, therefore, the content of it can not be altered or added to in the substitute place.
- Numeral one can be modified by submodifiers, such as *just one*, *only one*, not one, *pretty one*; while Substitute one can be modified by demonstratives, such as *this one*, *that one*, *those ones*, etc.

Ⅱ. Can you tell whether the *one* in each of the following sentences is the numeral *one*, the pronoun *one* or the substitute *one*?

(1) numeral  (2) pronoun  (3) substitute  (4) numeral  (5) substitute

## 16. Cohesion in English Text

**Task 1**

Comparing the two texts, we can find that some connections like *however*, *what's more so* and *as a result* are used between sentences in the second text to keep it cohesive.

**Task 2**

Some transitional words or phrases like *although*, *also* and *finally* are used to show the logical cohesion in the text.

**Task 3**

We can find 3 types of grammatical cohesion as follows:

A. Tense-aspect Cohesion

The present tense is employed from the beginning to the end in the text to show the current state of the gases on the moon.

B. Reference-based Cohesion

there: on the moon, It: atmosphere, they: gases

C. Substitution

atmosphere: exosphere, one another: gases

**Task 4**

(1) **Logical Cohesion**

when, until, for instance, for example, because, either … or, because, though

(2) **Grammatical Cohesion**

A. Tense-aspect Cohesion

the present tense and the present perfect tense

B. Reference-based Cohesion

The moon is the easiest celestial object to find in the night sky—when it's there. Earth's only natural satellite hovers above us bright and round until it seemingly disappears for a few nights.

How much of it we see depends on the moon's position in relation to Earth and the sun.

The moon is a bit more than one-fourth (27 percent) the size of Earth, a much smaller ratio (1:4) than any other planets and their moons. This means the moon has a great effect on the planet and very possibly is what makes life on Earth possible.

# Appendix 1: Solutions to Tasks

C. Ellipse-based Cohesion

For instance, calendar months are roughly equal to the time it takes to go from one <u>full moon</u> to the next (full moon).

D. Substitution

The <u>moon</u> is the easiest celestial object to find <u>in the night sky</u>—when <u>it</u>'s <u>there</u>.

<u>Earth</u>'s only natural satellite hovers above us bright and round until <u>it</u> seemingly disappears for a few nights.

<u>For example, the moon always shows us the same face.</u> <u>That</u> happens because it takes 27.3 days both to rotate on its axis and to orbit Earth.

How much of <u>it</u> we see depends on the <u>moon</u>'s position in relation to Earth and the sun.

<u>The moon is a bit more than one-fourth (27 percent) the size of Earth, a much smaller ratio (1∶4) than any other planets and their moons.</u> <u>This</u> means the moon has a great effect on the planet and very possibly is what makes life on Earth possible.

(3) **Lexical Cohesion**

A. Repetition of the Same Words

Moon is repeated dozes of times in the text.

B. Synonyms or Antonyms

synonyms: moon, natural satellite (moons), a satellite of Earth, solar system and sun, hover above and obit

antonyms: bigger, smaller

C. Hyponyms

satellite: Moon, moons

planet: Pluto, earth

(4) **Other Devices**

Comparatives and superlatives are employed.

The moon is the <u>easiest celestial object</u> to find in the night sky—when it's there.

Though a satellite of Earth, the moon, with a diameter of about 2,159 miles (3,475 kilometers), is <u>bigger</u> than Pluto. (Four other moons in our solar system are <u>even bigger</u>.) The moon is a bit <u>more</u> than one-fourth (27 percent) the size of Earth, a much <u>smaller</u> ratio (1∶4) than any other planets and their moons.

# Appendix 2: Glossary

## A

abbreviation 缩略词
abstract noun 抽象名词
active non-finite verb 非限定动词的主动式
active voice 主动语态
adjunct 修饰性状语
adjective 形容词
adjective complementation 形容词补足语成分
adjunct 修饰性状语
adverb 副词
adverbial 状语
adverbial clause 状语从句
adverbial of purpose 目的状语
affirmative sentence 肯定句
affix 词缀
affricate 塞擦音
allomorph 词素变体
amorphous sentence 无定形句
analytic form 分析形式
anticipatory it 先行词 it
anticipatory subject 先行主语
antonym 反义词
apostrophe [表示所有格和复数] 撇号(即')
appositive 同位语
appositive clause 同位语从句
article 冠词
assertive determiner 肯定限定词
attribute 定语
attributive clause 定语从句
auxiliary 助动词

## B

bare infinitive 不带 to 不定式
base form of a verb 动词原形
basic pattern 基本句型
be-subjunctive be- 型虚拟式
bound morphemes 粘附词素

## C

cardinal numeral 基数词
causative verb 致使动词
central adjective 中心形容词
central determiner 中位限定词
clausal ellipsis 分句性省略
classifying attribute 分类性定语
cleft sentence 分裂句
closed class 封闭词类
cognate object 同源宾语
cohesion 粘着性，衔接
collective noun 集合名词
Commentary adverbial 评注性状语
common noun 普通名词
comparative degree 比较级
complement 补语
complementary adverbial 补足性状语
complement clause 补语从句
complex clause 复杂分句
complex sentence 复杂句
complex transitive verb 复杂宾语及物动词
complex verb phrase 复杂动词词组
compound adjective 复合形容词
compound-complex sentence 并列复杂句
compound noun 复合名词
compound sentence 并列句
compound word 复合词
concession 让步
conjunct 连接性状语
conjunction 连词
conjunctive adverbial 连接性状语

conjunctive determiner 连接限定词
constraint 限制性
content word 实义词
coordinate construction 并列结构
coordination 并列关系,并列句
coordinator 并列连词
coordinating conjunction 并列连词
copular verbs 系动词
countable noun 可数名词

## D

declarative sentence 陈述句
dependent clause 从属分句
deep structure 深层结构
definite article 定冠词
dependent of the verb 动词从属成分
derivative 派生词
derivative noun 派生名词
derivative affix 派生词缀
descriptive adverbial 修饰性状语
descriptive attribute 描绘性定语
determiner 限定词
determinative attribute 限定性定语
did-hypothetical did- 型假设
direct object 直接宾语
disjunct 评注性状语
disyllabic word 双音节词
ditransitive verb 双宾及物动词
double genitive 双重所有格
double negative 双重否定
durative verbs 持续动作动词
dynamic verb 动态动词

## E

-ed participle 过去分词
ellipsis 省略
elliptical sentence 省略句
emotive verbs 情感动词

emphatic 强调的
equal footing 同等位置
exclamatory sentence 感叹句
existential sentence 存在句

## F

finite verb 限定动词
finite clause 限定分句
formal subject 形式主语
formulaic expressions 公式化语句
fraction 分数词
free morphemes 自由词素
free verb phrase 自由动词词组
fricative 擦音
function word 功能词

## G

general act 一般行为
general ordinal 一般序数词
generative linguistics 生成语言学
genitive noun 名词属格
gerund 动名词
gradable adjective 等级形容词
grammatical cohesion 语法衔接
grammatical concord 语法一致
grammatical ellipsis 语法省略
grammatical hierarchy 语法层次
grammatical form 语法形式
grammatical inversion 语法倒装
grammatical marker 语法标记

## H

hyponymy 下义词

## I

imperative mood 祈使语气
imperative sentence 祈使句

implied conditionals 隐含条件句
indefinite article 不定冠词
indefinite determiner 不定限定词
independent clause 独立分句
independent element 独立成分
independent genitive 独立属格
indicative mood 陈述语气
indirect object 间接宾语
individual noun 个体名词
infinitive 不定式
inflectional affix 屈折词缀
-ing participle 现在分词或动名词
intention 意图
interjection 感叹词
interrogative determiner 疑问限定词
interrogative sentence 疑问句
intransitive verb 不及物动词
irregular verb 不规则动词

# L

lexical cohesion 词汇衔接
linking verb 连系动词
loan word 外来词
locative adverbial 地点状语
long vowel 长元音
logical cohesion 逻辑衔接
logical subject 逻辑主语

# M

main verb 主动词
main clause 主句
material noun 物质名词
modal auxiliary 情态助动词
momentary verb 短暂动作的动词
monotransitive verb 单宾语及物动词
monosyllabic word 单音节词
mood 语气
morphology 形态学

multiplier 倍数词
mutation 元音变化

# N

negative determiner 否定限定词
negative sentence 否定句
nominal-adjectival complement 名词性-形容词性宾语补足语
nominal clause 名词性分句
nominal ellipsis 名词性省略
non-assertive determiner 非肯定限定词
non-gradable adjective 非等级形容词
non-finite verb 非限定动词
non-finite clause 非限定分句
non-progressive aspect 非进行体
non-referring "it" 非指代性"it"
non-restrictive attribute 非限定性定语
notional concord 意义一致
noun 名词
noun phrase 名词词组
number 数
numeral 数字

# O

object 宾语
object clause 宾语从句
object complement 宾语补语
obligatory adverbial 不可缺少的状语
open class 开放词类
ordinal numeral 序数词

# P

parenthesis 插入语
participles 分词
passive non-finite verb 非限定动词的被动式
passive voice 被动语态
passive infinitive 不定式被动态
past reference 照应过去
past tense modals 情态助动词过去时形式

performer 执行者
peripheral adjective 外围形容词
person 人称
phrasal verb 词组动词
positive / absolute degree 原级
possessive determiner 物主限定词
post-attribute 后置定语
postdeterminer 后位限定词
postmodifer 后置修饰语
pre-attribute 前置定语
predeterminer 前位限定词
predicate verb 谓语动词
predicative 表语
predicative adjective 补语形容词
predicative clause 表语从句
predicator 谓词, 谓语
prediction 预见
prefix 前缀
premodifier 前置修饰语
preposed element 前置成分
preposition 介词
present reference 照应现在
present progressive 现在进行体
primary auxiliaries 基本助动词
process verbs 过程动词
progressive aspect 进行体
pronoun 代词
proper noun 专有名词
proximity 就近原则

# Q

quantifier 量词
quasi-coordinator 准并列连词

# R

receiver 接受者
reciprocal pronoun 相互代词
reference 照应, 所指

reflexive pronoun 反身代词
register 语域
regular noun 规则名词
regular verb 规则动词
relative clause 关系分句
relative determiner 关系限定词
reporting clause 引出直接引语或间接引语的分句；转述分句
restrictive attribute 限定性定语
rhetorical ellipsis 修辞省略
rhetorical inversion 修辞倒装
root 词根

# S

segmentation 切分法
semantic difference 语义区别
semantic intention 语义意图
semantic relations 语义关系
semi-auxiliary 半助动词
sentence expansion 句型扩大
sentence pattern 句型
sentence transformation 句型转换
short vowel 短元音
silent -e 不发音的-e
simple clause 简单分句
simple noun 简单名词
simple present 一般现在时
simple sentence 简单句
simple verb phrase 简单动词词组
simple word 简单词
single-word verb 单词动词
source language 源语言
specific act 特定行为
stative verb 静态动词
subject 主语
subject clause 主语从句
subject complement 主语补语
subject-dependent inversion 主语-动词从属成分倒装
subject-operator inversion 主语与操作词倒装
subjunctive mood 虚拟语气

subordinate construction 从属结构
subordination 从属关系，从属句
subordinate clause 从句
subordinator 从属连词
subordinating conjunction 从属连词
substitution 替代
suffix 后缀
superlative degree 最高级
superordinate 上义词
synonym 同义词
synthetic form 综合形式

# T

temporal adverbial 时间状语
transformational-generative rules 转换生成规则
transitional verbs 位置转移动词
transitive verb 及物动词
transitory verb 短暂性行为动词

# U

uncountable noun 不可数名词
underlying pattern 基础句型
unit noun 单位词
universal determiner 通用限定词

# V

verb 动词
verbal complement 动词性宾语补足语
verbal ellipsis 动词性省略
verbless clause 无动词分句
verbs of perception 感觉动词
vocative 呼语
voice 语态
voiced consonant 浊辅音
voiceless consonant 清辅音
vowel 元音

## W

were-subjunctive were- 型虚拟式
willingness 意愿

## Z

zero article 零冠词

# References

Bas, Aarts. (2011). *Oxford Modern English Grammar.* New York: Oxford University Press.

Biber, D., Johansson, S., Leech, G., Conrad, S. & Finegan, E. (2000). *Longman Grammar of Spoken and Written English.* Beijing: Foreign Language Teaching and Research Press.

Cowan, R. (2008). *The Teacher's Grammar of English.* New York: Cambridge University Press.

Eastwood, J. (2002). *Oxford Guide to English Grammar.* New York: Oxford University Press.

Edward, P., Corbett, J. & Connors, R. (1998). *Classical Rhetoric for the Modern Student.* New York: Oxford University Press.

Huddleston, R. & Pullum, G. K. (2002). *The Cambridge Grammar of the English Language.* New York: Cambridge University Press.

Kolln, M. J. (2009). *Rhetorical Grammar* (6th ed). *New York*: Pearson.

Leech, G. et al. (1982). *English Grammar for Today.* London: MacMillan.

McArthur, T. (1998). *Concise Oxford Companion to the English Language.* New York: Oxford University Press.

Quirk et al. (1973). *A University Grammar of English.* London: Longman Group Ltd.

Richards, J. C., Platt, J. & Platt, H. (2000). *Longman Dictionary of Language Teaching & Applied Linguistics.* Beijing: Foreign Language Teaching and Research Press.

Seth, Lindstromberg. (2010). *English Prepositions Explained* (2nd ed). Amsterdam/Philadelphia: John Benjamin Publishing Company.

Swan. (1980). *Practical English Usage.* New York: Oxford University Press.

Zhang, Z. B. (2003). *A New English Grammar Coursebook.* Shanghai: Shanghai Foreign Education Press.

薄冰. 高级英语语法. 北京:高等教育出版社,1990.

陈新仁. 英语语法实用教程. 苏州:苏州大学出版社,2009.

戴炜栋,何兆熊. 新编简明英语语言学教程. 上海:上海外语教育出版社,2002.

何桂金,高纪兰. 新英语语法教程. 北京:外语教学与研究出版社,2002.

吕叔湘. 中级英语语法. 北京:北京出版社,1981.

徐立吾. 当代英语实用语法. 湖南:湖南教育出版社,1980.

张道真. 张道真英语语法. 北京:商务印书馆,2002.

赵俊英. 现代英语语法大全. 上海:上海交通大学出版社,2008.

章振邦. 新编英语语法教程. 上海:上海外语教育出版社,2009.